Mary Gilliatt's
INTERIOR
DESIGN
COURSE

Mary Gilliatt's
INTERIOR
DESIGN
COURSE

Watson-Guptill Publications/New York

Contents

First published in the United States in 2001 by
Watson-Guptill Publications,
a division of BPI Communications, Inc.,
770 Broadway, New York
New York 10003

Publishing Director: Lorraine Dickey
Senior Editor: Muna Reyal
Editor: Alison Wormleighton
Americanizer: Eleanor Van Zandt

Creative Director: Leslie Harrington
Designer: Mary Staples
Picture Editor: Jo Walton

Production Director: Zoe Fawcett
Production Controller: Alex Wiltshire

Library of Congress Catalog Card
Number: 2001086529

ISBN 0-8230-3046-6

First published in the United Kingdom in
2001 by Conran Octopus Limited,
2–4 Heron Quays,
London E14 4JP

Printed in China

First printing, 2001

For my three special children:
Sophia Gilliatt, Annie Constantine and Tom Gilliatt,
not forgetting my dear Sophie, David and Phoebe.
And for my four (so far) equally special grand-
children: Olivia, Georgia and Iona Constantine
and Freddie Gilliatt.

INTRODUCTION

Almost everyone at one time or another has to create a home, whatever their circumstances or space …

Curiously, the basics of designing interiors and the art of making a home are rarely taught to anyone but aspiring professionals. For some reason it seems to be tacitly accepted that decorating or renovating a house or apartment should be done by intuition. But although some people seem instinctively to possess such useful abilities and a natural sense of style, the fact remains that even the greatest flair or aptitude has to be backed by practical knowledge and honed by experience.

Trial and error, which is the best way to gain meaningful experience in most fields, can be a depressingly expensive process when it comes to renovating, decorating, and furnishing. In short, if you want to become competent enough to design your own home, whatever its size, in a pleasing and practical way, with the minimum amount of stress, you will need to understand fully the fundamental tenets of the subject.

It is a truism that as far as possible your home should be an extension of your personality, or at least a solid expression of your tastes and preferences. But, more importantly, I think, your home also has to be a comforting haven, a place for relaxation. If a home—however elegant it is, however

visually stunning, however fashionable—is not welcoming, not really comfortable, not suited to your lifestyle, it can seriously undermine your whole outlook. In other words, learning how to create a home that is both good-looking and practical is important to your actual well-being.

To achieve this, you will need to have a good working knowledge of all aspects of decoration. How else can you really get to know the most efficient way to plan, how best to choose among the myriad choices, how to buy sensibly, and what design and decorating standards to use? Even if you can afford to employ an architect or a designer (or both), it will still be necessary to brief them succinctly on what you want, what your ideal home includes, and the way that you hope to live in it.

In most cases, rooms or homes to be designed or redesigned already contain certain ingredients, like carpets, rugs, pieces of furniture, soft furnishings, and accessories. Some of these will have to be incorporated into any new design, or at least rethought, refurbished or re-covered. Indeed, it makes the process easier, by giving you a starting point. On the other hand, it is exciting to be able to plan a room, or a whole home, from scratch.

HOW TO USE THIS COURSE

Whichever situation applies to you, it is obviously extremely useful to learn about imaginative ways to utilize a given space: effective lighting methods; potential (and practicable) decorating styles; possible treatments for walls, ceilings, floors, and windows; furniture and soft-furnishing options; and the sensitive use of color and texture, scale and balance, contrast and harmony.

That is why I have prepared this course, which, if followed step-by-step, should give you a thorough grounding in the whole subject of interior design. It is the distillation of all my own hard-won knowledge and various writings on the subject.

My hope is that the course will actually be followed from the first page to the last, and that it will then go on being useful as a reference source. The aim is to take you through the entire procedure of planning a room, or a complete home, in a simple and logical order—the order that any good designer or decorator would follow—and, in the process, give you as much knowledge of the subject as is practicable. Above all, I want this course to engender ideas that could act as a springboard to inspiration for your own home. If I can achieve that, I will have achieved much.

Good design is the art of making something work well and look good. Since one of the most creative and rewarding achievements in life is the satisfying design of a home, it is clearly important to try to succeed at this as well as one possibly can. This course is therefore structured in such a way that, by the end of it, if you have thoroughly absorbed and understood the content, you should feel confident enough to tackle or mastermind any style of room or apartment or house.

I have divided the course into two main parts: **The Basics** and **The Specifics**. Both of these main headings are broken down into separate sections, each leading logically into the next.

Thus, **The Basics** begins with *General Planning* (which will help to determine your needs, finalize the budget, get the framework right, draw up plans and specifications). This is followed by *The Elements of Design* (covering lighting, storage, color, textures and pattern, scale and balance). *Style*, the third section, asks what is really meant by style and goes into the distinguishing features of the most popular style-periods. In addition, a chronological chart puts each style into its historical context, giving dates, reigning monarchs, and concurrent period-styles of other countries.

The second part, **The Specifics**, is just that. It starts with *Walls and Ceilings*, which goes into the finer points of decoration using paint, paper, fabric, and alternative coverings. *Floors* includes the full range of hard, flexible, and soft floorings, including antique carpets. The next section in this part, *Windows*, offers an extensive survey of drapery, shade, curtain, and blind styles, as well as how to deal with difficult window shapes. *Furniture* covers both modern and antique furniture, relating the latter to the style-periods covered in *Style*.

Finally, *The Finishing Touches* reveals how to acquire an eye for detail and accessorize skillfully.

Vocabulary pages appear throughout the book, explaining the technical terms for Lighting, Color, Decorating Styles, Paints, Carpets, Fabrics, and Period Furniture.

As you progress through the course, you should always keep in mind the following three headings:
- function
- mood
- style

The first is to remind you of the function of a room (what it is needed for; how it will be used, and by whom). The second refers to what mood you need to create (calm, restful, stimulating, warm, cool, and so on, depending upon the function of the room and the climate in which you live). The third refers to the style of the room or home (traditional, eclectic, contemporary, Early American, English country house, French provincial, Gustavian, etc.).

I very much hope that this course will provide a useful grounding in design. Remember that although assimilating it all is going to be hard work, doing so will provide its own rewards—in particular, confidence in your own taste and the knowledge that you are making the right choices.

PART ONE

THE BASICS

SECTION ONE

Some people take years to plan the contents of their ideal home and know exactly how they want each room to look and feel. Too many of us, however, apart from having a few particular likes and dislikes, plunge unprepared into the process and have to learn on the way, mostly through expensive mistakes. That is why I have gotten into the habit of trying to plan a home like a campaign. Really thinking about all possible needs from the beginning, finding out about costs beforehand, making endless lists and drawing up plans—all this can be tedious when you are impatient to get on with the job. But it is worth putting up with for the long-term gain. Major redecorating jobs rarely come without their attendant upsets, but at least you should feel in control. And, in fact, much of the planning and anticipation can be both creatively satisfying and exciting. Best of all, you should not be disappointed with the result.

General Planning

Planning Essentials

To ensure that the interior design of a room allows it to function to best advantage, you first have to go back to basics. This involves deciding how the space can be apportioned into different zones; what should be done about the wiring, lighting, ceiling, floor, walls, and windows; what can be improved and how. The results of this analysis will form the framework on which you can add whatever mood and style you choose.

Good interior design is as much about practicality, comfort, and detail as it is about mood and style. However beautiful the window treatments, however original the color schemes, however splendid the furnishings, no one is going to thank you if the room as a whole is not comfortable to live in or does not function as it should.

QUESTIONS TO ASK

Any competent designer who is asked to improve a home or to plan one from scratch would start by finding out his or her clients' tastes and the factors that make them feel most at ease, how they live their lives, how they would *like* to live their lives in an ideal world, and how much they are prepared to spend. To start with the optimum requirements and to work backward from there, in the light of the money available for the project, is as good a way as any of getting priorities right.

When designing for yourself, you should take a similar approach and be equally clear about your budget. The questions listed on the right are what a designer would ask you, although they would vary according to whether the work involved redoing a room or a whole house or apartment, or completely starting from scratch. The questions cover the four main aspects of the work: function, practicalities, aesthetics, and budget.

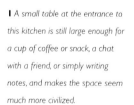

1 *A small table at the entrance to this kitchen is still large enough for a cup of coffee or snack, a chat with a friend, or simply writing notes, and makes the space seem much more civilized.*

2 *Old molds make a pleasant wall decoration in a dining room, which has been designed with both eating and working in mind.*

3 *A home office has been created in this small house. The winding stairs are simple but sculptural.*

Function

1 How long do you expect to stay in this home?

2 Are there, or are there likely to be, children in the household? If there are children now, how many are there and what are their ages? (This affects room planning.)

3 Are there any pets, and if so, what kind? (This affects the finishes and surfaces used.)

4 Are any elderly relatives living or staying with you, or likely to be?

(If so, you will need to think about good light for stairs, corridors, and hallways; non-slip bathroom floors; grip rails for bathtubs, showers; etc.)

5 How many people are at home for all of the day? (This might affect colors and lighting.)

6 What are the respective needs of each member of the household? Are these needs likely to change?

7 Where does the family feel most comfortable eating?

8 Who uses the living room most?

9   How often do you entertain and how?

10 How many people do you generally entertain at once?

11 In what rooms do you entertain the most?

12 If your children have friends in, where do they entertain them? (This affects space and surfaces.)

13 Do you feel that, in general, the overall space in the home is inadequate, or capable of being put to better use if you could only think how?

14 What is the minimum number of rooms you think you need? Can these be found from existing space (such as the attic, basement, or garage)?

15 Is the room in need of total rethinking as well as redecoration? Have family circumstances or interests changed since you first arranged it? Could your present facilities be improved? (To allow for the pace of technological change, you will need maximum flexibility, which affects wiring and lighting.)

16 Where do you and your partner like to sit most, and on what? Do you need different chair backs and seat heights? Where do you both like to work when paying bills, writing letters, etc.?

17 If you are redesigning the bedroom, what kind of bed and mattress do you both prefer? Is bedroom lighting as good as it could be?

part one: the basics

Practicalities

1   What is the state of walls, windows, woodwork, ceiling, and floors?

2   How up-to-date is the wiring? If you need to add any new electric outlets, will they overload the present system or be difficult to install? Does your wiring comply with safety requirements? Is it adequate for your present and future needs (again bearing in mind technological advances)?

3   Are there enough electric outlets in the right places?

4   Would it be an improvement to install long windows or French doors anywhere? (Obviously, they must not look odd or incongruous from the outside.)

5   Are any existing air-conditioning units unsightly, and if so, can they be improved, covered, or even removed from windows and resited in the wall?

6   Do you need to put in burglar, fire, or smoke alarms?

7   Does the existing hardware— such as door handles, light switches, finger plates, window catches, or faucets—need replacing, re-plating, or re-brassing?

8   Can you fit in another bathroom, shower room, or powder room? Do existing fixtures need replacing, or can they be resurfaced? Is everything in good order and likely to last some years without need of repair or replacement?

9   Are there good floorboards under the existing flooring? Can they be scraped and sanded? Do they need repairing or replacing? Would you like a different kind of floor, such as quarry tiles or marble?

1

2

If an answer to any of the previous questions will mean major work— such as rewiring or replumbing; re-flooring or stripping and sanding a floor; repairing damaged walls, ceilings, or floorboards; knocking down walls or adding new ones; changing air-conditioning units or putting in a new window—this obviously must be done before any decoration can be undertaken and should be allowed for in the overall budget.

Aesthetics

1   Is your taste in decorating and furnishing eclectic, traditional, modern, romantic, minimalist, or something else? Does it depend on the style of the house or room?

2   Do you and your partner share similar tastes or have decidedly different ones? Have you agreed to each have your own way in different rooms, or do you have to find some sort of compromise?

3   Do you know what color scheme you want? Are you open to suggestion?

4   What colors are you and your partner happiest with? Are there any colors either of you particularly dislikes?

5   What styles do you admire? What style would you like for this room or house?

6   Is it possible to include existing furniture, if any?

1 *Steel doors and handles make an elegant contrast to the polished wood floor, as well as leading the eye to the piano and bust in the room down the hallway.*

2 *There is a deliberately cool and tranquil air about this hall. The two rugs and the few carefully chosen pieces work harmoniously together and are well lit at night.*

3 *Optimum use of space has been made in this two-level room. A sofa is tucked away against the wall while the tall steel filing cabinet doubles as a side table as well as visually balancing the steps to the book area.*

Budget

1 What is the maximum you can spend on your project, bearing in mind that you should always keep a contingency sum in hand?

2 Are you truly comfortable with this budget? Have you researched current prices for merchandise and services?

3 If you could list the ten luxuries that would make your home seem more attractive to you and/or work better, what would they be?

4 What must be spent? Where can you save? Can you form a long-term plan so that urgent things can be implemented now and others later?

5 Can you make sensible compromises on items that could be recycled to less important rooms if better things can be afforded in the future?

Once you have gone through all these questions a few times, you should have a clearer idea of your ideal home, of

the jobs that most need doing, and of what it will cost. Some of the questions might sound elementary, but in the enthusiasm or the confusion of the moment, with so many things to think about, it is all too easy to forget the most basic elements of a home. Nevertheless, I cannot stress too strongly how important it is to take the time to find out for yourself the essentials that will make a room or home look and work better.

part one: the basics

Floor and lighting plan

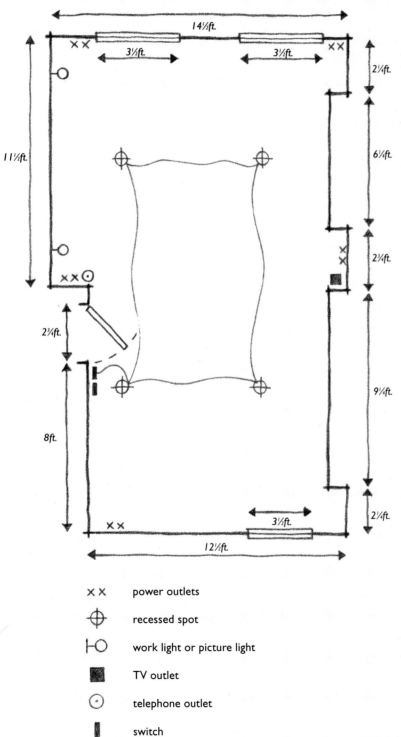

This rough floor and lighting plan is nevertheless drawn accurately to scale. This makes it easier to plan the space, as well as to allow an electrician to see exactly what lights and outlets you want positioned where and what lights (like the central recessed spotlights) you want working from what switch. Such a plan will save much expense later, when far too many people realize, after the decoration has been done, that nothing has been planned for overall lighting and lamps or, for that matter, power outlets and telephone.

FLOOR PLANS

Drawing accurate floor plans is an important part of any designer's work, whether professional or amateur. Quite apart from the usefulness of these floor plans for working out any changes, they are invaluable for deciding on the positions of new electric outlets, lighting, and furniture.

To draw a floor plan, or sketch plan, first make a preliminary plan of the room. Using a well-sharpened pencil, roughly sketch the shape on plain paper, then use a good-sized retractable tape measure to mark the dimensions of the main structural elements on the sketch. These should include the length of walls, the width of doors and other openings, the size of windows and any fixtures, the thickness of partitions, and the distance of fixtures from one another. Also mark

Furniture arrangement plan

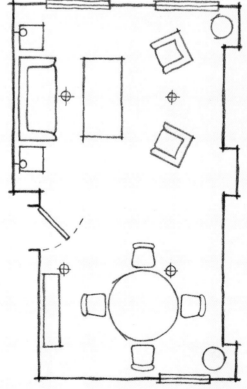

The same accurately scaled plan will also save you from making furnishing mistakes, like impulse-buying pieces of furniture that are too big for the space or will not fit through doors. Lighting has been included again in this plan, to show, for example, how art placed on the walls can be lit by recessed spot-lights in the ceiling and how the small side tables by the sofa can be left uncluttered by table lamps because of the lamps on extend-able brackets fixed to the walls above them.

✕ ✕	power outlets
⊕	recessed spot
⊢○	work light or picture light
■	TV outlet
⊙	telephone outlet
▌	switch

the positions of any outlets including those for television aerials and telephones; radiators, grilles, permanent heating appliances, and air conditioners.

To draw up the plan properly, you will need some graph paper; if possible, choose the kind with invisible perforations, which help you to draw straight lines. If measuring in inches and feet, choose graph paper with the 1-in. squares divided into eighths, and make two of these ⅛-in. squares equal to 1 ft.; a 1-in. square will equal 4 ft. This scale will work for all rooms except kitchens, bathrooms, and utility rooms, for which a scale of twice this size is better. If using metric measurements, choose metric graph paper with the 2-cm. squares divided into tenths, and make one of these 2-mm. squares equal to 10 cm.; a 2-cm. square will equal 1m.

With the sharp pencil, and also a ruler if the graph paper does not have invisible perforations, draw the perimeter of your room to the chosen scale on the graph paper. It is important to do this absolutely accurately.

Erase any door openings, marking their clearance (or swing, when opening) with an arc drawn to scale, then mark in fixtures or odd corners, windows, radiators, electric outlets, television and phone outlets and air conditioners, incorporating the appropriate symbols shown in the key opposite and using the sample plan as a guide.

Make sure that everything is accurate, as the slightest deviation can have disastrous consequences. If you will be taking delivery of large pieces of furniture, make notes of the measurements of windows, door openings, and staircases, especially at any turns, as well as the width, height, and depth of any elevators, to make sure they will fit.

DECORATING SCHEDULES

Another essential aid to decorating is a decorating schedule for each room, which will serve as a reminder of exactly what is to be done. If you are employing any contractors, type up copies for everyone involved so that there can be no misunderstandings or mistakes. Decorating schedules can be prepared at the same time as sample boards and kept with them for daily reference.

Head the paper with the name of the room, and then down the side of the paper write the following headings, leaving enough space between them for clear descriptions:
• Walls
• Floor
• Ceiling
• Woodwork
• Moldings

• Lighting and general wiring (phone and television outlets, doorbell, stereo, etc.)
• Window treatments
• Hardware (switch plates, dimmers, door handles, faucets, shower heads, etc.)
• Bed treatments (if applicable)
An example of a similar decorating schedule, for part of a house rather than just a single room, is shown below. (It includes only five of the above headings, because the other headings are not affected by the redecorating.)

If you prepare a mock decorating schedule for every room in your own home, it will soon become second nature to you–so much so that you will automatically conjure up those headings in your mind when looking at a room to be redesigned. This way, you will never forget to provide for small but essential parts of the room.

SAMPLE BOARDS

The other essential aid to decorating is a sample board for each room. Also known as a color board, this will help to clarify your scheme and act as a blueprint. You will need several sheets of thick posterboard, preferably in a color such as gray, dark blue, green, khaki, or sludgy brown, since white or cream can distort the effect of colors. They should be cut to a size of at least 24 in. (60 cm.) square. A larger size–say, 30 in. (75 cm.) square, or 30 x 36 in. (75 x 90 cm)– might be more useful, but the smaller size is easier to transport.

Gather together small samples of your proposed paint colors, wallpaper, fabric, and flooring. Cutting them out with pinking shears will prevent loose threads and untidy edges, but ordinary scissors can be used. The samples should ideally be large enough to show the designs, but if necessary you can have backup samples to show very large designs and also pattern repeats. You could make the size of each one roughly in proportion to its use in the room, to create a more accurate impression of the final effect, but this is not essential.

Arrange the samples on the board, using paste or double-coated tape to stick them down. With a black pen, caption them clearly, with their name and number, colorway, sources, and price. Print the name of the room at the top of the board.

If you wish, protect the board with a sheet of acetate the same width as the board but a little longer. Wrap it over the board, sticking it down at the back. Another attractive presentation, if you plan to keep your samples permanently, is to make the sample board out of two sheets of posterboard bound together, with windows cut out of the top sheet to frame the samples.

SAMPLE DECORATING SCHEDULE

• All painted surfaces to be properly made good and prepared with primer or undercoat, and two coats of paint, or three where necessary.
• If applying wallpaper, walls to be properly prepared and lined.

HALL

Walls	Latex flat, off-white no. 552
Floor	Blue, wool/nylon blend frise pile carpet
Ceiling	White latex flat paint
Woodwork	White semigloss finish
Moldings	White latex eggshell paint

LIVING ROOM

Walls	Pale terracotta rag-rubbed finish (see sample); undercoat of Gardenia eggshell alkyd paint
Floor	Saxony carpet no. 224
Ceiling	Latex flat white with tinge of terracotta
Woodwork	White satin finish
Moldings	White latex eggshell paint

MASTER BEDROOM

Walls	Wallpaper: no. 9671 col. blue & white
Floor	Axminster carpet no. 66
Ceiling	White latex flat paint
Woodwork	White satin finish
Moldings	White latex eggshell paint

CHILD'S ROOM

Walls	Wallpaper: no. 5890 col. pink-orange-white
Floor	Stripped, varnished floorboards
Ceiling	White latex flat paint
Woodwork	White gloss paint
Moldings	White latex eggshell paint

part one: the basics

SECTION TWO

In the context of this course, the elements of design are the factors that are part and parcel of every room–the aspects that give a room its initial character before the finishing touches are applied. These are lighting, storage, color, texture and pattern, scale and balance. All of these elements, along with styles and specifics like paint, wallpaper, fabrics, and window treatments (dealt with elsewhere in the book), have to be thought about in detail before any decoration can begin.

The Elements of Design

Understanding Light

Good lighting can alter the apparent size of a room, enhance good features or diminish ugly ones. It can add glamor, sparkle, and drama or a warm, comforting glow, at the turn of the appropriate dimmer switch. Lighting is as essential to the success of a room as it is to theater or film, yet it is often the least planned of all decorating elements. How often do people not even bother thinking about the lighting of a room until long after the decoration is underway and it is too late? If only they had considered it before, it might have been possible to install a useful and flexible system for comparatively little expense.

Many people think of artificial light as the counterfeit of daylight and treat them as completely separate issues. However, for an effective lighting system that will provide comfortable light at all times, a balance must be struck between the two types of light, with one discreetly boosting the other whenever necessary.

MAKING THE MOST OF DAYLIGHT

Daylight has, of course, all the advantages of variety. It alters in intensity through the seasons and even from hour to hour. And it changes in color, from the intense blue of clear skies to the dull gray of overcast days; from the clear light of early morning to the lavender glow of dusk; and from the burnished golden light of high summer to the white dazzle cast up by winter snow.

During each phase, the interior of a building will look subtly different (which is why it is useful to see a room in as many lights as possible before deciding on a color scheme and furnishings). Small windows should be left as uncluttered as possible, to make the best of what light there is, while large windows should have blinds, shades, or sheer curtains, which can filter any overabundance of daylight.

Daylight does not, however, have great qualities of penetration. In an average room, about one percent of the available daylight will reach the areas farthest from the windows, compared with as much as ten percent near the windows. That is why, for large periods of the year, demanding visual tasks like working at a computer screen, reading, writing, drawing, painting, or sewing can be done only close to a window.

Many rooms in buildings with a narrow frontage, or in buildings surrounded by other buildings, will have poor lighting at most times of the day. A good many rooms will therefore always need the boost of artificial lighting for some purposes, and in deep buildings, dark central areas that are used as kitchens, bathrooms, and laundry rooms, as well as halls and passageways, will need constant artificial light.

USING ARTIFICIAL LIGHT

Artificial background light used during the day is less depressing if you do not notice the source, so conceal any booster lighting behind valances or cornices over windows, around the perimeter of a room, or behind large pieces of furniture. In other words, try to keep it literally in the background.

Background lighting is just one kind of artificial lighting, which can be divided into three distinct types:

- general or background lighting
- local or task lighting
- accent or decorative lighting

Ideally, every room should be a combination, to a greater or lesser degree, of at least two of these, and they should meld into each other to form a harmonious whole.

1 *The entire window wall in this bedroom has been hung with elegant, thin-slatted Venetian blinds to filter and soften the daylight that would otherwise flood the room.*
2 *Diamond-shaped panes set into this old arched window crisscross and pattern the shafts of sunlight that glance through the glass. The role of artificial light should be to provide just such gentle drama.*

2

part one: the basics

21

TYPES OF LIGHTBULB

The lightbulb (or lamp, as it is somewhat confusingly called by the trade) is just as important a consideration as the type and position of a light fixture. The three main types of bulb used in the home–incandescent, halogen, and fluorescent–vary in their energy efficiency, their average lifetime, and the quality of color they lend to whatever they illuminate.

Incandescent

The incandescent bulb, which has a tungsten filament, is the most common domestic light source. Compared with daylight, incandescent light has a warm, yellowish tone; it is good for interior use because it does not much alter color relationships and it provides good tonal contrast. Tinted incandescent bulbs are also available in a range of colors, with pink the most popular.

Incandescent bulbs come in different sizes, wattages, and designs, to suit different kinds of fixtures. In addition to ordinary bulbs, there are strip lights, spots, globes, candle shapes, and bulbs with silvered backs or crowns to alter the manner in which light is spread. Incandescent bulbs have a relatively short life and they do not make efficient use of electricity, since they generate a lot of heat.

Halogen

This type of bulb is increasingly used in the home, giving a cool, crisp light that is whiter and brighter than incandescent. Like incandescent, halogen is effective at color rendering and at revealing contrasts, but it also has a particularly attractive sparkling

1 Colored lights installed above these archways space, cast a roseate glow onto the ceiling, in warm contrast to the predominantly pale green scheme.
2 Recessed downlights set into the partition wall illuminate the shelf below. Tiny low-voltage spots like these can also be tucked into comparatively small recesses between the ceiling and floor for additional illumination.
3 An elegant sculptural halogen floor lamp creates a dramatic curved light in this minimal living room.

quality, which makes it useful for up-lights, downlights, spots, and accent lighting in general. In a tall, sculptural floor lamp, it gives a great punch of light. A halogen bulb should ideally be used with a dimmer switch, and must never be touched with the bare hands or it will be ruined.

Fluorescent

Because fluorescent light is long-lasting and efficient and therefore less costly to run than incandescent lighting, it is much used in commercial and industrial buildings. It has a bright, even light, and in the past was not very sympathetic for domestic use. Modern fluorescents, however, are improving all the time. Some produce a passable imitation of daylight, and special diffusers are available to make the light quality more sympathetic.

ROOM-BY-ROOM LIGHTING

Every room has different lighting requirements. Here is a brief guide to the best lighting for each.

Living rooms, libraries, and studies

General or background lighting will seem more subtle if it comes from

well-placed downlights (or from wall-washers, track lights, or wall lights, if ceilings are made of concrete or have scant recess space above). Use them either on their own or with floor-standing uplights, which can be concealed behind plants, furniture, or decorative objects like sculpture or urns. This kind of lighting will give a soft wash of light, which is most definitely preferable to the bland and often all-too-harsh light that comes from the still ubiquitous central ceiling fixtures.

If you are going to rewire the room, it is a good idea to have all the portable, plug-in lights on a separate circuit, so that they can be operated from the doorway. This will obviate a lot of switching on and off. If this is impossible, try at least to have kick switches on each uplight, so that

part one: the basics

they can be turned on with a touch. Separate dimming capability is also an advantage.

Local, or task, lighting is provided by table lamps and floor lamps placed alongside sofas and chairs for comfortable reading or, if there is not much floor space, by swing-armed or other adjustable wall lamps set just above seating areas. Desk lamps are used for writing and general work. Very close work might benefit from a strategically positioned recessed downlight in the ceiling.

Accent or decorative lighting often comes from spotlights recessed into the ceiling–surface-mounted on it or mounted on lengths of track or a tensioned cable system–which are angled to highlight paintings, objects, tabletops, and so on. It also comes from pools of light cast by table lamps, concealed lights in bookshelves and cabinets, uplights set in or on floors, and good old-fashioned candles.

Dining rooms and dining areas

These look best, and more romantic, by candlelight, backed up by discreet, maneuverable background light. But candles should be either above or below eye level, so that they do not flicker directly in the diners' eyes.

Supplement the candlelight with a downlight or two, controlled by a dimmer switch. A pendant rise-and-fall light with an opaque shade will cast a pleasant light on the table but, again, should be attached to a dimmer switch and placed so as to avoid uncomfortable dazzle.

The serving area should be lit separately, perhaps by a well-angled spotlight or downlight or by an incandescent (not fluorescent) strip discreetly concealed behind a pelmet on the wall above the serving area.

Halls and staircases

Far too many halls and staircases have hopelessly inadequate lighting. They should be well lit at all times, with light on the floor to show changes in level or surface, and light on the walls to show switches and door handles. The ideal is to have a separate circuit of low-level lights that can be left on at all times, but this is seldom achieved except when starting from scratch. Instead, you could plug in small night-lights to prevent total darkness.

Bedrooms

Bedside lamps should be high enough to shine directly onto a book. The bottom of the light should be in line with your shoulder when you are in a semi-reclining position, and the lower edge of the shade at eye level. Wall lamps on brackets are excellent: not only is the light in the right position, but they save space on bedside tables. They are also useful for beds with side curtains. Bedside lamps should be on a dimmer switch, to obviate glare as well as being kinder to a sleeping partner.

Light above a mirror used for makeup is, contrary to custom, less helpful than light placed at either side. Also, lights that are positioned to shine outward are better than those that shine on the mirror itself. The same applies to full-length mirrors, where the light should be directed onto the viewer rather than onto the glass.

2

1 *Lights placed at either side of a bathroom mirror give better lighting for applying makeup, as here. However, if the mirror is used only for shaving, a light above the mirror, or small lights recessed into the glass, might be preferable.*

2 *Downlights illuminate stair treads in addition to lighting up the display niches around this sculptural staircase.*

3 *Lights set on top of cabinets, as well as underneath them, illuminate both ceiling and work surface in this well-planned kitchen, its spare lines softened by trailing plants.*

Children's rooms

In the rooms of small children, all wall outlets should be childproof and all light fixtures well out of reach, which means that table and floor lamps cannot be included. Wall lights are good, as they will give a softer light than ceiling fixtures. For children who are afraid of the dark, dimmer switches are useful, as the light can be turned down to a low level; alternatives are the very low-wattage night-lights designed to just cut the darkness. Older children need good light for homework, computer work, hobbies, and reading in bed, so adequate lighting should be provided on work tables and above beds.

Bathrooms

Small bathrooms may need only one ceiling light, and preferably that should be recessed. In a larger bathroom, a couple of downlights are preferable, with one of them set over the bath, or shower in a waterproof fixture. If a mirror is used for both makeup and shaving, lights should be fixed on each side, but if it is to be used only for shaving, a light should be positioned just above the mirror. An alternative is to recess small custom-made lights right into the glass.

Kitchens

All kitchens should have good overall light, plus booster light for any precise activity like reading cookbooks, chopping, mixing, assembling ingredients, and rinsing or washing dishes. Well-placed general diffusing lights fixed flush to the ceiling, inset spots, or a mixture of downlights and angled spots produce a good background light. Supplement this with striplights concealed under high-level cabinets to shine down on the work surface. Any fluorescent lights should be deluxe warm white, or any new variety that is geared to making food look more appetizing (and complexions more attractive) than earlier fluorescent versions did. Try also to light inside storage closets.

part one: the basics

25

canister on the mantelpiece, or use a directional spot aimed from below. Uplighting the painting in any of these ways will prevent reflection in picture glass or the glossy surface of an oil painting.

If you use a conventional picture light mounted on a frame to light the picture from above, it should have a rotating, or adjustable, reflector. If the frame is thick, the picture light will need to be adjustable from the wall.

For wall hangings fixed near floor level, floor sculpture, or plants, use uplights or small adjustable floor spots, concealed behind the plants, in corners or next to the objects to be lit. These will bounce light up or graze the object with light. Again, for convenience, try to get such lights switched from the door.

FLOOR AND TABLE LAMPS

People are often beguiled by the look of a floor or table lamp into purchasing it without thinking much about what the lamp achieves in the way of light output. A lamp should be

LIGHTING ART

For a whole wall of pictures, prints, wall hangings, or other art, the ideal is to use recessed wall-washers set into the ceiling about 2 ft. (60 cm.) from the wall. They will literally bathe the surface with light. If this is difficult, use a surface-mounted strip such as Plugmold, which can be bought in any length with any number of sockets on which to attach lights, or use track or a tensioned cable system. These make it possible either to light individual paintings or to wash a whole wall with light, depending on the desired effect.

The best spotlights for illuminating individual paintings and objects are framing projectors—also known as profile spots or pinhole projectors. They are extremely

expensive but worth it for serious paintings. When their lenses and shutters are adjusted accurately, they will focus exactly on an object, painting or sculpture, with no overspill of light. Framing projectors should be recessed into the ceiling 36-42 in. (90-105 cm.) from the wall. Alternatively, use surface-mounted fittings in conjunction with a track or mounted individually on a ceiling or beam.

Low-voltage halogen fixtures give an excellent light. If it is difficult to install recessed lighting or surface-mounted lights and you want to illuminate a painting over a mantelpiece, uplight it from low-voltage halogen spots, which are very small and portable. Alternatively, conceal a halogen light in a vase or small

1 *In a series of display shelves, an adjustable spotlight is set right into one of the niches to highlight a photograph. Small downlights can also be recessed into shelves to shine down on objects, or uplights can be recessed to do the opposite.*
2 *A judiciously placed lamp shines down on the objects on this table, as well as highlighting the handsome marble top.*
3 *An adjustable floor lamp set between a sofa and a pair of chairs can be swung either way for easy reading. It could also, of course, be angled upward to shine on the painting. This type of floor lamp is nicely versatile.*

as functional as it is good-looking, providing generous light for tasks and reading, as well as adding a comfortable feeling to a room.

Another area in which many people go wrong is the height and position of lamps. A good rule of thumb for table lamps is that the lower edge of the shade should be at eye level when someone is seated on an easy chair: that is, about 38-42 in. (97-107 cm.) from the floor.

Floor lamps should be 40-49 in. (102-123 cm.) from the lower edge of the shade to the floor. For reading, the lamp should be placed behind the reader's shoulder. This obviously is not possible when a chair or sofa is against a wall, so in this situation use adjustable floor lamps. Wall lamps on extendable brackets are also handy for

reading in small rooms where the seating is close to the walls and in rooms where a pair of lamps is wanted and end tables are of unequal height.

In a table lamp for reading, use a soft white-pink bulb of at least 150 watts, and in a floor lamp a soft white bulb of 150–200 watts. (Ensure they do

not exceed the shades' maximum recommended wattages.) Fit a tabletop dimmer, or one that fits onto the socket, to vary a lamp's level of light.

part one: the basics

Vocabulary of Lighting Terms

Three small vases on the shelf of a recess are lit so well, as is the picture above, that they stand out three-dimensionally to quite dramatic effect.

Accent lighting: Used to highlight color, form, and texture in objects and art, accent lighting is a key element in any kind of creative lighting design. It can range from a narrow beam to a broad SPOTLIGHT or WALL-WASHER.

Ambient lighting: General or background lighting that is unfocused, indirect, and, hopefully, unobtrusive.

Amp: An abbreviation of ampere, the base unit of electrical current, measuring the speed at which it flows.

Baffle: The device attached to a light fixture to lessen or prevent glare. Baffles on DOWNLIGHTS and SPOTLIGHTS are usually formed with concentric black grooves on the inside of the cowl.

Ballast: A part used in the control apparatus of a discharge lamp or bulb to control the flow of current and so prevent overheating.

Barn doors: The adjustable hinged flaps attached to the front of some SPOTLIGHTS to control the shape of the BEAM.

Bayonet bulb: A type of INCANDESCENT BULB, found in Europe, which has two lugs to attach it to its holder (as opposed to a screw bulb).

Beam: The spread of light from a FLOODLIGHT, SPOTLIGHT, or REFLECTOR BULB.

Cable: A covered or sheathed bundle of insulated wires used to carry electrical circuits around the home.

Candela: The SI unit of light intensity.

Cable system: A pair of tensioned CABLES that support LOW-VOLTAGE, tiny TRACK LIGHTS which can be moved along the length of the cables.

Ceiling rosette: Normally, a circular housing that projects from the ceiling and holds the connection between a PENDANT light fixture or a chandelier and the electricity supply.

Circuit: The path of an electric current which passes along the supply CABLES to light fixtures and electric outlets.

Circuit breaker: A special switch in an electrical consumer unit that carries out the same function as a fuse. In other words, under abnormal or potentially dangerous situations, it will cut off the current flow of the CIRCUIT.

Color rendering: The effect of a light source on the appearance of a colored surface, normally judged by comparison with its appearance by daylight. Some bulbs are given a Color Rendering Index rating (CRI) between 1 and 100. The higher the number, the truer the colors.

Contrast: In lighting terms, this is the difference in brightness between two points of a visual field—that is to say, the area that can be seen in front of us when our heads and eyes are still.

Cool beam bulb: A type of PAR BULB that reflects visible light but transmits infrared radiation so that the heat of the BEAM it transmits is greatly reduced.

Diffused light: Light that is filtered through a translucent material like a fabric shade.

Diffuser: Some sort of translucent screen used to shield a light source, soften it, and distribute light evenly.

Dimmer switch: A control switch that allows the lighting levels of bulbs to be lowered or raised. Most lights benefit from this sort of control.

Direct lighting: Lighting provided directly from a light fixture without bouncing off surfaces like ceilings or walls.

Directional lighting: Lighting designed to illuminate a surface or a task from a particular direction. This is generally provided by SPOTLIGHTS or desk lights, which are normally adjustable.

Discharge bulb: A bulb whose light is produced by an electric discharge through a gas, a metal vapor or a mixture of gas and vapor.

Downlight: A fitting that is usually ceiling-recessed, ceiling-mounted, track-mounted or wall-mounted and that throws light vertically (or at least steeply) downwards. It may be either TUNGSTEN or HALOGEN.

Eyeball spot or downlight: An adjustable recessed SPOTLIGHT that looks somewhat like an eyeball.

Filament: A thin, usually tungsten, wire in an INCANDESCENT BULB that emits light when it is heated to incandescence by an electric current.

Flexi-arm: An adjustable arm on a lamp, usually consisting of metal links, which can be used to position the light at a variety of angles.

Floodlight: A spotlight containing an incandescent REFLECTOR BULB to produce a powerful, wide BEAM.

Fluorescent bulb: A kind of DISCHARGE BULB in which the light is produced by the excitation of fluorescent phosphors by ultraviolet radiation. More energy-efficient than an INCANDESCENT BULB or a HALOGEN BULB, it is much cheaper to run and lasts longer. It now gives a wide variation of color rendition, although in the past it had too harsh a white light for most domestic situations.

Framing projector: Also known as a profile spot or pinhole projector, this is a spotlight designed to illuminate a painting, sculpture, or other work of art. Its attachments allow absolutely precise control over the shape and focus of the BEAM. Though expensive, it is the best and most accurate way to light art.

Glare: The discomfort and interference with vision that arise when some parts of the visual field are much brighter than their surroundings.

Ground: A necessary connection between an electrical CIRCUIT and the earth. Its purpose is to conduct electricity out of harm's way if there is a fault in the wiring, such as a break in a circuit cable or insulation, which would otherwise make a light fixture or an appliance casing become lethally live.

Halogen bulb: A special type of bulb containing a tungsten filament surrounded by halogen gas, which extends the bulb's life. Also known as a quartz halogen or tungsten halogen bulb, it gives a brighter, whiter punch of light than an ordinary incandescent bulb of the equivalent wattage.

HID bulb: A high-intensity DISCHARGE BULB, used for outside lighting.

Incandescent bulb: Term normally applied to the ordinary domestic lightbulb. It contains a tungsten filament (hence its British name, "TUNGSTEN BULB") which, when electrified, produces heat and light. This was the original lightbulb, invented by Thomas Edison. Technically, a HALOGEN BULB is also incandescent, as it contains a filament, as well as halogen gas.

Indirect lighting: Lighting reflected off a ceiling or walls.

ISL bulb: An internally silvered lamp, usually known as a REFLECTOR BULB.

Kick switch: A highly sensitive switch installed in the base of some modern light fixtures, which permits them to be switched on with merely a touch.

Lamp: The trade term for lightbulb.

Lenses: Accessories that can be used on fixtures to achieve different lighting effects. For example, a frosted lens produces a more even wash of light.

Low voltage: A low-voltage bulb is an excellent choice for lighting art and accenting objects, but it must be used in conjunction with a transformer. Available as either INCANDESCENT or HALOGEN BULBS.

Lumen: The SI unit of luminous flux, which means the amount of light given off by a source or received by a surface.

Luminaire: The trade term for a light fitting – the housing designed for a bulb and bulb holder to protect the light source, to provide a means of connection to the electrical supply, and to direct and control the flow of light.

Lux: Lumens measured by the square yard or metre. The SI unit of illuminance, which is a measure of the light leaving a surface in a particular direction.

Neon bulb: A bulb containing neon, an inert gas, at low pressure which throws off a red or pink glow when VOLTAGE is applied.

Opal finish: An internal coating of silica on the glass exterior of a bulb which gives it a milky or opalescent appearance.

Overspill: See SPILL LIGHT.

PAR bulb: A Parabolic Aluminized Reflector is a sealed beamed bulb with a front of tough, heat-resistant glass. The back of the bulb is parabolic in cross-section, and the bulb is internally aluminized to throw off a powerful BEAM of light. Especially useful outdoors, as it needs no protection from the weather.

Pendant: A light fixture designed to hang from, or project from, a ceiling.

Phosphor: A substance that can emit visible light when bombarded with electromagnetic radiation. It is used for the inner coating of FLUORESCENT BULBS.

Quartz halogen bulb: Alternative name for a halogen bulb.

Reflector bulb: A bulb with an internally silvered surface, used for SPOTLIGHTS or FLOODLIGHTS.

SI: Système Internationale d'Unités, an internationally agreed system of scientific measuring units.

Side-lighting: The technique of lighting from one side, usually to emphasize the modeling or texture of an object.

SON bulb: A trade name for a high-pressure sodium bulb.

Spill light: Light that spills over from the main profile of a BEAM, as in the light that seeps outside a painting lit by a SPOTLIGHT or WALLWASHER. A FRAMING PROJECTOR can be set to light a painting exactly, so that there is no overspill.

Spotlight: A REFLECTOR BULB with a directional beam, used for accent or decorative lighting. It may be surface- or track-mounted on wall, ceiling, or floor.

Swing arm: A style of lamp featuring a jointed bracket, which can be adjusted to reposition the light source.

Task lighting: Lighting specifically used for facilitating a task like reading, writing, painting, or sewing.

Throw: The distance between a REFLECTOR BULB and the farthest object it can light.

Track lighting: Straight or curved track that can be mounted on the ceiling or walls and supports SPOTLIGHTS, which are either fixed in position (but can be angled and swiveled) or free, allowing them to be moved along the track. Both fixed and free types can be main-supply or LOW-VOLTAGE.

Transformer: A device to transfer electric current from one CIRCUIT to another, usually with an increase or decrease in VOLTAGE. It is essential to the installation of any LOW-VOLTAGE bulb but is usually small enough to be hidden in the fixture.

Tungsten bulb: British term for an INCANDESCENT BULB, named for the tungsten filament that such a bulb normally contains.

UL: Underwriters' Laboratories. This independent laboratory tests appliances to make sure that they meet certain safety requirements, and a stamp indicating its approval should be attached to any light fixture you buy. The UL stamp will also indicate whether or not the fixture is suitable for wet or damp locations.

Uplight: A light fixture that throws light up to be reflected back from the ceiling or walls. Floor uplights are extremely useful for backlighting both objects and plants and for providing indirect light when you cannot install recessed lighting. Uplighting can also be provided by floor

and wall light fixtures and by directional table lamps.

Visual acuity: The ability to distinguish fine detail when concentrating on a task.

Voltage: The pressure of electricity flowing through an electrical CIRCUIT—the greater the pressure, the higher the number of volts. Main-supply voltage varies from country to country; in the United States it is 120 volts; in Britain it is 240; and on the Continent it is 220. For LOW-VOLTAGE lighting, a TRANSFORMER reduces the power, usually to 12 volts.

Wallwasher: A DOWNLIGHT that bathes the wall in light. It is usually mounted on the ceiling (on track, on the surface, or recessed), 18-36 in. (45-90 cm.) from the wall, depending on the desired finished effect.

Lit from within, boxes made from Lucite (a thick, clear plastic) provide dramatic display areas as well as punctuating the space with arresting cubes of light. A directional low-voltage downlight highlights the painting on the far wall.

Watt: A unit measuring the rate at which electricity is consumed and indicating the power of the light source. Every light fixture you buy should specify a maximum wattage.

part one: the basics

Maximizing Storage

There are three unassailable facts about storage: you can never have enough of it; more space should be allowed for the purpose than you could possibly imagine; and any kind of storage should be as much in keeping with the basic feeling, style, and proportions of a room as is viable.

PLANNING AHEAD

Most American homes are amply supplied with closets, which will accommodate not only clothes and accessories but all kinds of miscellaneous items, from suitcases to vacuum cleaners. Over the years, however, most people find that their possessions outstrip their closet space and that they must buy, build, or improvise additional storage space to prevent

1 *When storage requirements outstrip available closet space, a movable rack and some canvas storage bags can provide a temporary solution. This particular arrangement has a certain raffish charm which complements the striped futon.*

2 *Sliding doors resembling shoji screens conceal a variety of belongings in a neat and airy way. This is an excellent idea for dedicated minimalists determined to hide their possessions as aesthetically as possible.*

their home from looking like a garage sale. Before things reach this point, it is a good idea to plan for your future storage needs. Even if you do not wish to pay for extra storage now, you should at least think where you would like to put it later on and have an idea of how much it would cost. If you intend to move in the future, you need to decide whether you will take with you any storage that you buy now and then to choose accordingly.

For anyone who intends to start a family, planning ahead means thinking where you would keep a portable crib, toys, and all the other things you will need. Determine how best to use the space you have and how much extra storage you can squeeze in—your foresight and organization will save you a great deal of irritation and time later on. If you already have a young family, cast your mind forward to imagine all the bicycles, skis, and other sports equipment, CDs, videos, books, files, clothing, luggage, linens, and quilts the children will accumulate.

If your children have grown up and you thought you had left all the detritus of a young family behind you, don't forget grandchildren (or incipient grandchildren). You may need to accommodate some apparatus for when they visit you, especially if you have moved to a smaller home.

ASSESSING YOUR NEEDS

The best plan is to analyze your storage needs room by room, to see not only how best to meet them but also how to fit in the storage as aesthetically as possible. Clear your mind by asking yourself these questions:

1 Do you like traditional storage behind closed doors in cupboards and in chests of drawers, desks, and bookcases? If you possess this kind of storage already, can the interiors be improved or better organized? If you do not have it, can it be built in fairly easily and affordably? Do you have any recesses, corners, or old fireplaces that could be annexed for storage?

2 Would it make sense to convert a closet-less room or den to a bedroom—to give children more privacy, for example? If so, could you make do with purchased storage units, such as a shelving system or an armoire; or would it be worthwhile to have a closet specially built?

3 Have you considered a storage wall or entertainment units, or both, in your living room, to hold books, files, papers, computer, television, video recorder, music system, tapes, CDs, and so on? How many of these storage units will have to be bought, and how many can be improvised? (For suggestions for improvised storage, see pages 39–41.)

APPROPRIATE STORAGE

It is important that new storage does not look out of place. Before you choose it, take a hard look at the room, noticing proportions and architectural details particularly.

Bedrooms

In an old building, bedrooms with high ceilings and good-looking moldings might be best served with old free-standing armoires. Big pieces, often beautifully fitted inside, or capable of being specially fitted, can often be bought gratifyingly cheaply nowadays, since so few people have the space for them. Be sure to check the depth, however: many old pieces are too shallow for clothing to be hung in the conventional way. Ideally, they should be at least 24 in. (60 cm.) deep.

If you decide that you want built-in storage in a room that has fine proportions and moldings, you must first determine where it can be sited without spoiling the harmony of the space. Make sure that any storage that takes up a whole wall will not make the room seem too narrow for its height. If the bedroom has a fireplace with natural recesses on either side, the storage could perhaps be fitted in the recesses. One way of building in a lot of cabinets without losing a sense of perspective or depth is to fit them around doors or windows (see page 35 for more about this).

You will almost certainly need to spend money on an excellent carpenter, who should continue the same moldings and baseboards around the newly built pieces. It is of prime

importance to avoid an unsightly gap between the top of shelving systems and the ceiling in such a room, unless your carpenter builds a pediment or you can place objects on top.

Instead of investing in custom-built storage, you could buy ready-made unfinished-wood units. Have them fitted by a carpenter, who could then add moldings if necessary, to help them blend in. If you want to disguise them altogether, get flush doors with magnetic catches and either paint them or wrap any wallpaper or fabric around the doors,

1 Maximum storage advantage has been taken of the capacious bed platform in this splendidly spacious bedroom. Sliding-door closets above are balanced by deep drawers below. They are offset by bookshelves and recessed shelves in the room to display a diverse collection of objects.

2 This old chest of many drawers stores an enormous number of odds and ends as well as hosting a generous washbasin.

part one: the basics

the closets and install lighting underneath the cabinets. This creates a sleeping recess and will provide a practical function as well as giving a sense of perspective and depth.

If you have a large bedroom with only a small closet, you could perhaps cut a chunk out of it to create a walk-in closet or dressing room. Or you may be able to do this by slivering off extra space from a less valuable room or corridor adjacent to the bedroom. Another way to provide extra storage space is to build a half-height partition at one end of a bedroom, then add a cabinet on one side for storage and use the other as a headboard. With any of these ideas, the baseboard, and any other detailing should, of course, match the rest of the room.

In a room where you do not need to pay attention to architectural detail, you could create storage space by building a bed on top of a platform of low cabinets. When a bedroom is small or awkwardly shaped, however, the best option might be to fit cabinets just outside the door in a corridor or on a landing, in order to leave more space in the room itself. Another way to avoid cluttering up a room is to incorporate a dressing table into a wall of cabinets.

Living rooms and dens

Much the same rules apply to living rooms and dens as to bedrooms, especially where the rooms are handsomely detailed–if you want built-in storage, it is important that it not ruin the room's proportions and that the detailing match. For recesses on either side of a fireplace, you might find

1 *Interesting doors in this bedroom conceal closet space as well as the bathroom beyond. The top of the closets serve as a good spot for a collection of wicker baskets used for storing smaller objects.*

making sure they will still close. To prevent the paper from tearing or the fabric from fraying, you could install "reeding" (a thin piece of molding) around the edges of the doors. If the doors are paneled, they could be linked to the rest of the room with paint, paper, fabric, or trim. To make the units seem more like pieces of furniture, you could ask a paint specialist to "grain" them in a wood

finish. It is amazing how handsome and realistic graining can look if done by skilled hands.

A good way of providing storage in a bedroom without robbing it of a sense of space is to build closets on either side of a bed and a row of cabinets running over the top of the bed to join the two. If there is no space for bedside tables with this arrangement, build in shelves at the sides of

2

3

a deeper shelf with cabinets underneath for storage. Depending upon the size of the wall and the style of the room, the shelves could either have the cornice running in front, as in the rest of the room, or have a pediment, maybe with a light behind to cast a mellow glow at night.

If you want to create the look of wall-to-wall bookshelves, positioning the uprights for the bookshelves on either side of the windows and doors will make these openings look recessed and the shelving seem an integral part of the walls.

In a narrow room, glass shelves with uplights or downlights, or both, will add sparkle and take up little visual space. You can also set glass or wooden shelves across windows, to create more shelving for display and save the cost of a window treatment.

You may wish to consider a storage wall, or entertainment units built around the television screen. Remember that if you want to incorporate in the wall unit various appliances such as a television, computer, video recorder, music system, or perhaps even a small refrigerator and miniature sink unit for making drinks, you will need to ensure that they fit flush with the rest of the units. More expensive versions will incorporate most of these items anyway, or will at least specify what appliances, or other equipment will fit. The wall will have to be wired to provide power for these devices before the installation takes place.

In a living room that is really short on space, look to the windows: you may be able to provide extra seating and storage, as well as improving the look of the windows. Place uprights that are 18-24 in. (45-60 cm.) deep on either side of a window. If there are two or three windows on one wall, so much the better. Suspend a hinged seat between each pair of uprights, and

2 Glass-fronted drawers look elegantly airy but require disciplined tidiness. The empty frame set among the pictures on top of the chest echoes the serried panes of glass below.

3 Rows of numbered pockets set into this practical curtain provide a place for special toys and objects in a child's room, as well as looking both educational and decorative. Such inexpensive storage solutions are enormously useful for children's rooms. Similar holdalls are also handy for the backs of closet doors and in the kitchen, utility room or mudroom, and bathroom.

very tall old bookcases that will fit in well. These recesses are also natural places to build breakfront bookcases, as are the walls on either side of windows. Each bookcase can have a deeper shelf at waist height with cabinets underneath. If the shelf is deep enough and tall enough, it can take a television on a turntable, a video recorder, and a music system. The top of the bookcase can have a pediment or be finished off with the same molding or cornice as the rest of the room.

Alternatively, a large bookcase could be purchased for a long wall, or you could build in shelves running the length of the wall, again incorporating

build a cabinet underneath. Put tailored seat cushions on top of this lift-up window seat, and add scatter cushions. On the other side of each upright, build tall, shallow cabinets.

Children's rooms

Children's storage needs, for both clothing and equipment, seem to grow as fast as the children do, so you may well find that existing closet space is inadequate. Any additional storage should be full-size, but with rods positioned low enough for the child to reach it; later, the rod can be moved up to accommodate the growing child.

part one: the basics

Deep drawers under beds or bunks are useful, and there may also be room for a chest of drawers in the bedroom. My stock solution for inexpensive extra storage for the bedroom of any child–and for a master bedroom or a home office–is to buy two or three unfinished-wood chests of drawers, or a mixture of chests of drawers and low cabinets. Set them a kneehole apart, and top them with a long laminated top, to serve first as a play area and later as a desk. The units can be stained or painted.

Fragile toys and games are best kept on deep shelves behind closed doors or in deep drawers, so that toddlers cannot easily pull them out and dump them on the floor. Store sturdier toys in big boxes or chests for easy access. Keep inexpensive or robust books on windowsills and on low shelves within reach, but set more precious books on higher shelves which small hands cannot reach.

Kitchens

Keen cooks will want everything they use frequently to be within grabbing distance. Wooden spoons, spatulas,

1 *Storage doubles as decoration here with the curved shelves holding a miscellany of storage jars and scales, balanced by the herb box fixed below. Note how serving spoons, spatulas, and even a good old-fashioned meat grinder are clamped or otherwise attached to shelves and wooden brackets. The three striped eggcups and Thermos on the surface below make a nice counterpoint to the various strong stripes set above.*

2 *Simple dowels hold a series of glass goblets from their bases, at the same time forming an airily decorative frieze against the wall.*
3 *A practical wooden rack for storing dishes is fitted above the sink in a tiled recess of this well-planned kitchen.*
4 *A series of rods set above a long window behind the sink supports a batterie de cuisine as well as decorative bunches of drying herbs.*

slotted spoons, and similar tools can be kept in earthenware pots or pitchers. Saucepans can hang from an overhead rack or rod or be stacked on shelves within easy reach of the stove, their lids slipped into wooden or steel racks. Measuring cups and spoons, sieves, and colanders can hang from racks, from hooks on Peg-Board or from hooks fixed to the underside of wall units. Chopping boards must be near to hand, as should sharp knives, which can be stored in a wooden knife block.

Less dedicated cooks, however, will probably want all kitchen paraphernalia behind closed doors. There is an enormous choice of storage to suit all spaces and all budgets. Once again, unfinished-wood cabinets are a viable option, as they are inexpensive and can be stained, painted, or lacquered to match any decor.

Storage for a kitchen/dining room depends on whether the style of the room veers toward the rustic or the fairly sophisticated. For the rustic look, there are still all sorts of handsome old dressers to be found, rescued, and rehabilitated. These will usually hold and display a great deal. For a more sophisticated look, the whole area could be fitted with wall-to-wall, floor-to-ceiling cabinets.

Dining rooms
If you have a dedicated dining room, you will need practical, but attractive storage for glasses, china, linen, utensils, and possibly wine bottles, as well as after-dinner drinks, and probably some sort of display unit or units. The traditional sideboard, or its equivalent, can easily provide much of this, as can shelving units with cabinets and drawers underneath, depending upon the style of the room.

If, however, the dining room doubles as a library, study or home office, playroom, or guest room, then imaginative dual storage is clearly the answer. Screens, I find, are a good solution for such rooms. Not only do they look

- Make a desk by securing an unpaneled door to two, or even three or four, filing cabinets, leaving one or two kneeholes.
- If you do not want actual filing cabinets, use the innards in a window seat, or old trunk or chest, to hold suspension files.
- Neat wooden file frames on wheels can be pushed under tables or desks or into closets; and rattan boxes or plastic, lattice-sided crates, which also hold suspension files, can be stacked in closets, under tables, or even under beds.

For a home office in a bedroom, a drop-front desk is useful, since you can use the drawers partly for clothes, partly for papers and files, and then hide away any untidy paperwork when you close up the desk. There are also all kinds of cunning desktops and work surfaces that pull or slide out from wall units, as well as doors that fold down to reveal computer systems; when they are closed, the walls seem paneled. In this way, you can go from the functional to the serene in mere minutes.

decorative, but if they are sturdy enough they can have pegs or hooks at the back for clothes, should the room be used for occasional guests. Exercise equipment, luggage, baskets of toys, and all manner of other items can also be hidden behind them.

Studies and home offices

Since many home offices are part of another room, rather than entities in themselves, much of the storage has to be disguised. The chief problem is undoubtedly filing cabinets. They can at least be painted to fit in with the

I *Desk, file drawers, computer, and a hamper for files or papers are all tucked nicely below the stairs, turning an unused corner of a living room into a pleasant home-office area. The space under stairs is invariably useful, either for general storage, perhaps with doors, or for a desk or table.*

general surroundings (I have even had them painted to look like copper) and can be made to look decorative, with designs and patterns. There are also a number of ways to hide them:

- Conceal the filing cabinet under a skirt (see page 40).
- If you are building bookshelves with cabinets underneath, make sure the cabinets are tall enough and deep enough to take filing cabinets on small wheels or tracks.
- With the help of a good handyman or carpenter, adapt ready-made units to incorporate filing cabinets.

Bathrooms

Vanity units provide useful storage space underneath the basin and sometimes come with drawers down the side also. Or you can have them made to your own specification.

Bathroom cabinets of various sizes and degrees of grandeur are widely available, or you could fix shelves across any useful recess and then add a door with a mirror on it.

Glass shelves across a window will provide decorative storage as well as a degree of privacy.

IMPROVISING STORAGE

With a little thought, it's possible to improvise storage solutions that are as effective and good-looking as more expensive systems.

Baskets

Baskets in various shapes and sizes are useful for any number of small, and not so small, items. In one client's living room, where space was at a premium, I fitted glass shelves lit by uplights—the shelves were used for storing books, and large-handled baskets underneath them held mixer beverages and other bottles.

- Shallow, square, round or rectangular baskets are excellent for magazines and catalogs.
- Shallow, rectangular ones are good on large desks or work tables, or under side tables for work papers and files; on a hall table for hats, gloves, sunglasses, or letters; and on a kitchen worktop for a surfeit of spice and herb jars.
- Use laundry baskets to store anything from blankets, linens, or winter clothes to children's toys or cleaning materials.
- Deep, round baskets can be hung from pegs or hooks in a country-style bathroom to hold neatly rolled towels.

2 *Elegant shoe storage in this dressing room-cum-bathroom with its stylish glass basin, is nicely offset by a series of baskets filled with hair dryers, odds and ends such as brushes, small electrical appliances, and other grooming supplies.*

part one: the basics

Hooks and racks

Many people forget that the backs of doors can be used for storage. I always fix one or two double hooks to the backs of bedroom and bathroom doors on which to hang bathrobes, night-clothes, and items just back from the dry cleaner, as well as garment bags when packing or unpacking.

- In a small room or a vacation home, rows of large hooks on wooden or plastic boards, fixed high on a wall, can be amazingly handy for clothes storage when existing closet space is inadequate.
- Movable coatracks are also useful for clothes storage, especially in vacation homes and in halls and corridors.
- Small cup hooks can be fixed to the edges of shelves and to the underneath of wall-mounted cabinets to hold cups and small jugs, thereby freeing up space in cabinets for something else.
- Hooks on a Peg-Board are good for hanging up not just kitchen utensils (see page 37) but also home-office paraphernalia.
- Very large hooks can be used for suspending folding chairs.

Skirted tables

There is almost always space in a room for one or two skirted tables, which can hide any number of things. They do not, of course, have to be round. Rectangular tables covered in fabric, rugs, or throws look good as side tables, too, and hold more underneath.

- Use them in bedrooms to conceal electric fans, baskets of clutter, and even small pieces of exercise equipment such as weights.

- Fit a divided skirt to a table with a platform underneath, to hide the television. In order to see the screen, part the two sides of the skirt and hook them up.
- Conceal firewood under a skirted table in the living room.
- Hide a filing cabinet under one. If you want the table to be round, place a circular piece of MDF (medium-density fiberboard) on top, under the skirt.
- Stash luggage or other bulky objects underneath a large skirted table.

Shelves

Obviously shelves of different sizes are prime storage areas for almost anything, but there are a lot of places to put shelves that people do not think about.

- The space above doors is one good area. Depending on which room the door is in, use the shelf for display, books, or storage baskets.
- Run a shelf 6-12 in. (15-30 cm.) below the ceiling, all around the perimeter of a room. This was often done in the late nineteenth and early twentieth centuries to show off plates, trophies, and collections.
- Mount shelves or racks on the backs of closet or pantry doors to hold all manner of things. It is advisable for the shelves to have lips in order to prevent things from sliding off when the door is in motion; or mount wire basket shelves. Do the same on the backs of broom closet doors to hold polishes, dustcloths and general cleaning paraphernalia.
- Use wire shelves on the backs of closet doors to hold handbags, scarves, and other small, light items.

- Mount miniature shelves on the backs of kitchen-cabinet doors to hold jars of spices, herbs, and condiments and small packages.
- Make your own corner cabinet by fixing shelves across a corner, with or without a cabinet section underneath.

Under the bed

Do not underestimate what you can fit under a bed. In fact, if you are prepared to raise it a little higher than normal, you can store luggage, skis and other sports equipment, baskets, file boxes, blanket chests or out-of-season clothes. Beds can be bought with fitted drawers underneath, but if you do not have them already, you can get them made – say, one or two for each side of a large bed, so that you do not have to be perpetually crawling around to drag things out from the middle. Alternatively, simply buy a couple of large, shallow plastic boxes that are designed to slide underneath.

Under the stairs

Under-stair storage has always been practical and, if well organized, can be used for any number of purposes.

- Put a desktop mounted on filing cabinets there, with a chair on wheels to push under the desktop, and then build shelves all around the walls.
- If the temperature is fairly constant, use this space for wine storage. It is possible to buy wine racks specially designed to fit under the stairs, but any type could be adapted.
- Buy, build, or adapt a honeycomb of storage boxes to fit the space.

- Build bookshelves into the space, with or without some cabinets underneath.
- Turn it into a cupboard with shelf and hanging space, or just shelves, with doors to shut it all away.

If you are fortunate enough to have a wide flight of steps going up to an attic, or down to a basement, you can use one side of the steps to stash baskets or plastic crates, clearly labeled with their contents so that you do not have to keep searching through every container to find what you want. These are excellent places to keep office supplies, extra stationery, spare paper goods (paper towels, toilet paper, tissues, paper napkins, paper plates for parties), tool boxes, and any supplies you have bought in bulk.

Using fabric

Since draperies, curtains, and shades take up less space than doors, and certainly look less solid, they can be suspended across alcoves to create good clothes storage. Use them to conceal a movable clothes rack, a hanging rod, or shelves full of shoes.

An ingenious alternative to an armoire is the kind of freestanding tent wardrobe often seen at beaches. One of these, placed in a corner or alcove, would make a decorative storage solution.

I once saw a guest bed that was built on a platform under a window on a landing. Privacy was created by curtains across the window and draperies on the other side of the bed, both of which could be looped back or left loose. The bed had drawers underneath, and the walls at either end of the bed were mounted with shelves.

2

1 *Good-looking triangular plate-glass shelves are fitted neatly into a corner to provide a generous display area with barely any loss of space in the room. Such shelves could be lit from recessed downlights above, and some sort of uplight below, to provide maximum dramatic effect and sparkle–always a plus in any space.*

2 *Draperies hanging from a valance turn an alcove fitted with a bank of shelves into an attractive storage area. The draperies match those at the window in this small bedroom. An equally effective storage area could be created by suspending a drapery rod across a corner.*

part one: the basics

Using Color

Color is to rooms what light is to day–and is both the most noticeable and the most malleable element in decorating. Different combinations of color can make the same room and the same furnishings seem warm or cool, restful or stimulating, harmonious or jarring, welcoming or impersonal. It can even affect the apparent proportions of a room. In short, the choice of colors is a fundamental part of decoration. For that very reason, it is the source of a great deal of worry to most people, not least because the range of possible combinations is so vast and because the results when it goes wrong seem so conspicuous.

INSPIRATION

Some rare individuals can carry a color around in their heads and match it exactly. They look at a room and know instantly what will suit it and how it will look in this color combination or that. Most people, however, have to work at developing a color sense. The easiest and most effective way is to get into the habit of looking hard at any combination of colors that appeals, and to analyze the buildup of color within it.

Most painters develop the habit of patiently observing color, noting all the nuances in their subject. It is an interesting experiment to take a single item–such as a rug, a painting, or a piece of china or fabric–and to write down the various hues and tones in it. Note first those that predominate and then the various ancillaries that, together, form the whole.

Once you have gotten used to looking at and analyzing color, you can draw inspiration from almost everything that visually pleases you, particularly, of course, from nature. Think of the colors of the countryside,

forest, sea, or sky, or the buildup of tones in a Mediterranean village or a cottage garden. Most rural scenes contain innumerable shades of green, all blended and with accents provided by bright flashes of color from flowers, blossom, berries, or crops.

Similarly, an old-fashioned rose garden can show how to successfully blend pinks, yellows, and peaches with greens or terracottas. They create a scheme of equal tones against a background of the green tones of trees or the rose-terracotta tones of an old brick wall–or the grays of a crumbling old stone wall, come to that.

Another way to build up ideas for a scheme is through emotional response. People often have extraordinarily violent reactions to different colors for no logical reason. "I loathe green," they say–or, "I just can't tolerate anything pink." To make this intense response work in a positive way, take a favorite color and think of it in depth. Think, say, of yellow, remembering everything

1 The chunks of primary colors like the red wall in the foreground of this room and the bright chrome yellow by the window show up with almost psychedelic intensity against the deliberate pallor of the rest of this room.

2 The pitting of vibrant strokes of color against otherwise pale tones is also demonstrated in the room opposite. In this case, the yellows of the abstract painting seem to give a warm glow to the otherwise quite neutral color scheme.

floral and yellow, from the palest creamy yellow of honeysuckle or freesias to the vivid velvet of rose petals, through narcissi to daffodils, to crocuses, to marigolds, nasturtiums, and the centers of daisies. Or picture straw and dried hay, sand, heavy cream, the gold of stripped and waxed wood floors, lemons, honeydew melons, and thick honey.

If you consider blue in the same way, you might think of forget-me-nots and periwinkles, the fresh, sweet blue of hyacinths and bluebells, the intensity of delphiniums, irises, and lobelia, and the gentle, faded quality of dried hydrangeas and lavender. Then there are all those blues of the sky: the pale, blue-gray dawn, the azure of a clear summer's day, the grape blue of impending storms, the luminous blue of dusk, and the deep blue of a warm night. Think, too, of sun-dazzled water and of precious and semi-precious stones like aquamarines, sapphires, turquoise, and lapis lazuli.

Imagine other colors in the same kind of depth, and it should be easy to translate all these subtleties and variations of tone into interesting monochromatic schemes. Remember that the ingredients that make up a room—wood and wool; cotton, velvet and tweed; paint and paper—will all give varying depths of color.

If you are still unsure of the colors that you find comfortable to live with (and many people have a hard time with this), you should resort to the old trick that I recommend for color as much as for style. Buy as many decoration books and magazines as you can. Mark pictures in the books and cut out pages in the magazines illustrating rooms that appeal to you. Put them aside for a few days, then look at them all at once. You will almost certainly notice that the same color combinations reappear over and over. This will indicate, as nothing else does, the colors that are the most comfortable for you.

part one: the basics

MATCHING COLORS TO STYLES

It may be, of course, that you have set your heart on a particular style of decoration; or your home seems to demand a specific style, but you are concerned that the colors you like best are not appropriate. Again, don't worry. Specific colors are certainly connected with particular periods (for example, dark plums, reds, and greens with late Victorian style; bright green with the Empire or Federal period; orange, green, and cream with the 1930s). Indeed, colors are sometimes named after a period or style, such as Imperial purple, Pompeian red, and Adam green. But there is no need to feel rigorously bound by them–after all, many reputable fabric companies frequently change the colorways of their archive designs.

The textile ranges of both Liberty and Sanderson, for example, include recolored William Morris designs, which look good today without in any way sacrificing the William Morris late 1800s style. And many extraordinarily pretty chintzes have been revamped from old designs by Colefax & Fowler, Bennison, Pierre Frey and Braquenié, Cowan & Tout, Scalamandré, Boussac, Sanderson, Beaumont & Fletcher, and others. It is all a question of balance and proportion, and as far as your home is concerned, success will depend on the way you personally manipulate the style to suit your own taste.

BALANCED COLOR SCHEMES

Thinking up color combinations for a particular style of room is one thing, but achieving the right balance is quite another, and preparing schemes for a whole house or apartment is the most intricate exercise of all. There are, however, various ways to achieve an interesting balance.

One approach is to keep most of the room in shades and variations of one color, by using that color–say, a warm but pale cream–for walls, window shades, and carpet or rugs. Mix it with another color such as rose–for upholstery and draperies.

Then add accent colors–perhaps white (for chair frames), green (in plants and a stenciled design on the walls) and burnt umber (in a dried-flower bouquet).

Another approach is to keep walls, curtains and draperies, floor, and furniture in one color–perhaps white–and to achieve variety by varying the tones and textures. Alternatively, to the same basically white room, green and white cushions and masses of plants could be added to great effect.

A third approach is to use, say, a soft blue for walls, a slightly darker shade for the area under a chair rail,

crisp white paint for the woodwork, and touches of pale lilac. A variation here would be to add to these colors a chair or carpet in olive green.

It is important to vary surfaces and textures in the colors you choose, in order to make a play of light and shade and pattern. Picture, for example, a room papered in a blue and white wallpaper above lower walls of dragged dark blue paint over a lighter blue. Woodwork could be white, or a blue from the paper, in a semigloss finish. A dark blue and white throw could be placed over a sofa covered in off-white canvas or heavy cotton. Armchairs could be a medium-blue velvet or corduroy, or even damask.

1 Tonal variations add subtle interest to a corner of this yellow room. Lemon-painted walls are offset by the row of clear yellow flowers on the shelves, as well as the framed yellow-green ferns. The touches of silver, the pottery, even the pale wood of the chair, all aid the subtlety of the color buildup.

2 The room shown opposite illustrates a buildup of a much warmer yellow. The color of the walls is repeated in the rug and nicely grounded by the wide planks of the polished floor. The lampshade is yet another yellow.

2

1 *Blocks of red-oranges, yellows, and umber are teamed with—or, more precisely, calmed by—white and various natural wood tones in the closets, bed, and floor of this spacious bedroom. The overall feeling is one of interesting vivacity, rather than the hectic discord one might otherwise associate with such a deliberately unrestful scheme.*

2 *A basically all-white room is relieved here and there by flashes of color in cushions, a painting, and the frame of the coffee table; the black of the hearth and floor lamp; and even the laid-back silver of the television set.*

COLOR PLANNING A HOME

The way you go about color planning a whole house or apartment depends very much on the size of the home. If it is large, you can afford to have different schemes in every room, as long as you remember to take care with the meeting points of floor and wall finishes between rooms. You will also have to pay particular attention to corridors and open doors between rooms to make sure that differing colors, textures, and patterns work well together.

If the home is small, then it is sensible to create a harmonious whole, with an overall palette of colors that can be used in differing proportions through all the rooms.

For example, suppose you were particularly happy with apricot, dark blue, burnt umber, and green. You could use these colors throughout, varying the pace to prevent monotony.

In one room apricot walls would be combined with white painted shutters, a dark polished wood floor, a golden Afghan rug, and upholstery in dark blue and plain cream, accented with green plants and old needlepoint cushions in shades of yellow, apricot, and umber.

In another room you could have basically blue walls, overlaid with a dark apricot-umber glaze, and an apricot and blue paisley fabric at the windows and on chair seats.

Yet another room could have apricot and off-white wallpaper, used with plain deep-blue upholstery.

A fourth room could be off-white, with an apricot and blue border or stenciling, polished floorboards with a blue and apricot dhurrie or needlepoint rug, off-white shades with a double border of apricot and dark blue grosgrain ribbon, and a mixture of blue, off-white, and apricot upholstery, or blue or apricot bedspreads.

In this way, each room would seem entirely different and individual, but each one would also meld into the overall impression of the home without any discord.

MANIPULATING SPACE THROUGH COLOR

It can be seen from the foregoing example that a small apartment or house will seem more spacious if the same colors are used in different juxtapositions throughout. This is all the more true if the rooms have the same floor covering or polished wood floor. Similarly, the way in which you use color can alter the apparent proportions of a room.

- Strong or warm colors, like red or burnt orange, will make walls appear to close in and the space seem smaller.

- Cool colors will appear to stretch space, to push the walls out, particularly if the floor, walls, and ceiling all relate to each other and seem a harmonious whole.

- A corridor will look less long and narrow if the end wall is painted or covered in a warm color.

- A small space will seem larger if all the surfaces are painted the same light color and the walls washed with light.

- A high ceiling will seem lower if it is painted a darker color than the walls. This is the case even if the difference is slight.

- A ceiling will look higher if it is painted a lighter color than the walls, or if a cornice is fixed all around the perimeter of the ceiling and painted a darker color than the ceiling.

- A too-high ceiling can be made to look lower by adding a chair rail at waist level all around the walls and painting the wall beneath it a darker shade than the walls above, suggesting a dado.

part one: the basics

COLOR
AND ATMOSPHERE

Color will also immediately change the feel of a room, so when choosing a scheme, consider what atmosphere you want to achieve.

- Rooms painted in deep, warm colors like rust-red will seem cozy and comfortable and are perfectly appropriate in town or country, in any location with long winter months to get through.

- The same room painted white, pale yellow, blue, or light grass-green will seem airy and cool in a hot climate, especially if filled with plants and white wicker furniture, with perhaps yellow, blue, or green and white cushions or upholstery.

- A dark, rich room can be brightened by accents of more intense color and either lightened by white woodwork or given a jewel-box atmosphere by painting the woodwork in the same color as the walls.

- A light, somewhat bland room can be given more character by staining the floorboards a very dark brown and adding large plants in over-scale (very large) baskets or terracotta pots. Large pieces of furniture will look smaller if covered in a fabric of the same color as the walls; a smaller piece of furniture, covered in an accent color, can then balance it.

1 *Apricot and cream* trompe l'oeil *paneling adds warmth and interest to a pale and airy room. The same shades are picked up in pillows on the chaise longue and in the flowers.*

2 *"Greenery-yallery" curtains and a matching pillow are an interesting contrast to the plaid bed linen. Note how they are brought into sharp focus by the yellow pitcher.*

3 *Warm, rust red-orange walls in an attic bathroom brighten up a somewhat awkward space, as do the large mirror and the nice-looking old ceiling fixture.*

COLOR IMPRESSIONS

- Dark, warm colors make rooms seem not only comfortable but also distinguished. In addition, they have the knack of making a room look more furnished, or finished, than it actually is.

- Use light, airy colors in a light, airy room. If the room is small as well, the light colors will seem to push out the walls and make the room feel far more spacious.

- It is a fallacy that white, or very light, walls will make a dark room look lighter. In fact, they usually just end up making it look gloomier. Choose rich, warm colors, or creamy yellow, apricot, or a singing soft blue instead.

- If you have white cornices, they will stand out better if you paint the ceiling a much paler version of the walls.

- If the walls and ceiling are light, paint the moldings a contrast color. Alternatively, in a subtly colored room, drag the top of a dry brush, lightly dipped into a brighter color, over a white base coat so that you get just a hint of color. For example, if the walls are painted a honeysuckle-yellow and the ceiling is cream, you could drag the moldings with grass-green.

part one: the basics

HOW MANY COLORS CAN YOU PUT TOGETHER?

People often worry about whether they are using too many or too few colors. I feel that *major* areas of color (walls, floors, window treatments) should be restricted to three, at most, but that there need be no limit to the number of *accent* colors that can be used (for cushions, trims, moldings, accessories, flowers, etc.).

For example, in a room with glazed yellow walls, the carpet could have a creamy yellow ground with occasional touches of blues and rose-terracotta. The draperies could be in a yellow and white striped fabric, with glass curtains in creamy white. One sofa and one armchair could be cream and another sofa yellow, and a second armchair could pick up the blue in the carpet. Two other occasional chairs could have frames painted in soft terracotta and seats in faded blue-green, again to pick up some of the colors of the carpet. Strewn around

the various upholstered pieces could be old needlepoint cushions which match a third chair. A final color would be provided by the greens of plants.

MIXING AND MATCHING COLORS

When you are still finalizing a color scheme, it helps to collect together samples of all the "ingredients" you might use in a room (such as the flooring, wall covering, paint, draperies or curtains, blinds, tiebacks, trims, tablecloths, bedspreads, and dust ruffles). Put them on a table, if possible in the room in which you are going to use them, and have a good squint at them with narrowed eyes. By squinting at all those assembled colors and textures, you will see what colors go best with each other and in what proportion, as well as what stands out too harshly, and what patterns and textures provide the most harmonious whole.

Sometimes you might have a color in mind for walls or window treatments but you cannot find it in any store. The best thing to do is to keep an eye out for it in magazine features and advertisements, stationery, wrapping paper, clothing, fabric scraps, etc. As soon as you see the color, take it along to a hardware store to get the shade mixed. Or you could show it to a decorative painter, who might be able to achieve exactly the same subtlety by tinting a glaze and over-painting a wall, or by painting in different layers and rubbing the paint off by various methods to achieve the desired effect.

Similarly, you might find precisely the right color for a drapery fabric in a dress-fabric department. It will be a

1 *Purply lilacs in the painted wardrobe, checked upholstery, cushions, lampshades, and some of the ceramics make a harmonious contrast to the yellows in the room, highlighted by the occasional but telling touches of red.*

2 *Blue and yellow have always been a happy combination. Here, the floor harmonizes beautifully with the blue walls and upholstery of the living area, with the blue cabinets of the kitchen and with the yellow walls in the zone between these two areas. Note the rug and cushions, which, along with the floor, unite the three spaces.*

part one: the basics

I

2

narrower width, and probably also a lighter weight, but it may well be worth it to you to get the exact shade you want. Do not forget about antique textiles and old fabrics in general. It is often possible to find beautiful old curtains and linens in thrift shops, as well as antique shops.

Finally, do not neglect serendipity—happy accidents—or think that once a room is done to your satisfaction, it is finished. Rooms develop and, hopefully, mellow, like people. A jacket left over the back of a chair might provide a color juxtaposition that you had not thought of, which could be produced simply by adding a throw or some flowers. You might suddenly see a new (or old) fabric that seems to go perfectly with an antique rug. All you have to do is make a cushion with it, or an over-cloth for a table, and again the room has a new dimension.

tip

YOU DO NOT HAVE TO TAKE INFINITE PAINS OVER MATCHING COLORS EXACTLY. THEY ARE NOT, AFTER ALL, CAREFULLY MATCHED EDGE TO EDGE IN NATURE. ALL YOU HAVE TO DO IS THINK IN TERMS OF FAMILIES OF COLOR, AND, AGAIN, HARMONY. IN THIS WAY, YOUR ROOMS WILL HAVE THE MELLOWNESS THAT IS SO ENVIABLE TO OTHER PEOPLE AND COMFORTABLE FOR YOU.

I *Another blue and yellow combination, this time allied to white and made even airier by the white-painted open-screen room divider at the back.*

2 *An otherwise rather nebulous staircase space has been made warm and interesting by a play on roses: a darker rose on one wall is offset by a paler rose on the other, while the carpet is a grayed-down plum shade.*

Vocabulary of Color Terms

Accent colors: Used in a scheme to add a little sparkle and variety, accent colors are often chosen from the opposite side of the SPECTRUM from the main color of the room. They are used only in small areas—for example cushions, lampshades, flowers, or picture mats.

Advancing colors: These are warm colors, such as reds, yellows, apricots, and oranges, and they appear to bring surfaces closer. Advancing colors may also make objects look bigger, and they are useful in large rooms to bring in walls and to lower ceilings. Dark shades of other colors have similar effects.

Color wheel: The seventeenth-century physicist Isaac Newton developed the original color wheel when he was studying the effects of a beam of light shining through a prism. A prism splits the light into the colors of the rainbow, and the color wheel is the prismatic spectrum set out in circular form. It comprises twelve colors, from which all of the other identifiable hues are derived, and is based on the three PRIMARY COLORS (red, yellow, and blue), spaced equally around the circle. Between these are the SECONDARY COLORS (violet, green, and orange). The remaining six colors in the wheel are TERTIARY COLORS. All other colors are variations of these basics, mixed either with each other or with black or white.

Complementary colors: Each PRIMARY COLOR has a complementary color, or complement, produced by mixing the other two primaries in equal amounts. Complementary colors are opposite each other on the COLOR WHEEL. The complement of red is green (a mixture of blue and yellow), the complement of blue is orange (red and yellow), and that of yellow is violet (red and blue). When equal amounts of two complementary colors are mixed, they form gray. In design terms, however, the phrase "complementary colors" generally means colors that go well together.

Contrasting colors: Technically, a contrast is what you get when you put a SECONDARY COLOR against a PRIMARY. But in common usage the term means colors that are not near each other on the COLOR WHEEL. Contrasting color schemes include complementary schemes (using COMPLEMENTARY COLORS) and triadic schemes (using colors equidistant from each other on the color wheel). They generally work best if one color (usually the RECEDING COLOR) predominates. Small amounts of a contrasting color are often useful as ACCENT COLORS in a room scheme.

Cool colors: See RECEDING COLORS.

Equal tones: Successful decorating schemes are often formed from a mixture of colors of equal tone—in other words, colors having approximately the same brightness, depth, and lightness or darkness. Pastel pinks, yellows, and peaches, therefore, look harmonious and well balanced together, as do combinations of strong reds, yellows, and blues. In nature, the quality of the light often has the effect of reducing colors to equal tones—the pale colors of early dawn, the soft colors of dusk—while in decorating, white, gray, or black is often added to colors to produce a similar effect.

Harmonious colors: These colors are close to each other on the COLOR WHEEL and as a result are close in warmth or coldness. For example, a harmonious MONOCHROMATIC SCHEME might be composed of a light tone like pearl gray, moving through middle tones such as flannel gray and ending with a deep tone like charcoal.

Hue: A pure color to which neither black nor white has been added.

Monochromatic scheme: This type of scheme utilizes one basic color in a variety of TONES, though it will usually benefit from the addition of one or two ACCENT COLORS. Textural interest is also important here.

Neutral colors: These range from black to white, taking in grays from the palest silver to charcoal, and also including off-whites and browns, from creams and camels to tans and nutmegs. (Theoretically, however, black and white are non-colors—see SPECTRUM.)

Palette: This refers to the assortment of colors that are used by an artist or designer for a particular picture or room scheme.

Pastel colors: Pastels are soft, gentle colors that are produced by adding a great deal of white to other colors and their many hues: for example, pink (from red), lilac (from purple), or apricot (from orange).

Primary colors: The three primary colors—red, yellow, and blue—are pure colors and cannot be produced by mixing others. All other colors are derived from them.

Receding colors: Blue, violet, and green, or colors to which these have been added, are known as receding colors. Also referred to as cool colors, they can make rooms seem larger, because they make surfaces appear to move away from the eye.

Saturation: The intensity, brightness, or purity of a color. The opposite of a saturated color is a muted color, often referred to as "dirty" or "knocked back." Sometimes in a muted scheme it is a good idea to add the occasional spot of saturated color, which will almost sing out. However, it is not necessarily a good idea to add knocked-back color to a saturated color scheme.

Secondary colors: An equal mixture of two PRIMARY COLORS produces a secondary color: red and yellow make orange, blue and red make violet, and yellow and blue make green. Each secondary color is a COMPLEMENTARY COLOR of the primary color not used in its making.

Shades: These are the TONES produced by adding black to a HUE. In common usage, the term can also mean the colors produced by adding gray or white or small amounts of other hues to a color.

Spectrum: A beam of light when shone through a glass prism is broken up into its constituent wavelengths, represented by bands of red, orange, yellow, green, blue, and violet, just like a rainbow. Studying this phenomenon led the

The blue-painted frame and deep recess turn this window into a kind of painting, showing off the leafy landscape outside.

physicist Isaac Newton to develop the COLOR WHEEL. White is produced by a balanced mixture of all the colors of the spectrum, while true black is a total absence of color.

Tertiary colors: These are the colors made up of equal parts of PRIMARY COLORS and SECONDARY COLORS—for example, lime green is composed of yellow (primary) and green (secondary).

Tints: The TONES of a color, which are produced by the addition of white. Tints are often only marginally different from the principal color in a scheme.

Tones: These are the gradations of a color from its weakest intensity to its greatest—for example, the range from pale pink to dark red.

Warm colors: See ADVANCING COLORS.

part one: the basics

Playing with Texture and Pattern

Texture and pattern are much more crucial in a room's makeup than you might think. Colors are so radically changed by differences in texture and pattern that a monochromatic, or one-color, room can be as lively and as memorable through its subtlety as a vividly contrasting room.

TEXTURAL CONTRASTS

Textures need to be considered as carefully as the process of color building. They may not elicit such emotional reactions as color, but they are just as evocative. The name of a known texture can conjure up an almost tangible surface. Just as thinking about one color can evoke many depths and variations, so, too, do different textures engender their own imagery.

Bamboo
Boarding
Brick
Burlap
Cashmere
Ceramics
Corduroy
Cork
Denim
Felt
Glass
Lace
Leather
Linen
Marble
Patent leather
Plaster
Quilting
Rope
Rush matting
Silk
Sisal
Steel
Stone
Suede
Tweed

Take a little time to picture the textures shown in the box below left. Think about these one at a time, and you will discover that it is possible practically to *feel*, as well as see, the various textures in the mind's eye. Pick out some of them and imagine how they would look when appropriately distributed among walls, ceiling, floor, and furniture. Contrast their qualities; weigh up their surfaces; juxtapose them in your mind.

Obviously, some textures are more in keeping with each other than others. Rough clearly goes with smooth, and matte with gloss–but what rough with what smooth, and what matte with what gloss, are questions of taste and situation. For example, brick walls would probably look better contrasted with linen or cotton, or the smooth white finish of shutters, than with silk, velvet, or moiré. If you are very sure of yourself and your tastes, you can get away with some unconventional contrasts. Like other aspects of decoration, there are no real rules for this–only sensibilities.

To gain confidence, try to collect as many different textural samples as you can. Shop around. *Scrounge* around. Bring back samples of brick, tile, paint chips, carpet, matting, silks, velvets, other fabrics, glass, vinyl. Experiment with them and try out various contrasts.

1

Even when a room seems finished, the introduction of yet another contrasting texture, like adding another accent in a color scheme, might make all the difference to the liveliness and interest of a space. As already mentioned with regard to color, one often does not see this until some chance incident points it out–a velvet coat thrown over a cane chair, for example, or a basket or flowerpot left on a floor. Then suddenly the surface that previously had not even been considered seems just right, effectively delineating all the other colors and surfaces in the room, and one cannot imagine why it was never thought of before. But this is what interior decoration is all about, after all–the relaxed and gradual accretion not just of possessions but also of experience.

1 *Note how the cane seat on the chair, the somewhat rustic frame, and the nubby rug on the wood floor all contrast well and in an appropriate manner. Such a chair placed on, say, a velvet pile carpet would have looked out of place, although it would be fine on brick or tiles.*

2 *The same pattern has been used on practically every surface except the floor in this bedroom and adjoining dressing room. Another effective approach would have been to cover the chair, chaise longue, and bed in a smaller-scale design with much the same coloring, or in a checked, striped, or plain fabric.*

MIXING PATTERNS

Many people find it rather frightening to combine patterns, while others go overboard in mixing up scales and colors in a wholly inappropriate way. Again, it is less a question of rules and more a matter of training the eye and the sensibilities.

One way to go about it is to think of the patterns that are already being formed by your possessions. Books, with their various covers and jacket designs; the way pictures and prints are hung on a wall; the arrangement of objects in a storage unit or on a table; the jagged edges of plant leaves against a plain wall; the play of light and shade; the shapes of different pieces of furniture–all these form patterns in their own right. As a result, one more fabric pattern, more or less, cannot jar as long as–and this is important–its scale, tone, and proportion are right.

Large patterns that look interesting in some public place are often more suitable for just that sort of setting, unless you possess a very sure sense of scale. Similarly, you should remember that very small patterns often merge into one color when they are used for wall coverings or draperies.

A play of pattern, however, can be very effective, enriching the whole scheme. Properly used, it will give added depths to a room.

Here are some important points to remember when mixing patterns:

- It is best not to use more than one large-scale design in a room (or two at the most if they are similar in scale, feeling, and color). You can, however, use several different small-scale patterns with a large design. Small-scale repeats, in upholstery or soft furnishings, of a large pattern on a wall or in a window treatment can give a good sense of perspective and depth.

- The same pattern in two different colors can look good, and so can the same pattern reversed—say, green on white predominating, with white on green predominating.

- Similar patterns in the same colors can be used together to good effect, as in draperies and carpet or rugs with plain painted walls or a textured wall covering.

- Patterns with the same feeling, if not design, can also be used together effectively. Examples include paisleys in the same coloring with similarly colored florals; ethnic fabrics or batiks with heavily patterned oriental rugs; densely patterned, slightly oriental designs with oriental or needlework rugs; mini-prints of all sorts with small geometrics; and small Liberty-type prints with revived nineteenth-century designs in the same colors.

- Don't forget the subtle effect of sheer fabrics, printed with the same design as the draperies or with an allied pattern that is either a simplified version in one color on white (or white on white) or a toned-down version of the same coloring.

- Many companies now produce coordinating collections of papers and fabrics, using, say, one larger, predominant design in both paper and fabric. These may be grouped in various ways: with smaller-scale

1 *The parquet floor, black-painted cast-iron bathtub, plaster walls, steel faucet, shaggy chair covering, and large mirror in its gilt frame provide a variety of textural contrasts in what is actually a very simply decorated room.*

2 *The unadorned brick wall, large sailcloth or "duck"-covered sofa, rough wood coffee table, smooth wood-strip floor, and pair of curved iron sculptures combine rough with smooth, crisp with soft, comfort with hard edges.*

3 *A silky smooth wood cabinet set within a reeded frame contrasts with the black steel and glass of the desk, the tweed upholstery of the chairs, the latticework of the box on the desktop, and the wide planks of the polished floor.*

4 *Venetian blinds give textural interest to the uncluttered wall, just as the black upholstered chair contrasts the softness of the fabric with the hard shine of the floor tiles. The scheme could hardly be more monotone, but the severe contrasts in materials creates an arresting visual effect.*

geometric, fish-scale, or basket-weave patterns; with smaller-scale versions of the main design; with a single motif from the main design, used on a plain background in a fairly open manner; or with a monotone, pared-down version of the larger design. If you study these carefully, you will soon be

able to form your own groupings from different sources. They will be all the more interesting if you can mix them with an old design or two, perhaps from needlepoint or embroidered cushions or throws, antique quilts or old needlepoint rugs, in the same kind of coloring as the fabrics or paper.

Study the illustrations for examples. Collect a lot of samples of fabrics and papers, and look at them against your own furniture, walls, and objects, and in different lights. See what you think works well together. Try making up various groups of your own. You will soon become confident in playing around with pattern.

Controlling Scale and Balance

The other main elements in a room's makeup – scale and balance – are often overlooked, but they are very important. Acquiring a good awareness of these aspects will allow you to choose and arrange furniture and furnishings so that the height, visual "weight," color, texture, and pattern of each piece contributes to an overall feeling of harmony in the room.

BALANCING FURNISHINGS

If you think about balance, you automatically have to think about scale. It would look awkward, for example, to have one very large piece of furniture, like a huge sofa, in a room with a lot of small pieces and rugs; or only one tall object with a lot of low pieces. Conversely, it would look dull to have all furnishings of the same scale or the same height.

If, on the other hand, you can visually balance a large piece of furniture, like the aforementioned sofa, with a big desk, a sofa table, or work table, the piece will look in context with the room as a whole. It will become one of the anchor pieces, around which the rest of the furnishings revolve.

Equally, you should balance a tall piece, like a bookcase, storage unit, armoire, or secretary, with another large piece, a big painting or print, a group of paintings or prints, or a large mirror on another wall. However, do not choose a piece of art or a mirror that is actually bigger than the chest, side table, or other object beneath it or the effect will be top-heavy. Likewise, too small a painting, print, or mirror on a long expanse of wall will look puny and lonely.

You could offset a tall piece of sculpture, or a pedestal or a screen in one corner of your room with a large plant or a plant standing on a column or pedestal in another. Always try to vary the height of furnishings. Have at least one or two taller pieces – such as large works of art, wall groupings or plants – in a room. And, in turn, offset large masses of furniture or art with generous rugs.

Practice these juxtapositions by moving around scaled cut-outs of furniture on floor plans drawn on graph paper (see pages 16–17). Cut out magazine pictures of rooms with

arrangements that seem particularly pleasing to you, and analyze the way they are arranged.

Color contributes to visual weight, too, so be aware of the balance of light and dark tones in a room.

GROUPS OF ACCESSORIES

The same principle applies to groups of accessories. Keep similar objects more or less of a size; or, since that is not always possible, balance the size of one object with a stronger color in another. Size does not matter so much with dissimilar objects, where the fascination of contrast is the main objective. (For more about arrangement, see pages 208–215.)

1 *A nice sense of balance is demonstrated by this composition. The mirror over the fireplace is just a bit smaller without being too small. The flowerpots are a casual contrast to the centrally placed bust, which, in turn, is a good counterpoint to the ornate carving at the top of the mirror above it and the elaborate carving in the center of the mantelpiece below.*

2 *The crisp lines of the simple desk beneath the window are echoed by those of the Venetian blinds, while the lamp on its three steel legs complements the chair.*

3 *The very tall mirror hung over the sofa is an excellent counterpoint to the floor-to-ceiling window, while the curved legs of the fauteuil contrast with the straight legs of the stool.*

SIMILARITIES AND CONTRASTS

Repeat the same color here and there in a room. The color of a chair at one end can be repeated in a painting, a cushion, or a rug at the other. colors in a patterned ceramic table lamp can be picked up in a plain ceramic lamp somewhere else. The tones of a painting can be echoed in the plain color of a carpet.

Look, and then look again, at your room designs, asking yourself the following questions:

- Where can the pace be varied more?
- What other shapes can be effectively juxtaposed?
- What flashes of color will be enhanced with a little repetition here and there?
- Are there any felicitous contrasts that can be made?

By stopping to think in this way, you will ensure that you always have visual balance in mind, whatever changes you are making to a room.

part one: the basics

SECTION THREE

Once the basics of any remodeling or decorating job have been decided upon, you need to finalize the style. When you are sure of your tastes and requirements, the way you order, arrange, or transform rooms can be as instinctive as the way you arrange your wardrobe, no matter how well informed you are about all the possible styles. I have seen people manage to create rooms that are indisputably charming and memorable, with almost no money and a generally undistinguished miscellany of possessions. This is what is meant by a sense of style.

Style

A Sense of Style

To possess a sense of style is to possess a sense of suitability: a feeling for what is appropriate in any given situation (unless you are so sure of yourself that you can turn suitability on its head and defy the conventional). In addition, it is an understanding of the sort of arrangements, juxtapositions, colors, and proportions that will all meld happily together. You also need to have a pragmatic rather than a slavish view of fashion. It is hard to ignore a prevailing look that you find sympathetic, but trying to follow every fad in home furnishings would be outrageously expensive as well as totally impractical, particularly as fashions change so fast these days.

CULTIVATING A SENSE OF STYLE

Many people who claim to have no assured sense of style themselves can often recognize other people's natural style and instinctive good taste, amorphous though these are. Yet while acknowledging that others can put together possessions and colors in an interesting way, they persist in denying their own abilities and fail even to attempt to analyze why some combinations look better than others.

Over the years, I have watched enough people develop an excellent sense of style, as well as a good eye for both the acquisition of possessions and their placement, to know that the cultivation of this skill is definitely possible. More often than not, if you really *look at* and analyze what both pleases and suits you, the development of your own sense of style follows quickly. And when you have gained confidence in your own tastes, have developed a good eye, and have attained a working knowledge of the various furnishing styles, all decorative possibilities will open up to you.

CREATIVE COMPROMISE

Just as you do not have to have been born with a natural flair, equally it is not a prerequisite to have unlimited funds to indulge any whim in interior decoration. In fact, a form of shorthand—a glancing reference to a style (like using a stenciled Gothic cornice in a bedroom or a Neoclassical pediment over a bookcase)—is often more lively and amusing than the serious and scholarly placement of all the proper ingredients.

1 *This home might be called modern eclectic, with its pale colors, play on textures, and interesting old pieces mixed with the modern. It looks somewhat spare, but there is a lot of charm about the room.*
2 *This is definitely country style, with its battered old plastered walls, brick floors, old or distressed dressers, painted chairs, scrubbed tables, and lots of old pots and earthenware.*

The Suitability Factor

Clearly, there are certain commonsense factors to consider about any home before deciding to impose a particular style or styles. Aspects like location, climate, setting, and architecture cannot be ignored.

LOCATION

Houses in the country look best when furnished for comfortable rural living. Even in this context, there are distinctions, since the furniture, surfaces, and colors that you might use in a farmhouse or cottage would look out of place in a more formal Georgian or Federal house. Similarly, although the airy, comfortable feeling of a country home, whatever its degree of formality, has much to commend it in a city, a sophisticated urban look in the country is generally as much out of place as someone going for a walk in the fields in high-heeled shoes.

The whole point of beach houses, ski chalets, and other predominantly

1 *If the kitchen on the previous page has all the main ingredients for country rustic, this room must surely sing out "summer house." Glass walls overlooking a large stretch of water, blue-painted woodwork to match the sky, white wicker furniture, an air of luxurious relaxation—what could be more evocative of the perfect summer place?*

2 *This room is the epitome of cool: the white floor, walls, ceiling, and stone bed bases all seem to meld into one. Soft grays and ivories provide the gentlest of contrasts.*

seasonal or vacation homes is that they should be relaxed, carefree, and easy to maintain. This guiding principle will dictate casual, practical, comfortable furnishings, with floor treatments and upholstery that are easily cleaned of sand, mud, or snow.

CLIMATE AND WEATHER

By the same token, houses in hot climates should obviously look and feel as cool as possible (with some kind of comforting provision for the rare cooler or wetter days). Equally, homes in wetter, colder, and grayer climates must, of course, look and feel warm (again, with some sort of provision for the rare hot days).

There is a lot to be said for the sensible habits of our forebears in seasonal climates: during the summer months, they used cool linen or cotton slipcovers to disguise winter upholstery and often took down heavy draperies and took up rugs. Today, lack of domestic help and inadequate

part one: the basics

A SENSE OF PLACE

If a house or apartment building already has a distinctive architectural style, or if it is very much geared to its surroundings or climate (such as a home by the sea or one that is in a spectacular setting or in the tropics), it is best to be sensitive to these factors. Even if you do not actually like the building or landscape, location or climate, they are such important and fundamental aspects of the home that they cannot be ignored.

This does not mean that a period house must be decorated exactly according to its period or that a house

1 Simple modern furniture and a white-and-black scheme are kept low-key, the better to show off the intricate nineteenth-century architectural details.

2 The height and light in this converted barn have dictated the colors (which have been kept pale and neutral) and the furnishings (large-scale but simple). Nothing is allowed to detract from the sense of lavish spaciousness.

3 Entirely appropriate colors and furniture have been well chosen for this large and gallery-like space.

storage are usually the reasons given for not making seasonal changes, but if the possibility exists for such summer and winter makeovers, it is certainly worth the effort.

ARCHITECTURE AND SETTING

Apart from the commonsense dictates suggested by location and climate, there is often some salient factor about each room in a new home

that will also help determine its treatment. It may be the view outside, or lack of it; or it may be the fact that a room is rather dark, or very light; spacious or tiny; high-ceilinged or low. A room may be beamed or elaborately detailed with cornices and moldings; it may be paneled or have a distinctive arched or stained glass window. Perhaps it consists almost entirely of glass walls or, conversely, looks out onto a grimy brick wall.

3

by the shore should be furnished with fishing nets and maritime artifacts. These attempts at authenticity can all too easily look stilted and museum-like or, alternatively, banal, however much knowledge, money, or zeal, or all three, are lavished on them. Instead, it simply means that you should go with the flow–be true to the feel of a place as best you can–and be attentive to proportions, architectural details, and terrain without being completely cowed by these parameters.

I have seen very old homes in Europe looking marvelous with predominantly modern furniture and paintings and only one or two antique pieces; and I have also seen successful modern rooms in the United States and Australia graced with old furniture and rugs alongside contemporary furnishings.

In addition, I have come across beautiful eighteenth-, nineteenth- and early twentieth-century homes complete with their original detailing, in

which the carefully chosen colors and mix of furnishings make them charming and totally of the moment.

The factor that all these rooms have in common is that the frame-work, whatever it is, has been kept intact, and the proportions matched by the proportions of the furnishings. There has been no slavish imitation of the past. All the rooms are a successful synthesis of the past and the present, with a sharp eye for both comfort and balance.

THE FEATURELESS ROOM

Although suitability, spiced with imagination, is all-important when a building or room has some architectural distinction, or when climate or location dictate the approach, there are also many examples of homes that are the opposite. This particularly applies to the numerous city or suburban buildings built between the 1940s and 1980s that are almost universally anonymous, featureless, and very often viewless, and where

1 *Nothing detracts from the view in this comfortable room. Furniture is kept low so that the trees outside can become a major part of the decoration, making the most of the stunning location.*

2 *A definitely Middle Eastern feel has been created in this space with its trellised arch, different levels, and piles of sumptuously colored cushions.*

3 *Similarly, a precisely organized oriental-looking space has been achieved with shoji screens and the stepped pyramid of storage drawers, along with the free-standing floor light.*

climate hardly seems to matter. In these homes, you can superimpose any style that your inclinations, possessions, and pocket may dictate, without any guilt about lack of aesthetic sensibility.

One of the most interesting jobs that I have undertaken as a designer was the transformation, at the request of the widely traveled owners, of two adjoining featureless Manhattan apartments into something more akin to a luxurious Tunisian villa, complete with arches and fountains. As a final detail, I masked the sight of Broadway, six floors below, by stretching bright blue chiffon behind pierced shutters at most of the windows, so that one seemed to be looking out on a hot blue sky. At night the chiffon looked realistically dark. The project cost nothing like what one might assume such a transformation would cost, and the finished apartment seemed neither out of place nor kitsch, but simply the oasis of calm the owners had specified.

part one: the basics

Influences on Style

There are a great many general styles with generic names like "country," "contemporary," "colonial," "eclectic," and so on, the most important of which are defined on pages 78–83. In addition to these broad styles, there are the styles that have become synonymous with particular periods in history. Even if you are not decorating a period house, having a clear idea of the main historical styles is undeniably useful for your decoration knowledge and skills. Interior designers have always drawn upon the styles of previous eras for inspiration, and today is no exception. The main style periods are described on pages 70–5, but to put them in context, study the table on pages 76–7.

Running through the successive style periods have been a handful of fundamental "themes," or basic approaches to decorating (and, indeed, to the arts in general), that have reemerged in different guises over the centuries, sometimes even co-existing side by side. These major influences are the Classical, the Gothic, the Baroque, and the Rococo.

THE CLASSICAL

Classicism is derived from ancient Greece by way of Rome. Based on Greek and Roman forms and mathematical laws of proportion, Classical style applies not just to architecture and fine art but also to interior decoration. In the fifteenth and sixteenth centuries, the unprecedented burst of creativity and experimentation of the Renaissance marked the end of the medieval attachment to all things Gothic and a return to Classicism. Roman motifs—such as wreaths, garlands, and festoons, arabesques and scrolls, vine leaves and grapes, acanthus and anthemion

(Greek honeysuckle), *putti* (cupids) and urns—became part of the vocabulary of Classical ornament from this point onward.

Classical ideas, as interpreted by the sixteenth-century Italian architect Andrea Palladio, provided the dominant theme for the British version of Palladian architecture, introduced by the British architect Inigo Jones in the early 1600s. However, the style did not really catch on until a century after that in Britain, and around 1750 in North America.

Later in the eighteenth century, the almost obligatory "Grand Tour" of Europe allowed the scions of the aristocracy to immerse themselves in the ruins of ancient Greece and Rome and the glories of Renaissance Italy. The Grand Tour, combined with news of the extraordinary archaeological discoveries made in Italy and Greece, particularly those at Pompeii and Herculaneum, led to the first truly international style—Neoclassicism. The Neoclassicism of the late eighteenth and early nineteenth centuries

1 *Chiswick House, in west London, is one of the great examples of early eighteenth-century Classical architecture and decoration. Built between about 1725 and 1729 by Lord Burlington with William Kent, it embodies all the qualities of noble proportions, rich but restrained decoration, and the wholesale use of ancient Roman detail that are typical of the best architecture of this period. In the gallery, shown here, the decoration of the cupola, the three arches incorporating the entryway, and two niches for life-size statuary combine in one space a great many of the elements of Classicism.*

2 *Note how the floor and ceiling reflect each other in this wonderfully proportioned entrance hall at Cairness House, Scotland, another superb Classical-style house. Built in 1789 and designed by the architect James Playfair, it has a noble simplicity in line, color, and ornamentation.*

3 *Detail of a cornice with typical ancient Roman architectural motifs.*

dominated architectural interiors all over Europe and in America. Cool restraint, symmetry, balance, harmony, and proportion, along with Classical decorative motifs, were all features of the "Age of Elegance." There was another resurgence of the Classical in the mid-nineteenth century with the Renaissance Revival and other Classically inspired reincarnations. In the last third of the twentieth century, Postmodernism incorporated Classical elements and proportions into contemporary buildings and interiors.

THE GOTHIC

The Gothic style was used initially for early ecclesiastical architecture in Western Europe, from the twelfth century to the fifteenth or sixteenth, when it gradually gave way to Renaissance Classicism. A layman's

part one: the basics

version of Gothic appeared in castles, fortresses, and some early domestic and university architecture at the time.

Gothic decoration thus originated in the decoration used in medieval churches and includes the trefoil and quatrefoil motifs, the pointed arch, and pierced tracery.

In the early eighteenth century, the Gothic inspired a good deal of domestic architecture, architectural details, and furniture, but in a much lighter and more graceful vein than the original. Much Gothic design of this period was spelled "Gothick" to denote a deliberate frivolity.

The Gothic style made a strong reappearance in the late eighteenth and early nineteenth centuries, initially as a light-hearted counterpoint to the Neoclassical movement, when Gothic follies and lodges in gentlemen's parks were highly fashionable. From the 1820s to the mid-nineteenth century, the Gothic revival was a serious force again in Britain, France, Ireland, Germany, the United States, South Africa, Australia, and New Zealand. The passion for all things medieval caused the style to be interpreted in a much more serious way than in the previous century. The French version was known

as Troubadour style, which became hugely popular for a few decades. Gothic revival furniture, applied architectural details, textiles, and wallpaper were all produced at this time in large quantities.

In the late twentieth century, there was a mini-Gothic revival, with a wave of Gothic-style furnishings, fabrics, and wallpapers.

THE BAROQUE

By the early 1600s, the Classicism of the Renaissance had evolved into the Baroque style, which emerged first in Italy and spread around Europe during the seventeenth century.

The Baroque style reached its apotheosis in France, first in the reign of Louis XIII, and then, most magnificently, in that of Louis XIV, the "Sun King." It spread to Britain in the second half of the century and later to the American Colonies.

The style was splendidly ornate, theatrical, even exuberant, with heavy forms, large-scale planning, and elaborate plasterwork, strapwork, metalwork, woodcarving, paneling (at that time, removable like furniture), pilasters, overmantels, and tapestries.

Grand though it was, Baroque was the first European style to treat a room as a place actually to live in, rather than just to admire in passing or to have receptions in. And it was the first time that pieces of furniture were made to go together in a room, as opposed to being part of the architecture, or otherwise monumental. Interestingly, in spite of being an

part one: the basics

offshoot of the Classical style, Baroque actually represented the reverse of Classical harmony, completely breaking the Classical rules.

Baroque remained the style of choice in Europe and the Americas for those who could afford its extravagances, until it was finally overtaken by the Rococo or, as in Britain and the Netherlands, by Neo-Palladian Classicism. In the mid-nineteenth century there was a revival of Baroque among the multitude of other style revivals of the period.

THE ROCOCO

Rococo style first appeared in Paris in the early eighteenth century, as a reaction to the formality and opulence of the Baroque. It had its most famous expression during the Régence and the first half of the reign of Louis XV.

1 *Claydon House, in Buckinghamshire, is one of the few examples of the English Rococo style. But what an ebullient example it is, with its amazingly complicated plasterwork and clear pastel colors.*

2 *Claydon House is very chaste compared with this extraordinary room in the Amalienburg Pavilion at Schloss Nymphenburg, a summer palace near Munich, built by the Bavarian architect Cuvilliés in 1734–39. The Germans loved the Rococo style and went on with its elaborations long after most of Europe had moved into Neoclassical mode.*

3 *The silk wall covering in this room is an example of the "Chinese taste," a mania for everything oriental, inspired by the merchandise imported by the East India companies. Like eighteenth-century Gothick, this was an offshoot of Rococo.*

Light and frivolous, Rococo was characterized by asymmetry in carved and painted decoration, plasterwork, paneling, and furniture. Rococo motifs included seashells, ribbons, and bows. Colors were a revolution for the time: clear pastels, like blues and pale greens, pale yellows and roses, were used with a great many mirrors and candelabra and sconces to dramatize the brilliance and light.

The style was enormously popular in Germany and Austria, as well as in France, and, to a lesser extent, in Spain, Portugal, Italy, Russia, Poland, and across the Atlantic in North America. But it never took serious hold in Britain or in the Netherlands (apart from its offshoot, the "Chinese Taste," or Chinoiserie, which became popular in Britain and on the Continent in the eighteenth century).

Eventually, the elegance of Rococo became overblown and quite outrageously extravagant, and toward the end of the eighteenth century it gave way to Neoclassicism.

It was, however, revived in the mid-nineteenth century, when it was a favorite of the rich, of whom there were many. In France, the Rococo revival led in turn to the development of the Art Nouveau style.

part one: the basics

75

	France		Italy	Germany/Austria	Belgium/Netherlands	Scandinavia
	PERIOD/MONARCH	STYLE	STYLE	STYLE	STYLE	STYLE
1500		Gothic	Renaissance	Gothic	Gothic	Gothic
1525	François I (1515–47)	Renaissance				
1550	Henri II (1547–59) François II (1559–60)			Renaissance	Renaissance	Renaissance
1575	Charles IX (1560–74) Henri III (1574–89)					
1600	Henri IV (1589–1610)					
	Louis XIII (1610–43)		Baroque			
1625						
1650	LOUIS QUATORZE Louis XIV (1643–1715)	Baroque				Baroque
1675				Baroque	Baroque	
1700						Late Baroque
	RÉGENCE (regency of Duc d'Orléans to Louis XV, 1715–23) LOUIS QUINZE	Early Rococo Rococo	Late Baroque			Early Rococo
1725	Louis XV (1715–74)		Rococo	Rococo	Rococo	Rococo
1750						
1775	LOUIS SEIZE Louis XVI (1774–93)	Neoclassical	Neoclassical			Neoclassical (Gustavian: Gustav III, 1771–92)
	DIRECTOIRE Directoire (1795–99)			Neoclassical	Neoclassical	
1800	EMPIRE Consulate (1799–1804) Napoleon I (1804–15) RESTAURATION Louis XVIII (1814–24)	Late Neoclassical (Empire)	Late Neoclassical (Empire)	Late Neoclassical (Empire)	Late Neoclassical (Empire)	Late Neoclassical (Empire)
1825	Charles X (1824–30) LOUIS PHILIPPE Louis Philippe (1830–48) Napoleon III (President,1848–52)	Rococo revival Neo-Gothic		Biedermeier Neo-Gothic	Biedermeier	Biedermeier
1850	SECOND EMPIRE Napoleon III (Emperor, 1852–70)	Eclectic	Eclectic	Louis Seize revival	Eclectic	Eclectic
1875	THIRD REPUBLIC (1870–1940)					
1900		Art Nouveau Belle Epoque	Art Nouveau ("stile Liberty")	Art Nouveau ("Jugendstil")	Art Nouveau	Art Nouveau ("Jugendstil") + Arts & Crafts (Larsson)
1925		Art Deco International	International	International	International	International

Year	Britain — PERIOD/MONARCH	Britain — STYLE	United States — PERIOD	United States — STYLE	Year
1500	TUDOR Henry VII (1485–1509) Henry VIII (1509–47)	Gothic			1500
1525					1525
1550	Edward VI (1547–53) Mary I (1553–58)	Renaissance			1550
1575	ELIZABETHAN Elizabeth I (1558–1603)				1575
1600	JACOBEAN James I (1603–25)		COLONIAL (1608–1720)	Renaissance ("Jacobean")	1600
1625	CAROLEAN Charles I (1625–49)	Early Baroque			1625
1650	CROMWELLIAN Commonwealth (1649–60) RESTORATION Charles II (1660–85)	Baroque			1650
1675	James II (1685–89) WILLIAM & MARY William and Mary (1689–94) William III (1694–1702)				1675
1700	QUEEN ANNE Anne (1702–14) GEORGIAN George I (1714–27)	Early Neo-Palladian ("Queen Anne")		Baroque ("William & Mary")	1700
1725	George II (1727–60)	Neo-Palladian — Slight Rococo inc. Gothick and Chinoiserie	GEORGIAN (1720–80s)	Early Neo-Palladian ("Queen Anne")	1725
1750	George III (1760–1820)	Neoclassical ("Adam style") — Neo-Gothic		Neo-Palladian — Rococo	1750
1775			FEDERAL (1780s–1810)	Neoclassical	1775
1800	REGENCY (Regency of Prince of Wales to George III, 1811–20) George IV (1820–30)	Greek revival / Late Neoclassical ("Regency") — Chinoiserie	EMPIRE (1810–20s)	Late Neoclassical (Empire)	1800
1825	William IV (1830–37) VICTORIAN Victoria (1837–1901)	Eclectic	GREEK REVIVAL (1820s–40s) VICTORIAN (1837–1901)	Neo-Gothic	1825
1850		Arts & Crafts		Eclectic	1850
1875		Art Nouveau — Aesthetic movement — Queen Anne revival		Arts & Crafts ("Mission") — Colonial revival — Aesthetic movement	1875
1900	EDWARDIAN Edward VII (1901–10) MODERN George V (1910–36)		MODERN (1901 onward)	Beaux Arts — Art Nouveau	1900
1925	Edward VIII (1936) George VI (1936–52)	Art Deco — Neo-Tudor International		Art Deco International	1925

part one: the basics

Vocabulary of Decorating Styles

Adam, Robert: Robert Adam (1728–92) produced, often with his lesser-known brother James, some of the most graceful and interesting furniture and interiors in the history of British decorative arts. He believed that a room's decoration and furnishings should all add up to a harmonious whole, and he perfected an approach to design that enabled him to fit his interior schemes into existing houses. Although people today think of Adam colors as soft pastels, his schemes were actually very colorful. His work deeply influenced not only other eighteenth-century architects and cabinetmakers on both sides of the Atlantic, but also students of design up to the present day. He is the epitome of late eighteenth-century taste.

Aesthetic movement: More of a late nineteenth-century philosophy than a real movement, this was inspired by the new cult of the Japanese aesthetic and by the Queen Anne revival. It prevailed only in England and America, with no counterpart on the Continent. The emphasis was on maximum light, comfort, and informality, with pale colors. Japanese symbols were a particular feature, as were stylized sunflowers, lilies, and peacocks.

American Colonial: See COLONIAL (AMERICAN).

American Country: A broad style not related to a particular period. Hallmarks include primitive furniture in sun-washed barn reds and dusty blues, stenciled motifs, patchwork, rag rugs, painted floorboards, floorcloths, and matchboard wainscoting.

American Empire: See EMPIRE (AMERICAN).

American Southwest: Spanish and Native American influences on American Colonial style; sometimes called Santa Fe style. Hallmarks include adobe walls, rough-hewn furniture, Navajo rugs, and other brightly colored Native American textile designs.

Art Deco: An architectural and decorative style that flourished in Europe and North America from just before the First World War up to the 1930s. It became increasingly decorative in the 1920s, when it blossomed into all sorts of shapes inspired by primitive Aztec, Mayan, and African art; Leon Bakst's costumes and decor for the Russian ballet, then performing to great acclaim in Paris; and archaeological discoveries in Egypt. Art Deco, a name coined much later, is short for Arts Décoratifs.

Art Nouveau: This style was fashionable on both sides of the Atlantic from 1890 to World War I, and is known for its sinuous lines, mainly derived from vegetal forms. Victor Horta and Henry Van de Velde in Belgium, Hector Guimard

and Émile Gallé in France, A. H. Mackmurdo and C. F. A. Voysey in England, and Louis Sullivan, and Louis C. Tiffany in the United States were just a few of its gifted designers. In Scotland, Charles Rennie Mackintosh and the Glasgow School developed an influential rectilinear version inspired by Celtic ornament.

Arts and Crafts movement: A nineteenth-century movement led by William Morris and C. R. Ashbee in Britain. The aim was to eschew mass-production methods and return to the individually crafted furnishings of the past. Though it was meant to be an egalitarian movement, its products were too expensive for the "masses" to buy. However, Morris's papers and fabrics were copied by manufacturers like Sanderson and Liberty, who have been reproducing them ever since. In the United States, the movement centered around MISSION style, and also the PRAIRIE SCHOOL.

Baroque: Opulent, grand, ornate seventeenth-century style that evolved from RENAISSANCE CLASSICISM. It has been described as a "piling up of decorative motifs into an unashamedly theatrical composition whether on canvas, brick or stone." It was used with handsome results all over the Continent of Europe, in Central and South America,

and, to a lesser extent, in Britain and the American Colonies.

Bauhaus: Twentieth-century German school of design, an extension of the Weimar School of Arts and Crafts. Founded in 1919 by Walter Gropius, it was the most powerful single influence in the development—and acceptance—of modern design. In 1925, the Bauhaus School moved from Weimar to Dessau, and the new office Gropius designed became a model for the contemporary "dateless" look that was the epitome of the INTERNATIONAL STYLE for decades after. Most of the school's principal teachers moved to the United States at the onset of Nazi rule.

Beaux Arts: Late nineteenth-/early twentieth-century American equivalent of the RENAISSANCE REVIVAL style popular in Europe and Britain at much the same time. It was named after the École des Beaux Arts in Paris, where many of its architectural exponents had trained. With the rapid growth of wealth in the United States, a great many new mansions were built based on French *châteaus*. Beaux Arts architects combined modern technology and its creature comforts with historically derived details, such as acanthus leaves twisting around electric light switch plates, and dolphin feet on bathtubs. Colors and details were rich and exotic, with lavish plasterwork, beautiful joinery, paneling and gilding, as well as much Japanese influence.

Belle Epoque: French term for the opulent and glamorously comfortable period at the turn of the nineteenth century and the beginning of the twentieth, when, for the rich, all seemed "sweetness and light" before the onset of the World War I.

Biedermeier: An Austrian and German (and contemporaneously Scandinavian) decorative style popular from the 1820s to the 1840s, often known as "the poor man's EMPIRE." Its simple, graceful furniture, mostly in golden-hued wood with ebony or black-stained ornamentation, is very popular today.

"Chinese taste": See CHINOISERIE.

Chinoiserie: European imitations of oriental decoration, furniture, and decorative objects. The "Chinese taste," for Chinese silks, porcelains, lacquerwork, hand-painted wallpapers, and other items, as well as items from Japan and India, swept Europe and the American Colonies in the eighteenth century after trade had begun with China. The demand was so high that European companies started making pseudo-oriental imitations, or chinoiseries.

Classical: Style based on the disciplined lines, mathematical laws of proportion, and ornamentation of ancient Greek and Roman art and architecture, revived during the Italian Renaissance. Various forms of Classicism have woven in and out of the centuries ever since. It is characterized by cool elegance and restraint, symmetry and balance, geometrical forms, clean lines, and Classical architectural detail (columns, pilasters, etc.) and motifs, like laurel wreaths, acanthus leaves, and anthemion (Greek honeysuckle). See also NEOCLASSICAL.

Classical orders: The five styles of CLASSICAL architecture—Doric, Ionic, Corinthian, Tuscan, and Composite, which appeared in that order. They are based on the proportions and decoration of different styles of column, but in Classical architecture, even the proportions of the different sections of a wall could be based on those of a column. Sometimes the cycle of all design is compared to the sequence of Doric (simple, spare lines), followed by Ionic (more ornamental), and then by Corinthian (highly ornamental), and in many ways the flow of design styles follows that order over and over.

Colonial: Although generally thought of as an American style—see COLONIAL (AMERICAN)—Colonial also evokes the eighteenth- and nineteenth-century colonial experience in stiflingly hot climates, with verandas, white-painted weatherboarding, clapboard, handsome porticoes and pillars, shutters, mosquito nets, slatted furniture, rattan, muslin, and bare floorboards.

Colonial (American): This covers the period between the early 1600s (when the settlers had to make do with furniture that was primitive or imported) and the late eighteenth century, when the Federal government was established.

Colonial revival: Highly popular 1880s (also 1930s) American style, mixing the painted wood paneling, stenciling, and so on, of AMERICAN COUNTRY, with the fluted pilasters, Windsor chairs, etc., of early FEDERAL style.

Country style: See AMERICAN COUNTRY, ENGLISH COUNTRY, and FRENCH COUNTRY.

Contemporary: In interior design this means "of today," with current furnishings, colors, and mixtures.

Cromwellian: The period of the Commonwealth in England (1649–60), when Oliver Cromwell was Lord Protector of England, prior to the RESTORATION of the monarchy. It was a rather stagnant time for architecture, decoration, and furniture.

De Stijl: The name for a group of avant-garde Dutch designers in the 1920s who worked only in right angles and primary colors. Members of the group included the painter Piet Mondrian and the furniture designer Gerrit Rietveld.

Rietveld's architectural masterpiece was the Schroder House in Utrecht. With its clean-cut surfaces and metal-framed windows in continuous strips running up to a ceiling devoid of moldings, this was one of the model interiors for the INTERNATIONAL STYLE.

Directoire: French style, from the last five years of the eighteenth century, between the execution of Louis XVI during the French Revolution, and the *coup d'état* of Napoleon Bonaparte. This was really a simplified version of the last part of the LOUIS SEIZE style. The designs were elegant and simple, though the

1 *William Morris's bed at his house Kelmscott Manor, in Gloucestershire, England. Morris spearheaded the Arts and Crafts movement.*
2 *Design by Charles Rennie Mackintosh at the Glasgow School of Art. Mackintosh was a great exponent of the British version of Art Nouveau and was an international influence.*
3 *An Art Nouveau stair rail by the Belgian Art Nouveau designer Victor Horta.*

materials were of inferior quality to those of previous decades.

Eclectic: A combination of any number of styles and periods which, for this reason, is generally more idiosyncratic and interesting than any one style. The nineteenth century was a period of rampant eclecticism, when a number of style revivals coexisted.

Edwardian: The period between the 1890s and World War I. Design was much lighter and airier than the Victorian decoration that had gone before. The period encompassed the AESTHETIC MOVEMENT, ARTS AND CRAFTS MOVEMENT, ART NOUVEAU, and the QUEEN ANNE REVIVAL.

Elizabethan: Style during the reign of Elizabeth I of England in the second half of the sixteenth century. The period was one of great British prosperity, so there was an increased demand for more luxurious buildings and furniture. The style was based largely on the RENAISSANCE, as translated by the French and Flemish, so was actually quite idiosyncratic, with much carving and inlay. CLASSICAL architectural orders were used, though rarely in the proper proportions. Small wood panels were combined with pilasters and columns. In low-ceilinged rooms, the paneling generally rose from the baseboard to a primitive cornice. In grander homes, an oak dado was surmounted by a molding, then paneling, and finally an entablature. Flooring downstairs was most often flagstones or slates, and upstairs it was random-width oak planks.

Empire (American): The slightly more subdued American version of the French EMPIRE and English REGENCY styles appeared in the early part of the nineteenth century. Inspired by Greek, Roman, and Egyptian sources, the style encompassed many NEOCLASSICAL motifs together with lions'-paw feet, sphinxes, and Egyptian motifs, as well as the American bald eagle. Light cream or white woodwork was generally offset by red, green, blue, or yellow walls, or by European hand-blocked wallpapers with all-over patterns or scenic views. Either

2

3

part one: the basics

way, these backgrounds provided good foils for the mahogany furniture and the gilt mirror frames and details.

Empire (French): The Empire style was a French style of the early nineteenth century. Named for France's First Empire, it includes the Consulate (1799–1804) as well as the reign of Napoleon I (1804–15). Sometimes the reigns of Louis XVIII (1814–24) and Charles X (1824–30)–France's Restoration period–are also included. Motifs were strongly influenced by the discoveries of the ruins of Herculaneum and Pompeii and by Napoleon's Egyptian campaigns, hence the plethora of ancient Greek, Roman, and Egyptian motifs. Colors included Empire green, Empire ruby, lemon yellow, azure blue, amethyst, and pearl gray, all mixed with gold and white.

English Country: A broad, general style for which "benign neglect" and "faded elegance" are good descriptions. It is characterized by comfort, mellow colors, and slightly faded chintzes, rugs, and needlework cushions.

Etruscan: A decorative style based on Roman antiquity and Etruscan ornaments. ROBERT ADAM used many Etruscan motifs and ideas in his houses and, in turn, influenced the French, who called it *le style étrusque* and used it greatly in the late eighteenth century.

Federal: The term used to describe American architecture and design from the 1780s until the early nineteenth century, based on Neoclassicism. Highly prized in the United States, the style drew upon the designs of Sheraton and Hepplewhite, the early REGENCY in Britain, and the early EMPIRE in France. It used most of the familiar NEOCLASSICAL motifs, plus the American bald eagle as a symbol of the new federal government. Furniture was mainly mahogany or painted wood, and rooms reflected the abundance of new fabrics and French wallpapers in the country.

French Country: Also known as French Provincial, this style is characterized by Provençal print fabrics;

sunny color schemes of bright yellows, blues, pinks, and reds; whitewashed or colorwashed walls in soft tones of ocher, honey, rose, apricot, and russet; terracotta-tiled floors; and large, solid, unfussy furniture in either pine or chestnut, consisting of rustic, simplified versions of both LOUIS QUINZE and LOUIS SEIZE designs.

Georgian: A term applied to British architecture and design during the reigns of George I, II, III, and IV–i.e. from 1714 to 1830–a long period which went virtually from the PALLADIAN REVIVAL to the REGENCY. Sometimes called the "age of elegance," it was the golden age of British design in every field.

Gothic: The predominant style of ecclesiastical architecture in Europe during the Middle Ages, and one of the great influences on design throughout

the last millennium. The Gothic was much in favor in the eighteenth century as an antidote to rigorous CLASSICISM (when it was often spelled "Gothick"). It was enormously popular again in the nineteenth century, when it was called Neo-Gothic or the Gothic revival and was part of a reverence by the ARTS AND CRAFTS movement for all things medieval.

This revival interpreted it more seriously. Gothic decoration includes pointed arches, tracery, ogees, and medieval motifs such as the trefoil and quatrefoil.

Grand Tour: An almost obligatory part of the education for rich young men, particularly the British, who became known in Italy as *milordi*. They flocked to Italy, Greece, and, to a lesser extent, France, to steep themselves in classical antiquity. After two or three years of traveling, they returned laden with antiq-

uities, furniture, sculptures, paintings, and ideas on architecture, which greatly influenced the public taste.

Greek revival: An architectural movement that developed within the NEOCLASSICAL style stressing Greek rather than Roman and RENAISSANCE styles. It was at its height in Britain in the 1790s; and, in the 1820s–40s, it became equally popular in the United States, where it influenced many houses built at the time as well as a good deal of furniture. It was also popular in Europe, particularly Germany. Staircases became much lighter than previously, with splendid curves and slender stair rails. Painted, papered, and fabric-covered walls replaced wood paneling and were accompanied by handsome plaster cornices and beautiful mantelpieces.

Gustavian: A charming late eighteenth-century Swedish period style, named after Gustav III, who reigned from 1771 to 1792 and made the Swedish court a northern Versailles. The rooms were full of light from large windows, chandeliers, and mirrors. Walls, which were often hung with canvas, were painted with panels, swags, columns, or flowers. The style is typified by painted furniture; simplified Neoclassical designs; symmetry and understated elegance; cool colors such as blue-gray, straw yellow, muted pink, and pearl gray; checked fabrics; and distinctive tiled stoves.

High-tech: Also spelt hi-tech, this 1970s style was based on industrial components with a dash of MINIMALISM.

International style: Also known as Modernism, this was started by the BAUHAUS in the early 1920s. It advocated sleek lines, simplicity, natural textures, and pale, neutral colors. Gropius, Le Corbusier, and Mies van der Rohe were founder members of a style that has profoundly influenced architects and designers up to the present day.

Jacobean: The period style during the reign of the British king James I during the first quarter of the seventeenth century. (Sometimes it is extended to include also the Carolean period–the reign of Charles I, during the second quarter of the century.) Jacobean was essentially a more elaborate version of ELIZABETHAN style, but new ideas and proportions gleaned from the Palladian CLASSICISM of the Italian RENAISSANCE were better understood and were interpreted more accurately.

Louis Quatorze: During the long reign of the "Sun King," Louis XIV (1643–1715), France reached extraordinary heights of aesthetic splendor. With the magnificent Palace of Versailles as the seat of the French court, the opulent grandeur of BAROQUE style was allowed full rein. From that time till the first quarter of the nineteenth century, France was the leader of European taste. Bottle green or crimson velvet, tawny serge and damask wall hangings; embossed leather, sometimes decorated with foil, silvered, or gilded; tapestries; carved and gilded paneling (*boiserie*); marble or parquetry floors with Savonnerie carpets; gilt-bronze chandeliers, wall brackets, clocks, and other objects all typified the grandiose interiors of France in the *siècle d'or* ("golden century").

Louis Quinze: The French version of ROCOCO, which reached its height during the reign of Louis XV (1715–74). Colors were pale pastels with cream and white. Mirrors were used lavishly. They were set over console tables; were recessed into carved and gilded paneling (*boiserie*) opposite tall overmantel mirrors; and were used to disguise fireplaces in summer, as well as placed on ceilings and sometimes on sliding window shutters; occasionally entire walls were lined with them. Add to this the elaborately framed hanging mirrors, the hundreds of candles set into crystal candelabra and the *girandoles* (candlesticks set into mirrors), and you get a picture of the dazzle.

Louis Seize: The NEOCLASSICAL style that swept through Europe from the 1750s was known in France as *"le goût grec."* However, it is also known simply as Louis Seize, after the reigning monarch Louis XVI (1774–93), who presided over the full resurgence of Classicism in

France. Neoclassical motifs like caryatids, acanthus, and laurel wreaths appeared on furniture. Sky-blue cloud-painted ceilings and colors like terracotta and purple were added to the predominant gold and white, as Etruscan and Egyptian details began to be added to the Classical repertoire.

Mannerism: The transition between the RENAISSANCE and BAROQUE movements, in which designs included strangely attenuated human figures and "grotesque" ornament in the form of griffins, birds, and insects set within cartouches connected by strapwork designs. The term "grotesque" was derived from ancient Roman decoration excavated during the Renaissance, and had its roots in the word "grotto," or cave, rather than the current meaning. It was a deliberate reaction to the discipline of CLASSICISM and was particularly popular in northern Europe in the sixteenth and seventeenth centuries.

Minimalism: A 1970s, 1990s, and current movement which follows Mies van der Rohe's dictum that "less is more." All ornamentation is eschewed, along with clutter and most color. At its best, it is admirably clean-lined.

Mission: An 1890s/early 1900s American offshoot of the ARTS AND CRAFTS movement. Its exponents, particularly the Roycroft community and Gustav Stickley, believed they had a mission to promulgate utility of design. The name is also linked with the simple furniture of the early Spanish missions in California and New Mexico. The style is said to have begun when members of the congregation of a Franciscan Mission church in San Francisco made their own chairs to replace decrepit pews.

Modernism: See INTERNATIONAL STYLE.

Neoclassical: The first real international style and a major design force from 1760 to 1830. Originally a reaction against the frivolity and excesses of ROCOCO, it was the design equivalent of the Age of Reason. The style was influenced by the major archaeological discoveries of ancient Greece and of

ancient Rome at Herculaneum and Pompeii in 1738 and 1748, as well as Napoleon's Egyptian campaign. Motifs included acanthus leaves and lyres from Greece, lions' heads and paws, laurel wreaths from Rome, and crossed spears, swans' necks, sphinxes, and palmettes from ancient Egypt.

Neo-Gothic: See GOTHIC.

Orders: See CLASSICAL ORDERS.

Palladian and Neo-Palladian: Architectural style derived from the designs of Andrea Palladio, the great RENAISSANCE architect who based his pure, exquisitely proportioned buildings on the precepts of ancient CLASSICAL architecture. His designs were first introduced to Britain by Inigo Jones in the seventeenth century, and revived in the early eighteenth century. Interestingly, although Neo-Palladian (or Palladian revival) architecture was severely geometric, the furniture was rather BAROQUE in feeling. This is mainly because William Kent, the great eighteenth-century promulgator of Palladio's work, had no real model for ancient Classical

1 *A 1920s building by the Swiss-born French architect and furniture designer Le Corbusier, who was a leading influence on the International style.*

2 *A Swedish bergère with the gray-painted frame typical of the newly popular Gustavian style.*

2

furnishings, and so adapted the Baroque furniture he had seen in Palladian villas in northern Italy.

Prairie School: Designs by the American master architects Frank Lloyd Wright and Louis Sullivan, and a group of other architects and designers centered around Chicago from the late 1880s to the early 1900s; also known as the Chicago School. Its various influences were the low, rambling houses of the prairie, hence its name; the ARTS AND CRAFTS MOVEMENT from Britain; and the movement's American offshoot, MISSION.

Queen Anne: This gently simplified British adaptation of the BAROQUE was named for Queen Anne, who reigned from 1702 to 1714. Nothing much changed in room decoration from the WILLIAM AND MARY period preceding it, but furniture became fluid and beautiful, based on simple elegance, subtle curves and understatement. The vogue grew for CHINOISERIE and for "chinaware," which often covered every available shelf, as well as the walls. Wallpapers had a huge success with the middle classes, while the aristocracy were hanging Chinese silks. The style continued for several years after the monarch's death, till it gave way to the PALLADIAN REVIVAL style.

Queen Anne (American): In America the QUEEN ANNE style began to take hold just as it was waning in Britain (i.e., around 1720) and was influential until the middle of the eighteenth century.

Queen Anne revival: The so-called Queen Anne revival at the end of the nineteenth century in Britain had very little to do with the early eighteenth-century QUEEN ANNE style and was much more a mixture of NEOCLASSICAL designs, with the occasional nod to ROCOCO. It was led by the English country-house architect Richard Norman Shaw, who tried to reproduce this lightness of touch in revolt against Victorian heaviness.

Régence: Early eighteenth-century French style of richly gilded interiors during the transitional period between the magnificent BAROQUE of LOUIS QUATORZE and the full-blown ROCOCO of LOUIS QUINZE. It roughly coincided with the period when Philippe d'Orléans was regent to the young Louis XV.

Regency: The late NEOCLASSICAL British style named after the Prince Regent (later George IV), who was renowned for his expensive tastes. It was actually in favor during the first four decades of the nineteenth century and used Greek, Roman, Egyptian, French, Chinese, and Hindu motifs. One characteristic motif was the eagle, which appeared, for

example, in gilded window cornices, with the eagles supporting the curtains in their beaks. Also absorbed into the visual language of the style were pyramids, sphinxes, winged lions, and crossed-spear motifs, plus striped tenting and chairs with saber legs, all inspired by the military campaigns of the time against Napoleon, particularly in Egypt. Walls were often painted in intense colors like terracotta, maroon, or yellow. In addition to tented walls and ceilings, clouded ceilings were

fashionable. Curtains and draperies were elaborate and multi-layered, with outer draperies, under-curtains, muslin curtains, and shades, either on poles or with deep valances, and with complex trimmings.

Renaissance: One of the great watersheds of design, started in Italy in the great *quattrocento* (fifteenth century), the Italian equivalent to the glorious Greek fifth century B.C. The Renaissance, meaning rebirth, was the first revival of the CLASSICAL style.

It was most prevalent in the late fourteenth and fifteenth centuries in Italy, where the northern Gothic style had never really taken root, but it lingered until the seventeenth century. It spread to France in the first half of the sixteenth century and then to Spain, the Netherlands, and Germany. In England, a somewhat remote version resulted in the TUDOR style in the late sixteenth and early seventeenth centuries.

Renaissance revival: Also known as

Neo-Renaissance, this was a much favored style on both sides of the Atlantic in the latter part of the nineteenth century. Its heavy forms and elaborate decoration were actually taken from both the RENAISSANCE and the BAROQUE, and marked a return of interest in the NEOCLASSICAL style.

Restoration: The period after Charles II was restored to the British throne in 1660 following the CROMWELLIAN period. Restoration style was the first real English BAROQUE, impregnated with a sense of luxury and sumptuousness brought back by Charles from his sojourn at the grand court of Louis XIV. He imported Dutch, Flemish, Spanish, and French craftsmen, but the most famous craftsman of the period was the English woodcarver Grinling Gibbons. The taste for walnut started at this time, along with that for gilded gesso, silver decoration, and marquetry. Paneling, inspired by the *boiserie* at Versailles, ran from the dado to the ceiling, capped by a sophisticated cornice, with smaller, rectangular paneling set under the chair rail. Made from oak or walnut, it was left in its natural state and waxed, or was sometimes marbled. Tapestries were often hung within the larger panels. Softwoods were frequently grained to resemble the more expensive walnut or oak. Moldings and carvings were often gilded. If paneling was not used, walls were plastered and covered with damask or velvet. Cheaper alternatives were the new wallpapers. Oriental rugs began to be used on the parquet floors, rather than on tables. Adding to the richness were candle sconces in silver, brass, and iron, and the first crystal chandeliers.

Rococo: This movement originated in France around 1700. The style was particularly identified with the reign of Louis XV and spread all over Europe during the early eighteenth century, particularly to Germany, Austria, Spain, Scandinavia, and the Netherlands. It never reached quite the same heights of popularity in Britain and North America, although there were many Rococo pattern books in circulation. A reaction to the formal heaviness of the BAROQUE, it was a lighthearted, frivolous style. Its decoration relied on shells and flowers, its forms were curved, its furniture more comfortable, its colors pastel. Candles were reflected a hundred times by mirrors; windows were enlarged; the forms and motifs of CHINOISERIE were embraced, as well as anything to do with monkeys, often dressed up in human clothes.

Rococo revival: Also known as Neo-Rococo, this curvilinear, rather florid nineteenth-century style started in Britain, where French taste was once again vastly admired, in spite of the Napoleonic Wars. It was popular, too, in France, where it was known as *le style Pompadour*, during the reign of Louis-Philippe (1830–48). It reached Germany during the second half of the century and from there spread to the United States.

Santa Fe: See AMERICAN SOUTHWEST.

Shaker: A style loosely based on the simple, functional interiors of the Shaker sect, founded in 1774 but at their most populous in the United States in the first half of the nineteenth century. They are best known for their beautifully crafted, clean-lined wood furniture, much of it built-in, their stacking oval boxes with dovetail joints, and their habit of hanging chairs, brooms, mirrors, baskets, etc., on peg rails around the room, to keep the floors clear. They held that "beauty rests on utility"—a philosophy that was, in many ways, a precursor to the late nineteenth- and early twentieth-century doctrine of functionalism, and the American architect Louis Sullivan's famous tenet "Form follows function."

Troubadour: French, nineteenth-century version of the NEO-GOTHIC style, much influenced by the cult of medievalism. Gothic decoration was applied to furniture, tapestries, and small objects.

Tudor: Roughly the first half of the sixteenth century, this period style covers the reign of the English Tudor monarchs, apart from the ELIZABETHAN period of Elizabeth I. Gothic forms still predominat-

ed at the beginning of the period but were being slowly diffused by the gradual introduction of ideas from the Renaissance. Pargetting (decorative plasterwork), very often richly colored, covered the ceilings with Tudor roses, scrolls, cartouches, and fleurs-de-lis. Walls were generally paneled, and the field (center) of the panel was usually carved with a linenfold design.

Victorian: The umbrella title given to the period of Queen Victoria's reign in Britain from 1837 to 1901. In fact, the name was given to most nineteenth-century design all over the world during that time. It included an eclectic mixture of nostalgic revivalist styles, like Neo-Baroque, Neo-Renaissance, Neo-Rococo, and so on, as well as the avant-garde reactions to this selectivity, like the ARTS AND CRAFTS MOVEMENT, THE AESTHETIC MOVEMENT, and ART NOUVEAU.

Vienna Secession: In Germany and Austria, at the beginning of the

1 *William Palmer House in Michigan, USA, designed in the early twentieth century by the great American architect Frank Lloyd Wright, one of the "Prairie School" of architects.*

2 *The gasolier hanging down from the great dome in the Banqueting Hall of the Royal Pavilion, Brighton, England, includes a Chinoiserie dragon perching on the chain. The Royal Pavilion was designed for the Prince Regent by John Nash during the Regency period.*

twentieth century, the newly established Vienna Secession group began designing deliberately stark buildings with integrated interiors. Walls were plain plaster, devoid of cornices and moldings. These were the precursors of standardized mass housing.

William and Mary: This BAROQUE style, practiced in the late seventeenth century in Britain then in North America, was named after the joint reign in Britain of the Dutch William III (1689–1702) and his English wife, Mary II (1689–94). It was a more toned-down style than the exuberant Restoration period which preceded it, and a precursor of the splendid early eighteenth-century QUEEN ANNE style. William brought with him a team of Dutch craftsmen, as well as promulgating his own taste for the blue-and-white porcelain being shipped from China by the Dutch East India Company. At this time, too, many Huguenot craftsmen, among them the renowned cabinetmaker Daniel Marot, fled France for Britain by Louis XIV's revocation of the Edict of Nantes. This injected a whole new vigor into British craftsmanship.

part one: the basics

PART TWO

THE SPECIFICS

The walls and ceiling are the largest part of the framework of a room, and, although they are not necessarily as costly to cover as floors and windows, the ways in which you choose to treat them can either make or break the effect of the room. Historically, walls have always merited decorative interest and attention, and ceilings were almost always treated rather elaborately right up to the 1920s. Sadly, from then on, most of them reverted to a boring blankness. Yet, for both ceilings and walls, there is a great deal that can be done that can alter the whole atmosphere of a room.

Walls and Ceilings

Decorative Options

It is one thing to decide between paint, plain plaster, paper, fabric, mirror, or paneling for the walls and ceiling of a room—it is quite another to know the extent of all those options. Most people need an injection of ideas for what to do with such wide expanses, as well as advice on how to make the most of the plethora of techniques used today.

SPATIAL EFFECTS

As already mentioned in connection with color (see page 47), what you choose to do to the walls and ceiling can make a significant difference not just to its character, mood, and style but also to its seeming proportions and size. In fact, with the clever use of pattern, texture, and architectural details, as well as color, you could make it look smaller or longer, wider or narrower, cooler or warmer, lighter or darker and disguise any eyesores.

Of course, the *actual* space can also be altered, through structural changes such as adding walls or taking them away–which, unless they are load-bearing, is comparatively easy. By the same token, ceilings can be lowered physically, either to make proportions better or to form a deep-enough recess to install good lighting, especially for art and objects. Sometimes, too, ceilings can even be raised without too much expense, as long as there is enough space below the room above.

I *The elegant double doors and well-proportioned shelves in this room are actually cunningly executed* trompe l'oeil. *It is stunningly realistic.*
2 *A shoji screen has been used as a room divider between this kitchen and living space, letting light through and creating an attractive division where before there might have been an uninteresting wall.*

3 *A very grand trompe l'oeil drapery and tented ceiling are painted over and above the wide blue and white stripes in a tiled dressing-lobby area off a bathroom. The illusion is all the stronger for the propped processional lantern and the exotic gilded archway.*

part two: the specifics

3 An elaborately painted and plastered ceiling and painted wall panels give these two rooms a feeling of grandeur, even though the furniture and curtains are comparatively simple. The fireplace and the various bronzes are balancing features.

DECORATIVE CEILINGS

Decorative ceilings are a great source of pleasure in old houses and apartment buildings and are a source of wonder in some of the stately homes, châteaus, and *palazzi* open to the public. Ceilings have been a blank canvas, so to speak, for beams, moldings, *trompe l'oeil* effects, pictorial scenes, designs, and paint finishes for centuries. The eighteenth-century architect and designer Robert Adam used designs on the ceiling that were taken from a room's woven carpets.

Yet ever since the late 1920s and early '30s, ceilings have been more or less ignored. We have gotten into the habit of creating a smooth surface, erasing lumps, cracks, and stains as much as possible, and then simply painting them, most often in white.

1 A canopy of billowing, striped sheer fabric is threaded gently over the tops of beams in this bedroom, both to "lower" the double-height ceiling and to soften and lighten the spare four-poster bed and simple side tables. The white floor, ceiling, and walls make the lines of the furniture and the design of the bedspread stand out in sharp relief.

2 The sharply sloping ceiling in an attic kitchen has been painted to look like stretched and slightly wrinkled fabric, which gives the illusion of somewhat more space than there is. The glass shelf structure on the left of the room looks as if it is piercing right through the faux material.

part two: the specifics

In a well-proportioned modern room, I would agree with the dictum that "less is more." But it is the dull, unadorned whites and creams with no integral interest that we should do something to enliven. Occasionally one sees a cloud-painted ceiling, a mural, some tongue-and-groove paneling, or even a ceiling simply painted or tinted darker than the walls, but all these examples are rare. Yet uninteresting rooms can be made to look altogether more distinguished by giving the ceiling a special treatment. Possibilities include applying moldings or cornices, giving them a specialist paint treatment, using fabric to create a tented effect, or pasting up a striking ceiling paper.

In the box on the right are some recommendations for rooms of different heights, but obviously the choices

I This exceptionally high-ceilinged room also has extremely tall windows, so the deep squares formed by the beams draw your attention to the ceiling as well as helping the proportions of the room. The ceiling is further enhanced by the branch used as a fanciful chandelier.

you make will have to be governed by common sense, practicality, suitability, and, of course, cost.

All the same, there are so many new materials and new methods, and updated revivals of old techniques, that it is helpful to know something about the range of possibilities.

IDEAS FOR WALLS AND CEILINGS

If ceilings are a reasonable height:

- Edge the top of the cornice, if there is one, with strips of brass or with lengths of gilt picture frame molding fixed end-to-end.
- Paint the top stringing of a cornice (the part that edges out onto the ceiling) in a contrasting color, or cover it with gold or silver leaf.
- If your house or apartment is traditional in style—Colonial or Victorian, for example—you might add a cornice or crown molding and/or a ceiling rosette. Crown moldings are composed of several wood shapes or profiles, and their installation requires a skilled carpenter. Readymade plaster, resin, and carved wood cornices and rosettes can be purchased at relatively low cost.

If ceilings are too high:

- Install a picture rail about 18 in. (45 cm.) below the ceiling, and paint the wall above it in the ceiling color, to bring the eye down.
- Paint the ceiling a darker shade than the walls.
- Lower the ceiling and take the opportunity to install some recessed lighting, which will draw attention to what is on the walls.
- Add a chair rail and dado to break up the height of the walls. (For painted or papered dados, see page 107.)

If ceilings are too low:

- Vertically striped paper or painted stripes lead the eye up to give the illusion of more height.
- Install valances or window cornices just below the ceiling (rather than just above the tops of the windows) to make the windows appear taller, and so in turn exaggerate the ceiling height.
- Make tall, narrow panels for the walls using molding, paint, or paper, again to draw the eye upward.
- Use a shimmer paint on the ceiling.
- Install cool fluorescent tubes, and stretch voile or double-thickness cheesecloth just below, to light up the ceiling and make it appear to float.

2 Dark vertically striped paper makes a somewhat low-ceilinged room seem much taller—an illusion that is helped by the tall, skinny floor lamp and the large urns.

3 The kitchen ceiling is made to seem lower through the use of dark paint. The low-hanging light fixtures and gleaming floor also help to detract from the height.

4 Painted trim in this airy space is cleverly placed on the tongue-and-groove paneling to give the illusion of a tray ceiling. The same trim, used as coving, as well as around corners, window frames, and the French doors, makes the space seem very crisp and clean. Note the painted blue-and-white floor and how the blue is repeated in the sofa upholstery and the bench outside.

part two: the specifics

A Guide to Paint

Paint is a wonderfully versatile medium. Not only is there a huge range of colors available today, but virtually any shade can be mixed, whether by trial and error at home or by computer in a hardware store. It comes in a variety of textures and finishes, and in a choice of covering and protective qualities. Moreover, it can be used not just in the conventional way but also to simulate more precious surfaces.

PAINT VARIETIES

Paint basically consists of a pigment dispersed in some sort of binder, along with a solvent which makes the paint more workable and which evaporates when the paint dries. Some paints also contain resins or silicas to provide particular characteristics, such as quick-drying or anti-mildew qualities, textural effects, or special finishes that at one time could be achieved only by skilled decorative painters. For example, ranges are now available that emulate fabric, suede, leather, "wet looks," verdigris, and antique patinas.

Most paints are either water-based or oil-based. Both types come in several different finishes, which grade from dull to shiny, described by terms such as matte, flat, eggshell, satin, semigloss, and high gloss. Oil-based paints—also called alkyds—have lost some of their former popularity, overtaken by the increasingly versatile water-based paints. Known also as latex paints, these are combinations of resins (usually vinyls or acrylic) in water suspensions. Today's eggshell and satin latex paints, used in conjunction with acrylic primers or undercoats and with acrylic varnishes, are giving much the same professional finishes as those that used to be achieved with oil-based paints.

The main advantages of water-based paints over the oil-based variety are that water-based paints dry more quickly, leave no smell, and can be washed off hands and out of clothes. They used to be less hard-wearing, less easy to wipe down, and less attractive. However, all these disadvantages have been dispatched with the advent of the new colorwashes and varnishes. These can be applied afterward (and even on top of existing painted walls or woodwork), to give interesting translucent depths, as well as durability, to even the flattest of surfaces.

Non-drip paints

Both water- and oil-based paints are available in non-drip versions which do not need thinning or stirring, so that they can be applied immediately from can to wall or ceiling. Trays of "solid" latex paint, complete with a roller, are virtually drip-proof and so are especially useful for ceilings.

Epoxy enamels

These have a hard gloss finish which resists dirt and abrasion and can be used on ceramic tiles (as well as on masonry, metal, fiberglass, and porcelain). They are therefore ideal for painting over tiled walls in a kitchen or bathroom that is not to your taste. However, they do need careful handling and a long drying time, so follow the instructions on the can carefully.

Textured enamels

As they dry, textured enamels separate to give a "crazed" finish, so they are useful for painting wood paneling (as well as wood furniture and lamp bases), although a more subtle antique effect can be achieved in other ways (see page 101).

Distemper and milk paints

In recent years there has been a revival of interest—especially in Britain, but also in North America—in the paints that people used for decorating their walls before paint chemists discovered the decorative potential of latex. These early water-based or water-soluble paints, which could be made of various inexpensive, readily available ingredients, are called distemper. Today such paints are widely used in restoring old buildings.

One form of distemper, also called whitewash, consists of a chalk, known as whiting, dissolved in water and animal glue, with pigments added. It

America, where oil paints were hard to obtain and extremely expensive. It was made from skim milk, allowed to curdle, and then mixed with natural earth pigments and brick dust. Modern forms of these old milk paints, also known as buttermilk paints and casein paints (casein is the main protein in milk), are available from specialist paint dealers. They come in

lets walls "breathe," allowing moisture from damp walls to pass through it. But the main reason for its recent revival is its soft, subtle color ranges and lovely powdery appearance.

Another form of distemper, called milk paint, was used widely in Colonial

beautiful colors, including those that were used by the Shakers, and dry to a soft matte finish. Buttermilk paints can be thinned with water to produce a stain, and these paints can also be used to create a variety of decorative paint effects.

PAINT ALCHEMY

Many transformations can be produced through simple tricks with paint:

- Delineate a dull space with bands of color, by painting baseboards and/or moldings in a shade that contrasts with light-colored walls. Repeat the baseboard shade in the border of a rug or carpet.

- Paint two or three bands of subtle color in different widths on the walls, starting from just above the baseboard.

- Form a false cornice by painting one or two 2-3 in. (5-7.5 cm.) stripes immediately under the ceiling.

- For an interesting paneled look, stick rectangles of contrasting tape on plain painted walls, spacing them evenly.

- Disguise so-called eyesores—a confusion of unboxed pipes, off-center doors or windows, or too many breaks in ceiling levels (for example up a tall staircase)—by painting the area in a dark color so that everything melds together. Crispness can be regained with a pale floor covering.

- On the principle "If you can't beat 'em, join 'em," make a confusion of pipes look sculptural and interesting by picking them out in contrasting colors of paint.

1 A fanciful Middle Eastern feeling has been given to this bathroom by the painted motifs and borders on the walls as well as the exotic colored glass lights and the painted plaster-framed mirror. The sickle moons, candlesticks, and ceramics on the granite basin surround add to the Islamic influences.
2 Deeper yellow squares and rectangles make a most interesting abstract design, as well as confusing the angles on this wall.

part two: the specifics

TINTING AND APPLYING A GLAZE

When you tint a glaze, start with a small amount of tinting medium and slowly build up the amount of color until you get the shade you want.

- Squeeze a blob of artist's oil paint or tinting color into an old saucepan and stir in several tablespoons of turpentine or mineral spirit. Mix thoroughly until smooth. Test this mixture on a small area of wall prepared with your base coat.

- If you want to add more color or change the tone slightly, mix a bit more tint with some turpentine or mineral spirit in another old pan. Add this to the glaze and test again. Continue until you get the exact shade you want, but never add the artist's oil color or the tinting color straight from the tube, as it will not readily homogenize.

- Be sure the base coat is completely dry, and then apply the glaze evenly and confidently, using a sponge or rag and working in vertical strips. Keep it at the same consistency, and work quickly to avoid drips and clumps. Once the glaze is applied, it will dry fast.

- When the glazed finish has dried for 24 hours, you may want to varnish it. This will not only protect the glaze but also tend to darken the finish slightly, giving it a mellow look. Varnish is available in matte, semigloss, and gloss versions. Apply it with a roller, and brush it out with a large brush to get rid of any bubbles.

COLORWASHES

A colorwash is applied with a sponge or a paintbrush over a base coat of latex flat paint–even over existing latex flat on walls or woodwork–to give an attractive transparent finish of much greater subtlety than just plain paint. Colorwashes are available commercially, or you can make your own using a dye known as a tinting color. Or, you can simply mix small amounts of artist's gouache or acrylic color with water, and add the mixture, a little at a time, to soft-white latex flat that has been diluted with water in a proportion of at least three parts water to one part paint.

TRADITIONAL PAINT TREATMENTS

In previous centuries, paint colors had to be mixed individually, somewhat like an artist mixing tones on his palette. The inferior grinding of pigments would often give an uneven, textured quality to walls.

Early decorators practiced many special paint effects on walls, as well as on woodwork and furniture. At first, the techniques were used to simulate more expensive materials, such as rare hardwoods or marble, and were truly *faux* ("false") finishes, but soon they were also being used simply for their decorative effect.

Today these same techniques are enjoying renewed popularity, and they still fall into the category of either a decorative finish (such as dragging, stippling, stenciling, and so on) or a *faux* finish (which imitates other materials like marble, tortoiseshell, lapis lazuli, various woods, malachite, and ivory). Whether you want to experiment yourself or just commission various finishes, it is useful to know something about the main techniques.

GLAZES

Most special paint effects rely on glazes, which either are applied over a dry, opaque base coat, in order to give a

translucent effect or are distressed in some way to achieve a particular effect like dragging, ragging, or stippling.

A glaze is a transparent film, usually tinted, and it adds richness and depth to any wall treatment. If a glaze is tinted with a hue from the same color family as the base coat, the resulting shade will be a delicately deepened tone. On the other hand, if the glaze and the base coat are from different color families, the resulting color will be an entirely new one, with the additional richness of translucence.

Any glazing technique will look better with colors that are similar in intensity, or with a darker color over a

lighter one. A Sienna brown glaze over deep green, for example, produces a lovely terracotta; dark gray over Pompeian red looks like Moroccan leather; and dark green over medium green makes walls a subtle jade.

Glazing liquids, sometimes called scumble glazes, are available at good hardware stores. Traditionally, they were oil-based, but now water-based acrylic glazes are also available. You will need a smaller amount of glaze than you would of paint, because you will be applying a thinner coat. It looks like canned cream of chicken soup to begin with, but if it seems too thick, thin it gently with mineral spirit.

1 *Trompe l'oeil panels in sand and pale papaya counteract the elaborate white-painted plaster-work above them, as well as making an interesting background for the collection of ceramics on the chest.*

2 *A tracery of twiggy trees painted onto the yellow walls in this hall adds a softness in contrast to the diamond-shaped floor tiles. The door has been dragged with the same cheerful yellow shade.*

3 *Deliberately uneven-textured walls in this old bedroom have been stenciled with white fleurs-de-lis, which look good with the small but quite elaborate headboard.*

part two: the specifics

1 *Mint green loosely ragged over blue-gray (used on its own for the room next door) creates an unusual effect.*
2 *A painted dado, chair rail, and borders in 1930s colors look as ancient and worn as an Etruscan fresco, making an unusual background for the classic 1920s leather chair.*
3 *Printed leaf shapes (made by dipping real leaves in paint and patiently reapplying them to the wall) are strewn as thickly in this powder room as on an autumn path. Note how the mirrors have been painted in the same tones as the leaves, which look particularly mellow against the yellow walls and the various brass fittings.*
4 *Stippled apricot walls are paired here with a dragged umber-tinted cream doorway. Yellow stippled onto a red background makes a far truer apricot than any conventional or even specially mixed paint color.*

ADDITIVE AND SUBTRACTIVE TECHNIQUES

Most decorative finishes can be classified as either additive or subtractive. With additive techniques, a glaze or wash is applied in a broken film over a dry base coat using a sponge or a rag (the texture affects the finish). Additive techniques are the simplest, since the drying time of the glaze or wash is not critical, and you can work on your own. It is best to work in vertical strips. Once the first glaze is dry, you can always add another one on top or a second coat in a different shade.

With subtractive techniques, a glaze is rolled or brushed onto a dry base coat (usually an oil-based semi-gloss in soft white or cream) and then distressed with a sponge, a wad of tissue paper or of burlap, a soft rag, a stippling brush, a comb, or another tool of your choice.

Subtractive methods are a great deal easier if done by two people: one to apply the glaze and the other to distress it, since you have to work quickly before the glaze dries.

The effects you get with techniques like ragging, rag-rolling, sponging, and shading depend upon whether they are

3

done with a colorwash or a glaze, and they can be done using either additive or subtractive methods. Stippling, dragging, and combing are best done with glaze in subtractive mode.

DRAGGING

Dragging is achieved by applying a glaze of transparent color over a chosen base coat (semigloss so that the glaze doesn't sink into the surface) and then dragging a dry, wide brush through it before it dries. The glaze is

generally a darker shade than the undercoat, and the resulting softly textured look of fine, irregular vertical striations gives a distinguished look to a wall or woodwork.

STIPPLING

Stippling is a little less difficult than dragging but just as decorative. It is often used in conjunction with dragging–for example, dragged moldings and a stippled ground on paneled walls. It can look as soft as

chamois leather, or as pitted as orange peel, for stippled walls are dappled with flecks of color without emphatic definition, allowing the base color to become very much a part of the whole.

As with dragging, the tinted glaze is applied to the chosen semigloss base coat, and then removed with a professional stippling brush (which you can get from a specialist paint dealer) or with a scrubbing brush. You can also use a large sponge for a more muted look.

RAGGING

Ragging is a more free-flowing and irregular version of stippling, which is therefore easier to do alone. It is good in a small space because the somewhat cloudy effect creates an illusion of airiness and softness. Ragging is done with a bunched-up rag or piece of cheesecloth, burlap, or tissue paper. The coarser or crisper the material, the coarser or crisper the result.

Try rolling pastels over a creamy-white base coat. Alternatively, for an

part two: the specifics

extremely subtle look, use a tinted white over white, or an umber-tinted cream over cream.

LACQUERING

This ancient craft originated in the Far East. If done properly, the process is very time consuming, since up to 40 coats of lacquer are applied, each of which is buffed and burnished with a pad of steel wool before the next coat can be applied. But the effect is as deeply rich as it is rewarding, and the surface is extremely hard-wearing. Happily, there are a number of facsimile techniques which are less time consuming, although they still require a good deal of patience.

If you are lacquering walls (as opposed to a piece of furniture, which is where it is more often used), you have to start with an absolutely smooth surface. The simplest method is to apply a couple of coats of thinned-down semigloss or high-gloss varnish over two or three coats of oil-based flat or semigloss paint, depending on how shiny you want your surface. A more complex method is to apply a series of tinted glazes over a base coat.

The whole is then varnished for protection and increased depth. This creates an extremely pretty deep gleam rather than a high gloss. Remember that when you are applying varnish to any surface, the room must be totally free of dust.

ANTIQUING

Another very effective technique is antiquing. This artificially ages a surface, even one of the decorative surfaces described above, by applying either a "dirty" wash or a glaze tinted with a small amount of raw umber, burnt umber, or burnt sienna, which makes the surface appear softer and deeper and gently aged. You can either mix up your own or use a commercial "aging" liquid. Similarly, woodwork can be helped along to a distinguished old age by applying a light umber-tinted wash or glaze.

CRACKLE GLAZE AND CRAQUELURE

These products are applied to painted surfaces to reproduce the network of fine cobwebbing that often appears in old painted and varnished surfaces. They are used to give modern materials–such as MDF (medium density fiberboard), resin-manufactured objects, and modern unit furniture–the verisimilitude of graceful aging. Both products are available commercially. (An alternative method, which produces a realistic aged appearance, is to paint a surface with an acrylic or red oxide metal primer and contrast it with latex flat colors, followed by polyurethane varnish, perhaps topped off with an antiquing glaze.)

GRISAILLE

This technique utilizes shading and highlighting to trick the eye into supposing that a surface is raised or indented. It was usually executed in grays, black, and white, but it can also look effective in different shades of terracotta, or in umber and cream. It is effective for suggesting architectural details like panels, architraves, and moldings, but it also looks extremely good (if the application is skillful) in classical images like urns, caryatids, pilasters, columns, and *putti* (cherubs).

STENCILING

The ancient art of stenciling originated in China before 3000 B.C. and was apparently used in Europe from the sixth century A.D. It continued to grow as a popular form of decoration up until the eighteenth century, and was popular once again in the nineteenth century. It was favored by the early settlers in North America instead of more expensive wallpapers (and also on floors, furniture, and soft furnishings). Now many popular wallpapers emulate stenciling– *plus ça change*.

In any event, it is a useful and decorative art to practice and is fairly easy. Just remember that stencils look a good deal better in soft, slightly uneven colors that do not look too newly applied. Instant aging can be applied here, either by rubbing it with fine steel wool or by painting over the design with a thin wash of off-white latex flat or an umber-tinted glaze or varnish.

PLAIN PLASTER

Plaster, which used to be the main ingredient of an interior wall, should not be forgotten. Old-fashioned plaster walls were made by troweling layers of a mixture of lime and wet sand onto a wire mesh, which enabled walls to be curved and variously shaped, if so desired. After six months or so of waiting for the plaster to dry out, the wall was generally painted or papered, although its natural creamy pink color is a nice finish in itself, particularly if sealed or wax-polished. Today, comparatively few walls are made like this, but you can apply a skim coat of plaster to chipboard, MDF (medium-density fiberboard), or wallboard.

Plaster can be left natural, or it can be textured with marble or metallic powder for a sparkle, or, more roughly, with straw, wood chips, or sawdust. The purest finish of all is obtained by burnishing with kaolin (available from some builders' suppliers), which is used to whiten porcelain. Rubbed onto plaster, it makes it a gleaming white.

1 An interestingly decorated door is painted a patchy dirty yellow in subtle contrast to the sleek bathroom beyond.
2 A framed grisaille looks very handsome over this fireplace, against pale yellow dragged walls. The grays contrast with the soft roses and terracottas of the upholstery and the border, placed just below the ceiling line.
3 Painted trees, a black-and-white photograph of foliage, a vase of leaves, and a plant make an attractive corner without overly stretching the theme. Such visual puns are fun displayed here and there in a home.
4 Stenciled horses following the design of the bedspread are used to make a frieze around the bed in this child's room. Another cutout horse is framed in a darker gray and fixed to the wall above in a repeat of the pillow. The painted chair tones in with the general coloring, as does the otherwise alien bear in this principally equestrian world.

part two: the specifics

Vocabulary of Paint Terms

Old black-and-white framed photographs contrast well with a patchy, worn wall in an Indian palace. This look can be emulated by distressing or antiquing a wall, but here it is entirely genuine.

Acrylic colors: Quick-drying artists' colors, which are excellent for STENCILING. The PIGMENTS are mixed in a water-soluble polyacrylic base, resulting in clear, matte colors. Can be used diluted with water for a transparent effect or undiluted for an opaque effect.

Alkyd : A synthetic resin used in paint; another term for an oil-based paint used for interior or exterior painting. See also OIL PAINT.

Antiquing: Artificially aging paint, usually by rubbing over the new paint surface with a "dirtying" GLAZE or a COLORWASH of raw umber, burnt umber or burnt sienna. (On furniture, the surface may then be wiped over with a cloth, leaving the darker color in the crevices.) Antiquing also applies to rubbing off new paint with steel wool to give a patchy, worn look.

Badger blender: Finest badger-hair brush to blend and soften a COLORWASH or a GLAZE that has been applied with a different brush, a sponge, or a rag and is not yet dry. A DUSTING BRUSH is a less expensive substitute.

Bagging: Creating a textured finish by wrapping a rolled-up cloth in a plastic bag and then working over a newly applied oil-glazed surface, either in a particular pattern or at random. Never do more than 2 square yards (2 square meters) at a time, or the GLAZE will dry before it has been textured.

Base coat: Applied before topcoats of paint or glaze to give a good surface and coverage. If you are painting over a dark color with a light one, you may need two coats of base coat and one topcoat. (It is a good idea to thin the first coat with a little water.) If you are painting a dark topcoat over a light base coat, tint the base coat with a little of the topcoat, or buy an appropriately tinted standard base coat. A PRIMER is usually used on a new surface like wood or plaster before applying a base coat.

Broken color: Two or more coats of different-colored paint, in which the top layer(s) have been partially removed to reveal the color beneath.

Brushes: Many different specialized brushes are used in painting, depending on the method used. These include a BADGER BLENDER, , DRAGGER, DUSTING BRUSH, FITCH, FLOGGING BRUSH, MOTTLER, OVER-GRAINER, STENCILING BRUSH, STIPPLING BRUSH, and SWORD STRIPER.)

Buttermilk paint: See MILK PAINT.

Button polish: See SHELLAC.

Casein paint: A paint made from pigments in a casein (milk-curd) medium. It is opaque and powdery (though less powdery than DISTEMPER). Use it thinned with two parts water for a COLORWASH, or with white casein for cream and pastel shades. Tough, water-resistant, and inexpensive, but not widely available.

Chalkboard paint: Used for creating a chalkboard on a surface, such as on a portion of wall in a child's room or on a large piece of primed and undercoated board fixed to a wall.

Cissing: The reverse of SPATTERING, this is achieved by applying a GLAZE or COLORWASH to a dry base coat, and then, while the glaze or colorwash is still wet, spattering on mineral spirit or turpentine (for oil-based paint) or water (for water-based paint).

Colorwash: A delicate, transparent wash of color. It was traditionally achieved with watered-down, tinted DISTEMPER but today is generally done using a LATEX, GOUACHE, or ACRYLIC paint diluted with water.

Combing: Broken finish, or a pattern such as basket weave, achieved by dragging a coarse comb of specially cut stiff cardboard or plastic, or of wood or steel, through a wet GLAZE.

Crackle glaze: Obtainable from specialist paint dealers, imitates the effect of old, peeling paint. Crackle glaze is applied between two different-colored coats of water-based paint, producing a network of cracks in the top layer of paint through which the underneath layer is visible.

Craquelure effect: A method in which two VARNISHES that dry at different rates are applied to a painted surface to imitate the crazing that develops in layers of old varnish. It produces finer crazing than CRACKLE-GLAZE but is expensive.

Decorator's brush: Chiefly British term for any non-specialist paintbrush used for painting walls and other large, flat surfaces.

Distemper: Powdery paint, which can be mixed to make extremely pretty pastel colors and COLORWASHES. Also known as whitewash, it is made from animal glue, whiting, pigments and water. Also, any pre-latex water-soluble paint, such as MILK PAINTS.

Distressing: Making surfaces look older and time-worn through techniques such as BROKEN COLOR.

Dragger: A long-bristled brush which is used for DRAGGING.

Dragging: The process of dragging a dry brush, such as a DRAGGER or FLOGGING BRUSH, through a wet GLAZE or COLORWASH to produce an irregular, fine-lined effect.

Dusting brush: Used for small-scale stippling work, such as on a baseboard, but can also be used for softening and blending instead of a BADGER BLENDER, or for dragging instead of a DRAGGER. The soft, medium-length bristles should be very carefully cleaned and must never be immersed in solvent, or the bristles will drop out.

Enamel: Oil-based paint which is so dense that only one coat is needed; most often used for small areas of wood or metalwork.

Epoxy enamel: A tough oil-based ENAMEL paint with a hard finish that resists dirt, grease, and scratches. Ideal for painting over ceramic tiles, porcelain, fiberglass, masonry, and metal.

Fitch: A small, rather stiff-bristled brush used for small-scale work, such as detailed STIPPLING work and SPATTERING. Available in fan, angled, oval, and flat shapes.

Flogging brush: A long-bristled brush used for DRAGGING and GRAINING, as it picks up the GLAZE easily when pulled across the surface. The brush is used with a slapping technique.

Gilding: Adding a gold finish. Traditional gilding uses gold leaf, or some other metal leaf, which is fixed to a surface with GOLD SIZE. A gilt effect can be reproduced using bronze, silver, or aluminum powders.

Glaze: Traditionally a transparent oil-based finish (also known as scumble), but a water-based, acrylic glaze can now be obtained, which is much faster-drying. A tinted glaze has to be applied before any sort of broken finish can be produced.

Glue size: See SIZE.

Gold size: A rapid-drying oil VARNISH, usually used as an adhesive in traditional GILDING and as a medium for some quick-drying paints.

Gouache: Concentrated colors in a water base which give an especially clear, fresh, matte finish. Used neat to decorate paneling (or furniture) or use to tint water-based colors or COLORWASHES.

Graining: A highly specialized art reproducing every kind of wood grain using paint in a most realistic manner.

Japanning: Old term for LACQUERING, dating back to late seventeenth- and early eighteenth-century imitations of imported lacquerwork from the Far East.

Lacquering: A technique involving the patient application of many coats of VARNISH, one upon another, sanded down each time when dry before another coat is applied, to create a smooth, lustrous finish. The original lacquering technique, which was developed in the Far East, involved applying many layers of a lacquer made from the sap of the lac tree. Lacquering is used for furniture, but a lacquer effect on walls can be produced by applying semigloss or high-gloss varnish over paint (with a roller to avoid brushstrokes) or by using a tinted GLAZE.

Latex paint: Water-based paint consisting of pigment bound in a synthetic resin. It is available in matte or flat, satin or semigloss, and gloss finishes. Soluble in water, it is quick-drying and does not necessarily need an undercoat.

Liming: The process of "whitening" wood, particularly oak. Excellent for new paneling and for elderly, as opposed to old, oak furniture. Liming paste for producing this effect is available from specialist paint dealers.

Lining brush: A thin brush used to make narrow decorative lines. Artists' sable brushes work very well, or a SWORDLINER can be used.

Marbling: The technique of producing *faux* marble. This can either copy a particular type of marble as closely as possible or give the general effect of marble. The latter approach is sometimes known as marbleizing.

Milk paint: A simple CASEIN PAINT, in which powder colors are mixed with buttermilk or skimmed milk. It was widely used in Colonial America and produces lovely, clear colors and a smooth, flat finish. Protect with matte VARNISH.

Mineral spirit: A SOLVENT used to dilute oil-based GLAZE or paint and to soften old LATEX finishes.

Mottler: A brush used to mottle, highlight, or distress GLAZES when GRAINING.

Oil paint: This comes in three finishes: gloss, semigloss, or eggshell, and matte or flat. It is soluble in mineral spirit or turpentine and takes much longer to dry than water-based varieties.

Over-grainer: Very small brush with clumps of soft hairs like individual long-pointed artist's brushes. It is used to add fine details or a darker grain to a GRAINED surface—in other words, to delicately *add* color, rather than take it off, as most paint-finish brushes do.

Pigment: The coloring element of paints. It is available in many forms, including powder; compressed cakes or blocks; artist's oil, GOUACHE or ACRYLIC colors; and TINTING COLORS. In general, like should be mixed with like—SOLVENT-thinned pigment with solvent-thinned paint, and water-thinned powders with water-thinned paint—but tinting colors can be mixed with either oil- or water-based paints.

Polyurethane varnish: See VARNISH.

Priming: A primer is generally used on new surfaces (wood or plaster) to seal it before applying an UNDERCOAT and then the final finishes.

Ragging: Using rags to achieve a particular painted finish. The exact finish depends upon the type of fabric used.

Rag-rolling: Using a rolled rag to get the desired effect when RAGGING.

Rottenstone: Fine, gray abrasive powder, bought from specialist paint stores. Rottenstone is mixed with lemon oil, baby oil, or sunflower oil to form a paste, which can then be used to give the final polish to a wall that has been varnished.

Shellac: A quick-drying spirit-based VARNISH, available in "transparent" form (actually, a yellowish-brown), orange, white (which is almost clear), and brown. Orange shellac, also known as button polish, can be used to go over metal leaf to simulate gold.

Size: Also known as glue size, this serves as a medium to bind paint. In addition, it can be used as a sealant, instead of PRIMER, to prevent fresh plaster (and also unpainted wood) from absorbing too much paint when being painted, or too much paste when being wallpapered. Plastic-based sizes such as PVA (polyvinyl acrylic) are used with synthetic paints like LATEX PAINT, and animal sizes with natural paints such as DISTEMPER and CASEIN PAINTS. The best quality is made from rabbit skin.

Solvents: Used to dilute paint, GLAZE, or VARNISH and to clean brushes. MINERAL SPIRIT and TURPENTINE are both solvents for oil-based products, and water is the solvent for water-based products.

Spattering: A simple, BROKEN-COLOR technique that consists of spattering a dry surface with dots of color. It is an additive technique.

Sponging: This technique can either be additive (by sponging color onto a previously painted surface) or subtractive (by dabbing GLAZE off for a more subtly painted distressed effect). Either way, sponging is one of the easiest paint finishes to achieve.

Stenciling: The application, usually repeated, of paint through cutout shapes in a stencil, using a STENCILING BRUSH or sponge. A stencil that will be used on walls should be cut from oiled manila paper or acetate so that it will be long-lasting.

Stenciling brush: A short, plump brush with shorn-off hog's-hair bristles, which looks somewhat like a shaving brush. It gives a more interesting effect, with a crisper edge, than an ordinary brush.

Stippling: A good, soft finish for a large area. The effect is produced by gently dabbing a STIPPLING BRUSH against a wet GLAZE or coat of paint.

Stippling brush: A rectangular brush with long and short detachable handles. The long one is used for STIPPLING walls, the short for close work. It lifts off fine flecks of paint to produce the typical stippled and freckled effect very well indeed. Cheaper alternatives are a man's old hairbrush or an old clothes brush.

Sword striper: A type of LINING BRUSH used for making fine, thin lines, particularly in MARBLING. Its bristles taper to a point.

Tinting colors: Synthetic dyes, which are obtainable in good artists' suppliers and paint stores. They can be used for tinting paints and GLAZES. Tinting colors can be used for either oil-based or water-based paints.

Tossaway brush: An inexpensive brush, often used to apply varnish, which can be thrown away after use.

Trompe l'oeil: Literally, to trick or deceive the eye by painting illusionist effects, particularly using shading and highlighting and perspective.

Turpentine: A SOLVENT used for cleaning brushes, as well as for thinning artists' oil paints.

Undercoat: Standard paint to apply as a thin, dry coat before main coats of paint for a better finish.

Universal stainers: British term for TINTING COLORS.

Varnish: Final transparent layer to harden and protect a decorative finish. Varnishes come in matte or flat, semigloss, and gloss finishes. The quick-drying acrylic varnishes, which are water-based, are superseding polyurethane and oil-based varnishes.

Verdigris: The blue-green shade that copper and bronze turn with age. It can be replicated in paint on any surface.

Wash: See COLORWASH.

part two: the specifics

Wallpapers

Wallpapers, from cheerful stripes to the most opulent scenic papers, are quick to set a mood. They brighten up a dull room; change the feeling, style, and apparent proportions; and give a proper unity. They are also extremely useful for disguising flawed or uneven walls. An enormous choice of patterned, textured and plain, or almost plain, papers is available today, from the inexpensive machine-made variety to expensive hand prints. In addition, there are separate borders (which can be used on painted walls or on top of paper); borders that match or coordinate with papers; friezes; and papers in different scales of the same design to be used together. In fact, the difficulty is more one of narrowing down the choice than of finding a paper that is suitable within a price range.

VINYL WALLPAPERS

Vinyl wallpapers are waterproof and tough especially because they are made from polyvinyl chloride with a backing, rather than being just a paper with a plastic coating (as are ordinary "washable" papers). They can be scrubbed (with slight pressure) as opposed to the gentle washing which is all that washable papers can withstand. Vinyl papers are, therefore, a good choice for bathrooms, kitchens, and children's rooms, as well as halls and passageways, or anywhere that walls are likely to be touched a lot. However, they must be pasted on with a fungicidal adhesive, otherwise a disagreeable mold can form beneath.

TEXTURED PAPERS

These heavy wallpapers, with their embossed patterns are particularly useful for covering irregular surfaces. Designed to be painted over, they are most often used for dados in hallways because of their durability. Lincrusta is an example of this type of paper. The other principal type of textured paper is flock wallpaper, with a relief pattern that imitates cut velvet. Textured papers go in and out of fashion; they were very popular in the eighteenth century, at the end of the nineteenth century, and from the 1930s to the late 1950s, and are now often seen again.

Some colored and neutral burlaps, grass cloths, silks, linens, felts, and foils can be bought with a paper backing, which enables them to be hung like ordinary wallpaper. In fact, many firm materials that are suitable for covering a wall can have a backing applied to them, so that you can achieve the luxury of a fabric-lined room without the trouble of battening or upholstering the walls.

LINING PAPER

If your ceiling or walls are really uneven, lining paper will help achieve a good finish. The heavier the lining, the better it will hide defects. On walls it should be hung horizontally and stuck precisely edge-to-edge so that no bulge will show through when the decorative wallpaper is put on.

FACTORS TO CONSIDER

Before finally settling on a paper, spend time thinking about the effect you want to create. Pin a length of paper to the wall. Try it out with window treatments and upholstery fabrics, both existing and possible, before you make a final choice. Look at patterned papers carefully. It might not be apparent in a small sample that a floral design is actually in stripes, or ogees, or on a diagonal, but they often are. So get samples showing repeats, and always familiarize yourself with the overall effect of a design before finally choosing.

When measuring a room for wallpaper, bear in mind the size of the repeat in the design (this is almost always stated on the paper). Lengths of paper must, of course, be matched together perfectly.

1 *In an undistinguished room, an allover patterned paper, used literally all over walls and ceiling, can inject instant character. The fabrics on the daybed and at the window harmonize well, as does the painted chest-cum-coffee table.*
2 *A textured camel-colored grass-cloth wall covering makes a good-looking background for the dark furniture and the striped rug and dust ruffle in this bedroom.*

3 *"Print room" paper on a creamy-yellow background recreates the feeling of an eighteenth-century print room, when engravings were glued straight onto the walls and given exotic paper "frames."*

WALLPAPER BORDERS

Borders come in various depths and in every conceivable design, from florals, fanciful ribbons and swags, and children's motifs to china dogs and gardening and sporting themes; and from serious, seemingly three-dimensional copies of architectural moldings to narrow solid-color strips. No more than 2 in. (5 cm.) deep, the latter are useful for subtly delineating the perimeter and detailing of a room. Indeed, the chief roles of a border are either to define or to break up a given space, and either to take the place of missing architectural details or, if these exist, to define them further.

Borders at the tops of walls

The most common way to use a border is to buy one that coordinates with or matches your chosen paper and run it around the top of the wall, just below the ceiling or just below the cornice, if there is one.

Personally, I do not see the point of running a very deep border under an existing molding because I think it makes walls look top-heavy (unless a ceiling is inordinately high, in which case it will help to lower it visually).

If there are existing, fairly elaborate moldings, you might like to consider using one of the slim, solid-colored borders, instead of a border

CHOOSING WALLPAPER PATTERNS

The kind of pattern you choose depends entirely on personal taste and the proportions of the room. There are, however, certain guidelines that make the task of choosing patterns easier.

- In a living room, it is preferable to use a simple design or fairly plain paper (such as a paper made to look like a decorative paint effect). Strong or definite patterns can be distracting and do not make good backgrounds for paintings and prints. A border or frieze is a good way to set off the paper here.
- Dark papers generally make a room seem smaller.
- Vertical stripes will make a room seem taller.
- Horizontal stripes will seem to broaden out a space.
- Mini-prints, small geometrics, stripes, *faux* panels, linear prints, small florals, and gentle modern abstracts can be successfully used in bedrooms.
- Small prints are a good choice for small bedrooms.
- More open patterns look best in larger spaces.
- Scenic and geometric designs, florals, large abstracts, papers with borders, and trellis papers can be used to good effect in halls and corridors and on staircases. (Bear in mind that whatever you choose for the hallway in a house often has to go upstairs also.)

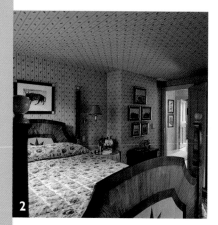

that has been made to go with the paper. If the wallpaper is a stripe or *faux* finish or is fairly plain, this border could be in a tone that is deeper than the paper or contrasts with it. Or, if the paper is patterned, the border could be in a color that appears in the paper. This will help define the demarcation point and will also draw attention to the molding without competing with it for attention.

More border ideas

Of course, a border does not have to be used just with wallpaper. Any border that seems appropriate can be used on plain painted walls, either to take the place of an architectural molding or simply to add a little pizzazz.

Borders can be run along the tops of baseboards, around windows or doors, or even vertically down the corners of rooms. They also look highly effective when defining the angles of the sloping walls in an oddly shaped attic room.

Use a border to make a false chair rail, and then paste a contrasting or coordinating paper below it, to create a false dado. Or do the same on a plain painted wall, with either wallpaper or a different paint finish below. When you meet a doorway, either stop the border at one side and resume it on the other, or run it around the door as well. Another idea is to paste a narrow border both above and below an actual chair rail.

Making your own borders

Although it is a tedious operation, it is often worthwhile cutting up wide borders and friezes to use in different ways around a room or in adjoining rooms or hallways. For example, if a border or frieze is many-edged, like an oriental rug, you can cut off some to form a narrow border to run around doors or windows. Or use them to form panels on a fairly plain background such as painted walls, leaving enough edge to frame the main border, which will go under the ceiling as usual.

Alternatively, buy extra border so that you can leave the main border alone and use the surplus to provide coordinating edges to define doors, baseboards, or the corners of a room, or to run around a corridor or bathroom off a bedroom.

Another way to create your own borders is to cut strips from any wallpaper that has the right linear design (such as side-by-side or vertical repeats or stripes). Or you can stick on ribbon, such as grosgrain, braid, cord, or thick yarn.

1 *A simple striped paper is hard to beat for instant elegance. This one, teamed with checked cotton upholstery in a similar shade of blue, makes a good background for the bordered creamware platters arranged on the mantelshelf.*
2 *A mini-patterned "little nothing" paper, again used on walls and ceiling, provides an effectively neutral background for a decorative bed and a print collection.*
3 *The deep, swagged border pasted over black marbled paper in a high-ceilinged hall, already complete with cornice, helps to reduce the apparent height of the space, thus giving the illusion of much better proportions than actually exist.*

part two: the specifics

MAKING A LITTLE PAPER GO A LONG WAY

If your taste runs to very expensive wallpaper, you can get much of the effect at much less of the cost by the following ploys:

- Use it below a chair rail only. If you do not have a chair rail, create one (at chair-top height) with an appropriate molding or a wallpaper border.

- Buy only one or two rolls, depending upon the size of the room, and cut the paper into panels (first working out the size of the panels on a plan of the walls drawn to scale on graph paper and then drawing them on the wall). Paste the paper within the drawn frames, and frame the panels with narrow wooden molding, picture frame molding, or strips of paper border.

- Use one roll of paper like a very large painting on an empty wall, framing it with molding or a paper border.

WALLPAPER FRIEZES

If a border is deep enough, it can justifiably be called a frieze. Some will even fill the entire space between picture rail and ceiling in a very high-ceilinged room, which will usually help to lower the height. If a high-ceilinged room has no moldings, you can create the appearance of a picture rail by using a slim molding in a coordinating or matching color and then pasting a frieze above. You can also buy embossed friezes which tend to emulate old and ornamental plaster cornices, or crown moldings, and are also generally deep enough to fill the gap between a picture rail and the ceiling. They need to be painted which can be done to imitate old plaster by "antiquing" the paint (see page 101).

ILLUSIONIST DETAILS

Apart from all the conventional and unconventional ranges of papers and borders, you can choose from ranges of cut-out paper architectural details, scenic papers, and wall paneling to create your own architectural fantasies, interior follies, and *trompe l'oeil* illusions. It is possible to buy elaborate paper swags and rosettes; columns (Doric, Ionic, Corinthian, or Tuscan), pilasters, cornices, and broken pediments; balustrades and balusters; arches and arched alcoves; urns, classical busts and statues; and scenic and sky papers.

Or you can use tongue-in-cheek "paneled," "book-lined," or "print room" papers, which are especially fun in powder rooms, small halls and corridors, dressing rooms, and walk-in closets. Hanging paneled paper horizontally below chair-rail level can create the effect of a dado.

2 *A cherubim grisaille border on gray craquelure-effect paper has been delineated with a plain blue band to match the gray and blue Classical-motif shades.*

3 *"Bookshelf" or "library" paper cut into a panel has been framed with a wood surround to make a tongue-in-cheek book collection.*

part two: the specifics

UNUSUAL PAPER
WALL COVERINGS

It is, of course, quite possible to cover the walls with other kinds of paper. Although by no means meant for the purpose, they can look extraordinarily effective, given the will, the time, and, in some cases, the skill.

Tissue paper

Once, in Spain, I saw a beautiful, ethereal room unlike anything I had seen before. The walls turned out to be covered in layers of pastel-colored tissue paper, stuck over each other like *découpage* and given a top layer of plain white tissue and several coats of eggshell varnish. The pale blues and roses, yellows and greens gleamed softly through the white, making the walls look opalescent. This is a charming and inexpensive idea for a bedroom, combined with, say, a bed dressed chastely in white linens and a pale wood floor bleached, stained, or painted white or gray.

Kraft or wrapping paper and newspaper

Rolls of caramel-colored, green, or blue kraft paper, or rolls of beige or caramel-colored parcel wrapping paper, used matte side out, also make handsome rooms. The texture of the paper is attractive and the cost is small. However, although wider— typically 36 in. (90 cm.)–than most wallpaper, it is somewhat thinner. Therefore, the wall will first need to be either painted in pale latex paint or hung with lining paper, because a bright paint color or a patterned wallpaper would show through. Another drawback is that you have to buy a whole roll of paper, and the

quantity on a single roll may be more than enough for several average rooms. You might like to give away, or sell, the extra, or you could cut it up for children's paintings.

You will need to cut out "drops" from ceiling to floor on as big a table as you can find, bearing in mind the paper's increased width. Paste the back of a sheet with wallpaper paste, handling it carefully, and position and smooth it out well with a clean, dry cloth. It is probably better to overlap the sheets slightly, rather than to join them edge-to-edge.

Another interesting effect can be obtained by similarly pasting up sheets of newspaper.

1 *Different-colored squares of paper have been pasted onto much larger, contrasting areas of color to turn these walls into an interesting abstract.*

2 *Sheets of newspaper on the walls of this bathroom have been protected by a couple of coats of polyurethane varnish, both to protect and harden the surface and to give it a feeling of age.*

3 *Plain blue walls in another bathroom have an unusual and striking border of silver-leaf squares. Marble floor tiles have been used to create a dado, but a similar effect could be created using squares of marbleized paper over chipboard.*

part two: the specifics

Alternative Wall Coverings

When deciding on wall treatments for main rooms and bedrooms, nearly everyone thinks first of some kind of paint or wallpaper treatment, but there are myriad alternative wall coverings that can look splendid, including fabric, mirror, and tiles.

FABRIC

Fabric has been used to cover walls for centuries, first in India, the Far East, and the Middle East, and then in Europe, at least since medieval times. By the late seventeenth century, fabric had been somewhat eclipsed by wallpaper, but it was never entirely replaced by it. Samuel Pepys, the famous seventeenth-century diarist, writes of visiting Cornhill in London and having a wretched time trying to buy his wife "a chintz, that is painted Indian calico, for to line her new study which is very pretty." John Evelyn, another diarist of the period, mentions "dining out in a room hung with *Pintado*," another name for chintz.

SHORTCUTS TO UPHOLSTERED WALLS

As a shortcut to achieving the softly luxurious effect of upholstered walls, you can use panels of polyesterfiber, which is quite soft. Obviously you will need to have measured the room and made a scale drawing of it (see page 16), in order to work out how many panels to get made. Don't forget the spaces over doors and fireplaces, over and under windows, and so on. You ill also, of course, need to work out the right amount of fabric. Allow extra for wrapping the fabric around the panels—about 1 yd. (1 m.) all around each one.

Wrap the fabric around the panels, securing it with staples, then either screw the panels to the wall or attach them with adhesive. You can conceal the joins if you want by covering them with braid, but the panels, if well-sized and fitted, can actually look quite neat in their own right.

There are also wall-upholstery systems, which rely on heavy-duty plastic tracks with adhesive backing. The panels of fabric are inserted into the channels of the track. For a really padded appearance, polyester batting can be placed on the panels before the fabric is stretched over them.

Upholstered walls

Today, fabric-covered, or "upholstered," walls are still very much in evidence, particularly in Europe, and especially in France, where a surprising number of hotels and private homes have soft

1 Dark green fabric and matching draperies make a distinguished background for a collection of paintings, as well as giving a timeless quality to these old rooms.

2 Green checked cotton above a plain painted dado looks agreeably crisp. The cotton is also used on the closet doors. The smaller red check on the charming painted chair creates a counterpoint to the green.

3 A large red check hanging looks arresting behind the table and striped chairs and contrasts with the flagstone floor. Note the empty picture frame on the table.

padded walls. I say surprising, because "walling" (as such treatments are called) in Britain, is both expensive and extremely labor-intensive.

The process involves fixing a framework of thin battens to the wall, lining between them with wads of fire-retardant polyester and then stretching seamed fabric over the battens. The results are often original and usually luxurious, as well as

1

1 *Lengths of white cotton sewn together are gently suspended from brass doorknobs fixed just below the ceiling, softening the walls in this otherwise graphic black-and-white bedroom. Curtains and bedspread are made from the same soft cotton; the quilt adds more texture.*

2 *In this subtly colored room, single widths of fabric are hung individually to lie on the floor in an unusually tailored manner.*

providing excellent insulation against both cold and noise.

Upholstered walls are something the inhabitants of medieval Europe would have found a great deal more comfortable than their paneling or their tapestry, wool, leather, and canvas hangings. Ironically, the method is similar to that employed in the late sixteenth and seventeenth centuries for displaying wallpapers. If only our ancestors had thought to do the same thing with fabric lined with sheep's wool, instead of just hanging it, they would have been a great deal warmer.

Hanging fabric from rods

Another way of using fabric on walls is to treat it like curtains hanging from just below the ceiling. As long as the fabric is fairly voluminous (it needs to be about three times each wall's width) and looks graceful, you can use cotton sheeting, voile, or muslin, which are not only inexpensive but can be taken down and tossed in the washing machine at intervals. Alternatively, you could use fabric, like a heavier wool, flannel, or camel hair, or sumptuous silk or velvet, which all need to be dry cleaned. The advantage of this

approach is that even if the fabric is not washable, it can at least be removed and cleaned.

Continuous rods on brackets are fixed all around the room at ceiling height. Each curtain, which should be long enough to just touch the floor or to "puddle" onto it, is made with a casing at the top, so that it can be slotted onto the rods. The curtains are allowed to hang loose, but the hems will probably need to be weighted.

Where there is a door, window, or fireplace, the curtains are simply held back with tiebacks. If the fabric is

length of fabric. The battens are then fixed to the walls just below the ceiling and above the baseboards, to keep the fabric fairly taut and tightly gathered or in neat pleats. Short panels are used above and below windows. Roller shades can be used at the windows, or the fabric can hang loose there and be tied back. Panels should be positioned so as to give easy access to light switches and electric outlets.

Pasting fabric on walls

If the fabric is firm, like good-quality felt, tweed or other wool, burlap, corduroy, or imitation suede, it can be stuck to the walls somewhat like wallpaper. As wide a fabric as possible should be used. It is cut into the required lengths, allowing for overlaps at top and bottom and any pattern matching. The paste is brushed onto the walls, and then each fabric length is unraveled, aligned to a plumb line, and gently smoothed down with a large roller. This clearly will not look as soft as walling, but it will still look distinguished and add an interesting texture.

Tenting

If ceilings are in a bad state of repair, or really undistinguished, or if you would like to finish walls covered in fabric in an exotic way, you could try tenting the ceiling. The idea is to allow fabric to hang in dramatic folds from a fixed point, or points; at the other end, each length of fabric is fixed to the angle of the ceiling and wall. You could use a circular rail, or a corona (designed for bed hangings), fixed in the center of the ceiling, and swoop from it however many lengths of fabric are needed to conceal the ceiling.

permanently tied back at the windows, roller shades could be used behind it, in a fabric that is matching, contrasting or "negative" (in the same two-color design, but with the colors reversed). Where fabric is tied back at the mantelpiece, the wall can be painted where the curtains part, or something large, like a mirror or painting, can be put there.

Hanging fabric from battens

An alternative way to hang fabric "curtains" on the walls is to slot battens of wood into hemmed casings at both the top and bottom of each

part two: the specifics

MIRRORING

Floor-to-ceiling mirror can be relied upon to give a room added length, width, and height, as well as extra light. It is a somewhat expensive way to gain this extra visual space, but there are tricks by which the effect of mirror can be maximized:

- Fixing mirror literally from floor to ceiling doubles the apparent size of a room by creating the illusion of an opening going through to another room.
- Used on one wall, preferably at right angles to a window, mirror will seem to double the size of the room, and the extra reflected light by day will be stunning. Draperies, curtains, or shades, when closed at night, will also seem to double in size.
- Fixing mirror in the space between two tall windows will make an enormous difference to light and brightness.
- Lining an alcove with mirror will increase the feeling of depth, adding perspective to a room.
- In a dark room, lining the recesses at either side of a projecting mantel with mirror will make a huge difference. If you stand tall, bushy plants in front of each, with uplights behind, the effect will be even airier.

Make sure to take accurate measurements so that the large piece, or pieces, of mirror required will fit through your doors and if necessary will go up the stairs (including being transported around any bend or turn in the stairs) or fit into an elevator. If the space to be mirrored is large, you will almost certainly be better off with panels of mirror.

Some people find blank mirror cold-looking. Tinted mirror glass is one way of counteracting this, and it will add to the room's ambience. Alternatively, glass shelves can be fixed across the mirror to display a collection of glass, or a mixture of books, *objets*, and small plants. The display can be lit from above by a recessed downlight, or from below by an uplight, or both.

I A door in this bedroom has been completely mirrored, to reflect and seemingly enlarge the space, as well as to provide good allover personal reflection. Note the round mirror placed on the wall to allow an efficient view of the back when the door is at an appropriate angle.

TILING

Tiled walls can look splendid, and not just in bathrooms and kitchens, as demonstrated by ancient buildings in the Far East, Iran, Turkey, Italy, Spain, the Netherlands, and South America.

No one can fail to be impressed by the magnificent completely tiled rooms (floors, walls, and ceilings) of the Alhambra in Granada, Spain, and the splendors of Istanbul's Topkapi

tip

OLD GROUT CAN GET VERY DIRTY, BUT LUCKILY THERE ARE SOME STAIN-RESISTANT VARIETIES TODAY WHICH LOOK MUCH BETTER, AND YOU CAN CAREFULLY MATCH GROUT COMPOUND TO TILE COLOR, OR TO THE BACKGROUND COLOR IF THE TILES ARE PATTERNED, TO MAKE THE GROUT ALMOST DISAPPEAR.

Palace and Blue Mosque, with its 20,000 blue-glazed tiles covering the inside walls.

In cooler climates, a wealth of tiled surfaces will generally seem too cold, but they can be used to good effect in smaller amounts. Many western and northern European countries used the tin-glazed, painted maiolica tiles produced by Italy and Spain from the fifteenth century onward. And the blue-and-white Delft tiles, first produced in Holland in the seventeenth century, were—and still are—as popular in the United States as in Europe.

Today there is an enormous choice of tiles, not just machine-made ones but also handmade or hand-painted tiles from all over the world. Moreover, it is still possible to find beautiful antique tiles, particularly Victorian examples.

Economical ideas

If you cannot find enough of a particular antique tile, or cannot afford many expensive tiles, you could always use them as a border, like a chair rail, or in a square or diamond shape, or as randomly placed tiles in a wall of plain, less expensive ones.

Inexpensive plain tiles can be effective without any adornment if they are laid on the diagonal or in a

2 Two separate designs of highly decorative blue-and-white tiles are used on the walls of this kitchen, cleverly divided by an edging of slim white border tiles. In contrast, plain white tiles with a dark bullnosed edging have been used for the worktop.

part two: the specifics

herringbone or basket-weave pattern. Or they can be delineated with a border of tiles in a contrasting color or special edging tiles.

Other decorative tiles

There are a great many pictorial tiles available—that is to say, tiles made to form part of a picture or design, like an urn of flowers, a fountain, an arch or bower, or some sort of landscape.

These need very careful measuring of the space they are to fill, to make sure that the design will fit, quite apart from expert tile-laying. (You could achieve a similar effect by getting an artist to paint a design on a wall of pale-colored plain tiles—see right for advice on painting on tiles.)

Don't forget about mosaic tiles and glass bricks, both of which can look highly decorative. Glass tiles can

also be found, though they are not widely available. Make sure that whatever you use is appropriate to the style of room.

Painting tiles

If you are stuck with tiles you hate, remember that you can disguise them with paint. A good paint supplier might recommend an epoxy enamel paint (see page 94), but an oil-based

paint should do, particularly if you apply a commercial tile primer first. You can either just paint them a solid color and leave it at that, or you can then embellish them with stencils or an allover design.

An alternative is to tile right over the top, provided they will not stick out too far; this is generally cheaper than ripping the old tiles off and starting all over again.

WOOD PANELING

Wood paneling looks good in virtually any style of interior, particularly as there are so many different ways to use it. It can be left unfinished, stained with a natural shade or a color, painted, or grained to make it look like more expensive wood.

If it is not already in place, new paneling can be added, either from floor to ceiling or to chair-rail or picture-rail height. Traditional fielded paneling can look good in a period home—architectural salvage yards are good places to look for this. Tongue-and-groove is a less expensive, widely available option, and even plywood can look good if given an interesting finish. Another option is the thin "matchstick" paneling that looks so charming in many houses on the East Coast of the United States.

Paneling needs to be hung by a carpenter, as it is fixed to a framework of battens screwed to the wall. New wood will need to acclimatize to your home for a few weeks before being installed, to reduce the risk of cracks and gaps opening up over time. If you are having new hardwood paneling installed, make sure that it is from an ecologically farmed plantation.

1 *Leather tiles look handsome with a similarly colored leather-covered stool and chair.*

2 *Multicolored tiles are used here for walls, ceiling, and floor, thus giving the impression to anyone entering the room of walking into a bright, hard-edged box of M&Ms.*

3 Light, modern paneling in different subtle tones resembles a series of shoji screens applied to the wall. There is certainly no need for art.

4 A dado of genuine old paneling in a hallway is repeated in paint in a room leading off. Note how the same sludgy green is used to paint the door architrave.

5 Tongue-and-groove paneling on a stairway is painted a cool gray and white. The effect is pleasantly cool in conjunction with the painted white stairs.

part two: the specifics

SECTION FIVE

Floors are the bottom line, so to speak, of any room and have tremendous decorative, as well as practical, potential. They anchor a scheme, hold it together, and give it a crucial steadiness, richness, simplicity, or glamour, according to the function, mood, and style of the space. Because they are also walked on, sometimes danced on, and very often sat or lounged on, they take a tougher beating than any other surface. The first choice in any space, however, is between hard, soft, and the in-between flexibility that vinyl or linoleum offers. Fortunately, you don't have to limit yourself to just one type—wood, tiles, or stone of any kind, softened by rugs or squares of carpet, gives you the best of both worlds.

Floors

Flooring Options

Whether you decide to go for carpets or rugs, hard floors or flexible flooring, or a combination, you need to consider your options first. In particular, this involves thinking about the existing floor and any future flooring–ideally, not just in the room (or rooms) you are decorating but in the rest of the home, too.

EXISTING FLOORS

Don't make any radical decisions on floor coverings before studying existing floors carefully. They might not need to be covered at all.

Wood floors

Parquet and other wood floors in reasonably good condition–without gaps, splits, and frayed, splintered ends –could just be polished and then either be left bare or have rugs laid on top, with some non-slip backing to prevent them from slipping.

If a floor is worn, the first task is sanding it down. This can be done professionally, or you can rent a sander with a dust-bag attachment and sand it yourself (which is messy and hard work, but a great deal cheaper). It can then be either stained a different color –say, much darker, or even a dark green or bronze–or bleached, or whitened.

An alternative is to paint it with a paint specially designed for floors or decks; or just with flat alkyds, acrylic, or latex paint. Or you can give it a more ambitious, decorative paint treatment, perhaps marbling it, combing it, painting it in checker-board squares, or stenciling it. In fact, an otherwise plain floor can look extremely effective with a stenciled border or design.

Whichever treatment you choose— plain, stained, bleached, or painted— the floor will need to be sealed with two or three coats of protective varnish afterwards. Acrylic-based varnish needs 12 hours' drying time, but for other types, each coat must be allowed to dry for 24 hours before being walked on. Besides protecting the surface, this will give it a sheen, with the degree of gloss depending upon the varnish, and it will bring out the graining (except on painted floors, obviously).

Vinyl and linoleum floors

These are best disguised using oil-based paints, instead of latex, which does not grip as well on their surfaces. (Even oil-based paint will eventually peel off from vinyl, but it is still worth doing, as it can simply be painted again when that happens.) Before applying any paint, it is essential to wash the floor thoroughly with a degreaser solution (degreaser is available through most good hardware stores and home centers) then rinse it well and allow it to dry completely.

Concrete floors

Paint is surprisingly effective on concrete floors. A floor and patio paint (from a specialist paint dealer or good hardware store) can be painted straight onto it. Alternatively, oil paint can be used; this provides a better choice of colors, but it must be applied over a diluted white-glue seal and then overpainted with an acrylic varnish when dry. In fact, with either type of paint, you should finish with an acrylic floor varnish.

I once saw what I thought was a splendid old flagstone floor in a converted barn. In fact, it was concrete that had been scored to look like flagstones, pitted here and there with a chisel, then rubbed all over with clear floor polish in many patient applications, and finally sealed. Patches of tan and reddish-tan shoe polish, artfully superimposed in random areas, provided realistic variations in tone. It was impressive.

Tiled floors

Existing tiled floors with unsightly stained or cracked grout can be pryed up, cleaned, and relaid with fresh new grout. Since grout comes in many tones and colors, choose one that will camouflage wear and tear and that will not be so noticeable that the grid pattern becomes too dominant.

JUXTAPOSITIONS

When planning flooring for a room, don't think about it in isolation. Remember the vistas that are constantly opened up in a home. Doors that lead off corridors and hallways are often left open, and glimpses of upper stories can be seen from stairways. For the space to flow naturally, the floor coverings need to be coordinated, at least in color. And of course, a small apartment or house looks better if one color is used throughout, though it need not be of uniform quality.

Where different textures or colors meet at doorways—say, carpet with tiling or parquet, or chestnut brown with apricot—the effect is neater if a threshold strip is inserted between the two. This is also practical, since it will protect the edges of the different materials, as well as delineating the contrasting areas.

1 Paint was used to make this concrete floor look like flagstones with a terracotta border and inlaid center design. Realistic pits and crevices were achieved by pressing sheets of newspaper onto wet paint and quickly removing them.

2 A pale-colored kilim softens an expanse of coir matting in this house. It is always best to use some kind of gripping device or underlay when adding a rug to any soft floor covering; otherwise it will bunch up or creep. Note how well the Arts and Crafts occasional table balances the staircase.

3 The wood floor in this kitchen with its interesting storage wall has been painted clear blue and protected by several coats of acrylic varnish.

part two: the specifics

Carpets

Besides being soft and warm underfoot, wall-to-wall carpet is very practical, providing good sound insulation and draftproofing and also hiding floors that are in poor condition. There is an enormous range of carpeting in every price, color, and texture.

Most modern carpets are either woven or tufted. Although woven carpet has a reputation for durability, good-quality tufted carpet will work well in any area of the home and is a good deal less expensive. The main aspects you should look at in either type are density and pile height.

DENSITY

A carpet's density is measured by the number of stitches per inch or centimeter, and is the most important aspect of carpet construction to understand. A very closely tufted or woven carpet will assure years of wear, whatever the height of the pile.

PILE HEIGHT

The term "pile" refers to the tufts or loops of pile above a carpet backing. They form the surface of a carpet, and although many people think that a deep-pile carpet looks more expensive, this is not necessarily so. In fact, high pile on a carpet often means that it is rather loosely woven and that the pile will flatten easily when walked on.

CARPET TEXTURES

The surface finish of a carpet depends on which type of pile it has. Here are some of the most common types.

Velvet or plush pile: A short, dense, and smooth finish. In this kind of pile, all the loops formed in the manufacturing process are sheared at the same height. Some people do not like it much because it can show footprints, while others like it because of the feeling of light and shade. Because the loops are cut, velvet does not have the resilience to dirt that a more tightly woven loop carpet will have. However, it does look particularly elegant and is therefore recommended for formal living rooms and rooms where there is not too much traffic.

Saxony pile: In this kind of cut-pile carpet the pile yarns are slightly more twisted than those in velvet or plush pile. The effect is exceptionally smooth and well suited to formal rooms.

Friezé pile: Another hardwearing, cut-pile texture, friezé is formed by twisting the pile yarns very tightly, so that they are almost curly. The appearance is somewhat textured. This is a good type of carpet to use in hallways and rooms that get a lot of traffic.

Loop pile: This pile is formed by loops of yarn. It looks good but can snag. An example is the elegant Brussels weave,

tip

WHEN CHOOSING CARPET, GIVE IT THE "GRIN TEST" BY FOLDING IT BACK ON ITSELF. IF A LOT OF THE BACKING SHOWS, THE CARPET IS NOT GOING TO BE VERY DURABLE. IN THE TRADE, THIS GLIMPSE OF BACKING IS KNOWN AS "GRIN" BECAUSE IT LOOKS A BIT LIKE A SMILE BREAKING THROUGH.

which can look extremely good in living rooms that do not get heavy traffic, as well as master and guest bedrooms. If the carpet does snag, you can either cut off the offending tag very carefully or, if the carpet is loose-laid, turn it back and pull the snag through the backing.

Cut-and-loop pile: As the name indicates, this is a combination of the two basic types of pile. If they are of different heights, this produces a sculpted effect; if they are of the same height, the effect is a more subtle contrast of textures. Multicolor effects are also possible.

Long or shag pile: This has an informal, rough-and-ready look. It is made in the same way as velvet—that is to say, tufted in high loops. But the loops are then cut through with a shearing knife (as if shearing a sheep's coat) to give it its distinctive thick, shaggy look. Shag pile carpet comes in many densities, and the less tightly the yarn is packed, the more it is likely to flatten. Because of its long length, it is not easy to clean. Since shag is difficult to look after, a good compromise is a similarly textured rug, like the Greek flokati, which is woven in a natural white.

CONSTRUCTION

Carpets are made by a variety of methods, the two main methods being weaving and tufting.

Woven carpets are the most durable, because the weaving process itself links the backing and the surface pile. They are also more expensive than tufted carpets. There are several types of carpet loom; among the most common types are velvet, wilton, axminster, and tapestry (sometimes called flatweave).

A velvet weave (which should not be confused with velvet texture) is the simplest kind of weave, producing looped and cut textures. But patterns are limited to tweeds and stripes.

Similar to a velvet loom, but capable of producing multicolored designs, is the wilton. The greater size of an axminster loom, along with its more complex construction, allows greater variety of color in patterned carpets than in wilton, where the number of colors in any design is limited to five. Thus, axminsters are generally patterned, while many people favor solid-color velvet wilton. In wilton, the colors not appearing in the surface pile are carried along the back, to form an extra pad of fiber that cushions against wear—hence wilton's reputation for hidden value.

Tapestry weave, also known as flatweave, is used mainly for kilims and dhurries.

Sisal carpets—and those made of other grass-like fibers, such as seagrass and coir—are available in many different kinds of weave, including herringbone, bouclé, and twill.

Tufted carpets are constructed by a method similar to sewing; a machine fitted with hundreds of needles stitch the pile through a backing material, which is then coated with latex to secure the tufts. Additional backing is added to strengthen the carpet.

TUFTING

Tufted carpets, in which the pile is punched into a backing and glued, are more common and less expensive than woven ones.

part two: the specifics

FIBERS

There are actually only four generic families of fibers generally used in carpets: wool, acrylic, nylon, and polyester. All the brands and trade names fall into one of these families. They can be mixed with each other, can be woven or tufted, and are available in any of the textures described above.

Wool not only is good-looking, hard-wearing, and warm but also resistant to water and stains. It has a natural resilience, which means that the pile springs back into place easily. It is also the most expensive fiber.

Nylon, in its various guises, is the strongest, but the average home does not require maximum strength. It is easier to clean than anything else and is less expensive than wool or acrylic. By itself, however, it does not adapt quite so easily to color, texture, and pattern. A favorite mixture is 80 percent wool, 20 percent nylon, because it has all the softness and subtlety of wool, takes dyes well, and is extremely hard-wearing.

Acrylics accept dye well, are very soil-resistant, and are getting softer to the touch all the time.

Polyester is the least expensive of any of the fibers. It soils more easily but takes dyes well and so comes in a rainbow of colors.

WIDTH

In the United States most carpet is woven to a width of either 12 ft. or 15 ft. (3.66 m. or 4.58 m.) and is called "broadloom." Berbers are usually woven in the larger width, because seams are relatively difficult to hide in this construction.

1 *Cord carpet is an effective construction for cheaper fibers.*
2 *Brussels weave is woven in much the same way as cord, with a recognizable crisp looped appearance.*
3 *Twist pile has a sturdy, hard-wearing finish and is good for stairs.*
4 *Axminster looms allow a greater variety of color in a design (as here) than Wilton.*

ALTERNATIVE FLOOR COVERINGS

Natural matting, such as sisal, coir, and seagrass, is an attractive alternative to carpet made of wool, nylon, and other conventional fibers. Available in broadloom and rug form, it has a traditional feel and can look very good in either the city or the country. An excellent background for rugs, matting is also a good common denominator for a mixture of furniture periods. However, it is tough on the feet and can be slippery on stairs, and its roughness makes it less suitable if young children will be crawling around. Yet, matting certainly looks more appropriate in the country than carpeting and is useful where wood floors are beyond redemption.

5 Loop pile carpet is the same construction as the elegant Brussels weave. The snag is literally that it can snag easily.

6 Seagrass has a nice crisp texture.

7 Coir makes a good background for furnishings.

8 A wool-and-sisal-blend carpet here contrasted with stone.

9 Sisal fibers can be dyed easily; sisal is available in herringbone, ribbed, and bouclé patterns.

part two: the specifics

Rugs

The popularity of area rugs is not surprising, given their infinite versatility. Not only do they provide a soft, comfortable surface underfoot, but they soften hard floors visually, too, and add color and texture to a scheme. They are particularly useful for helping to demarcate zones within a room and to draw disparate items of furniture together.

Another distinct advantage that rugs have over wall-to-wall carpets is their adaptability, since they can easily be moved around or changed, without having to be replaced as carpet does.

Oriental rugs are the aristocrats of area rugs. Equally elegant are the beautiful, large, antique needlework rugs like the French tapestry-woven Aubussons, as well as the excellent modern Romanian, Portuguese, and Chinese copies of these.

There are also the non-politically correct, but nevertheless striking, animal-skin rugs (though many people prefer the *faux* varieties) and dramatic contemporary rugs with their bold, often graphic designs.

A considerable number of ethnic rugs are widely produced around the world. Most of these fall roughly into one of three categories: ethnic cottons, such as traditional Moroccan or Greek weaves and Indian dhurries; dense woolen piles like Finnish ryas and Greek flokatis; and the luxurious, thick woolen weaves produced by the Spanish, Portuguese, South Americans, and Irish.

All rugs should be secured to prevent them from either slipping on a wood or tiled floor or "walking" when laid on top of carpet or matting. Use a non-slip mesh backing or Velcro, cut to the appropriate size.

tip

TO CHECK WHETHER A RUG IS HAND-KNOTTED, PART THE PILE AND LOOK FOR ROWS OF KNOTS AT THE BASE OF THE TUFTS. LOOK AT THE BACK, TOO—THE PATTERN SHOULD BE VISIBLE.

Handsome area rugs not only soften the polished stone floor but, with their geometric design, make a good foil for the eclectic collection of furniture, light fixtures, and other furnishings. They also define the sitting and working areas.

ORIENTAL RUGS

"Oriental rug" is the umbrella term for rugs, carpets, prayer rugs, runners, and kilims made by nomadic tribesmen and village craftsmen to furnish their tents. The rugs were draped over seating and hung on the walls, as well as being laid on the floors.

Antique rugs are the most prized, but oriental rugs are still produced today to the designs of the past, which relate to the area from which they come. Some of the rugs are handmade and others mass-produced in cooperatives based in towns and cities.

Kilims are made using the technique of weft tapestry weaving, in which long threads are woven in and out of the warp, covering it completely and forming the design. They therefore do not have a pile.

Other oriental rugs are produced by knotting short lengths of wool around the warp threads of a loom. Knotted rugs thus have a pile and are more durable than kilims.

Designs are all based on traditional patterns and reflect the life, culture, and customs of the Islamic and Far Eastern worlds. Most rugs or carpets have a central "field" or "ground," which is surrounded by a border. The designs in the center range from the geometric and abstract to the figurative and floral.

Experts can tell which small production center any rug comes from. The six traditional carpet-producing regions are Persia; Turkey.; Turkistan in Central Asia; the Caucasus; India; and China. The carpets from each of these regions have distinctive features, which are described on the following pages.

tip

AN ORIENTAL "RUG" IS REGARDED AS BEING SMALL ENOUGH TO HANG ON THE WALL AND SO IS LESS THAN ABOUT 6 FT. (2 M.) LONG; AN ORIENTAL "CARPET" IS LARGER THAN THAT. IN PRACTICE, HOWEVER, THE TERMS TEND TO BE USED INTERCHANGEABLY.

part two: the specifics

Persian rugs

These are considered to be the finest of all oriental rugs.

- Persian rugs are almost always rectangular or elongated, rather than square.
- They are generally woven in wool, using the special *Senneh* knot. (Exceptions are the rare, beautiful and extremely expensive silk rugs–which explains the old Persian saying, "The richer the man, the thinner the rug.")
- Their coloring is rich and often has a central field of crimson or indigo, with figurings of warm browns, greens, and yellows.
- The Persians were the only Muslim people to include realistically represented (in hunting carpets) humans and animals .
- Most designs, however, are based on floral motifs. Some of the most popular are used in the *garden* rugs and carpets, so called because they are laid out in the form of gardens with paths, flower beds, pools, and streams.
- *Vase* rugs are a more formal version of floral motifs, with vases holding flowers or plants.
- Other designs include prayer rugs with the pattern of a Moorish arch, sometimes pointed at the top, called *mihrab*; and geometric medallion pieces with a large central design and canted corners.
- Persian rugs made before the eighteenth century are usually classified according to their design: *garden, vase, animal, medallion*, etc. Only those made after then are attributed to specific towns, such as Feraghan, Schina, Herat, Heriz,

Silk Tabriz prayer rug, c.1890, from northwest Persia

Isfahan, Joshaghan, Kashan, Qum, Shiraz, or Tabriz.

- If you are lucky enough to see an early *animal* carpet, there is a very good chance that it came from Isfahan, just as *vase* carpets probably came from Joshaghan,

and *medallion* carpets from Herat. Herat carpets are considered to be the very best Persians and are particularly associated with small, recurring leaf patterns (sometimes thought to be fish) and rosettes.

Early nineteenth-century Turkish Ghiordes prayer rug

Turkish rugs

These come from the Anatolian region of the country and are often referred to as *Anatolians* by dealers. Popular in Europe long before Persian rugs, they differ from them not only in design and colors but also in the type of knot used. This knot is known as the *Ghiordes*, named after one of the major rug-producing areas. (Other centers of production include Bergama, Hereke, Kula, Kum Kapi, Kirsehir, Konya, Ushak, and Ladik.)

- The pile in Turkish carpets is almost always longer than in Persians, and fewer colors are used in Turkish carpets.

- Patterns are bold and tend to be geometric, but there are stylized flowers like the rhododendron, pomegranate, and hyacinth.

- In the *mihrab* mosque pattern on prayer rugs, there is a lamp, or ewer, suspended from an arch. This is sometimes flanked by two pillars of wisdom. More sophisticated versions have Arabic script.

- The most usual background colors are red and blue, although prayer rugs are sometimes woven in green, a sacred color.

- Some of the major rug-producing areas have their own distinctive designs. For example, rugs from Ghiordes—which makes the finest rugs, often considered the equal of the best Persians—have attractive arabesques, floral designs, borders, and stripes.

- Because most Turks are Sunni Muslims, they observe the Koranic prohibition against the depiction of people or animals, so you will rarely see these on Turkish rugs.

part two: the specifics

Indian carpet, c.1900, probably from Lahore

Chinese carpet

Detail from Chinese rug

More examples of various oriental rugs. The detail (left) of a dragon rearing up against a stylized blue sky is taken from an old Chinese rug, and the carpet (far left below) showing scalloped roundels containing imperial dragons is also Chinese.

Caucasian runner

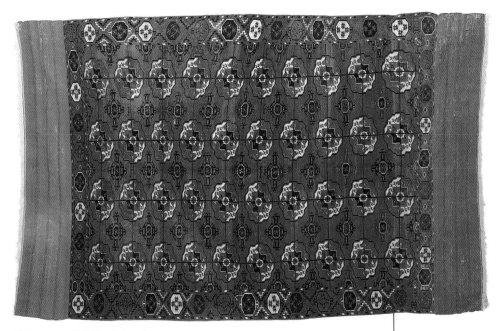

Tekke carpet, c. 1880, West Turkmenistan

Indian rugs

Though generally made in the Persian tradition, Indian rugs also have definite characteristics of their own. They were originally introduced to suit the royal tastes of the Indian princesses and of the merchants who set up the early workshops.

- Many designs feature animals, birds, trees, and flowers.
- The colors are lighter than those of Persian rugs, with an extensive use of rose.
- The pile is noticeably longer and coarser than in Persian rugs.

Chinese rugs

Knotted rugs were being made in China two thousand years ago in organized workshops, much as they are still being woven in factories today, although there was not a real rug industry until the eighteenth century.

- The colors are generally subtle blues, yellows, peaches, roses, and apricots, in complete contrast to the ubiquitous reds and greens of the Persian, Turkish, Caucasian, Turkoman, and Indian rugs.
- The designs incorporate the motifs common to most Chinese art. Buddhist and Taoist symbols are used extensively. The designs include animals, especially dragons, and flowers like the lotus, peony, daffodil, and pomegranate.
- They have a much longer pile and are tied with an asymmetrical knot, which is often cut around the edge of a motif to give greater emphasis to the pattern.
- The famous *pillar* designs are found only in China. They were made to wrap around a pillar, so the pattern is continuous.

Caucasian rugs

These come from the Caucasus, which is the mountainous area between the Caspian Sea and the Black Sea. Although the region is now part of Russia, it has been home to many different tribes from Turkey, Armenia, and Persia, all of whom have contributed to the region's rich heritage of rugs.

- The rugs are distinctively colored in red, blue, green, and beige.
- The designs, though varied, are always severely rectilinear.
- Animals, birds, flowers, crabs, beetles, etc., are highly stylized.
- Other designs include medallions, also composed in geometric arrangements, with decorated borders of stars, rosettes, or running dog patterns (the Caucasian equivalent of the Greek key pattern).

Turkoman rugs

Turkoman, or Turkman, rugs come from the region between the Caspian Sea and northwest China, which includes Turkmenistan, Uzbekistan, Afghanistan, and Pakistan.

- Red is the predominant color, although different tribes and areas can be identified by the various hues that they introduce into their designs. For example, rugs from the Beshire area of Afghanistan use yellow and green, as well as red. Baluchis use a lot of dark blue with rust reds, bluish mauves, and occasional touches of camel, ivory, and cream.
- Golden Afghan rugs are really the ubiquitous red rugs, washed until they have become a distinctive apricot gold color.
- Designs are almost always geometric, and generally feature the octagonal *gul*, or stylized rose motif.

part two: the specifics

Vocabulary of Carpet Terms

Acrylic: This synthetic looks a lot like wool and is nonallergenic, but is slightly less stain-resistant and resilient than wool. However, it is also lower-priced.

Axminster: Axminster is a woven carpet, named after the loom on which it is woven, which positions the pile tufts at the same time as it weaves the backing. Because the threads are not carried along the back of the carpet, it is possible to weave axminsters in a great variety of colors. Although it has a CUT PILE, it can be woven long and shaggy, stubby, or sculpted, as well as short or smooth. The strongest weaving quality is generally 80 percent WOOL, 20 percent NYLON, but it can also be woven in ACRYLIC or a blend.

BCF: Abbreviation for "bulked continuous filament," a yarn (typically nylon or polyester) with relatively long fibers, bulked up to resemble wool. See also STAPLE.

Berber carpets: These are traditionally made of natural, undyed sheep's wool, with a dense, looped pile, named after the original hand-woven squares made by North African tribes. They are now made by machine in white, cream, beige, fawn, gray, and dark brown and are often made of olefin. The term is also used loosely to refer to any multi-level loop carpet, either in a solid color or in a flecked color.

Body carpet: British term for a carpet woven on a narrow loom.

Bouclé: The pile formed by uncut loops of yarn in BRUSSELS WEAVE carpet.

Broadloom: The term describing the standard widths of carpet: 12 ft. and 15 ft. (3.66 m. and 4.58 m.), as contrasted with those used as runners, often woven on narrow looms.

Brussels weave: Tightly looped carpets with a neat, crisp appearance, which lend themselves to clean-cut and geometric designs. They do, however, snag easily, so loose ends need to be carefully snipped when they appear.

Carpet tiles: Squares of carpet, in woven, tufted, or bonded form and in various combinations of wool and synthetic fibers. They come in various sizes, ranging from 28 in. to 36 in. (96 cm. to 92 cm.) square. They do not require padding or underlay and are flat, thin, and comparatively hard-wearing, although they lack the softness underfoot of fitted carpet. They can be laid by amateurs quite easily, all in one color, or in checkerboard fashion, or made into random designs. Their advantages are that they are reasonably inexpensive and that, if one or two get stained or worn, they can be removed and replaced.

Coir matting: Increasingly a favorite for many rooms because it is a good background for rugs. Made from coconut-husk fibers, it is inexpensive and hard-wearing. Coir comes in area-rug sizes, mats, tiles, and BROADLOOM forms. It is available mostly in natural colors but is sometimes made from dyed fibers. Latex backing prevents dirt falling through.

Cord: A low-loop, woven carpet, used in Britain, which looks a little like corduroy. It is woven in much the same way as plain WILTON but is much cheaper and not particularly soft underfoot.

Cotton: Cotton rugs have the advantage of being machine washable and hard-wearing, but one drawback is that they get flattened easily.

Cut-and-loop pile: Also known as high-and-low pile, this is a combination of CUT and LOOPED pile, which gives it a sculpted or textured appearance.

Cut pile: As the name implies, the strands of yarn are cut rather than left looped. All AXMINSTER carpets and some WILTON carpets have cut pile.

Dhurrie: A TAPESTRY-WEAVE COTTON rug, the Indian equivalent of the KILIM.

Felt: Felt is a good option for short-term rentals or vacation houses, and infrequently used guest rooms, when it is bought in carpet thickness. It comes in a good range of colors and is not expensive.

Flatweave: An alternative term for TAPESTRY WEAVE.

Friezé: Hard-wearing carpets with tightly twisted yarns which form a thick, low-pile surface. They are good for stairs and any area that gets a lot of use.

Fusion-bonded: Fusion bonding produces a very dense CUT PILE available mostly in solid colors.

Hand-knotted: Oriental rugs (apart from KILIMS) and Native American rugs are produced in this way. The yarn is hand-tied with a woven backing, using individual knots. Since the process is labor intensive, it is expensive.

Heat setting: A process that sets the twist in pile yarns.

Indian carpet: This is always off-white, is comparatively inexpensive and can be bought in rug sizes and BROADLOOM widths. The WOOL PILE is looped and knotted into the backing, so it wears well.

Jute: The fiber of an Asian herbaceous plant, jute is used for matting. It feels relatively soft, compared, for example, to sisal, and looks almost silky, but it is not particularly hard-wearing.

Kilim: A traditional FLATWEAVE rug from Turkey or Afghanistan. The fiber is usually wool, and the pattern is geometric. The vegetable dyes used produce warm, rich colors that mellow with age.

Linen carpet: Found in Britain, this has an interesting texture and looks very handsome, with much of the natural feel of sisal and coir. It is expensive and not at all hard-wearing, so it is best for decoration rather than practicality.

Long pile: See SHAG PILE.

Looped pile: A surface formed from uncut loops. How well it wears depends on the density of the construction—i.e., the number of loops per square inch or centimeter. It can be shaggy or smooth.

Low pile: See VELVET PILE.

Nylon: The most popular man-made fiber used for carpeting. It is non-allergenic, resistant to water-soluble stains, very easy to clean, and easy to dye, taking color more clearly than wool. The latest nylons cost more than the older varieties as they have built-in static control and are more resistant to soiling.

Performance rating: A grading system indicating a carpet's suitability for the use it will receive. Most systems have a five-point scale: the higher numbers signify an ability to withstand heavy wear.

Pile: The tufts or loops of fibers above the backing of either a woven or a TUFTED carpet or rug. The quality of the pile is affected by the fiber size and weight, the ply of the yarn (the number of strands twisted together to form one strand), and the density of the tufts.

Plush pile: An alternative term for VELVET PILE.

Polyester: The advantages of polyester are that, like NYLON, it is nonallergenic and is moisture- and abrasion-resistant. It forms thick CUT-PILE carpets that have a luxurious feel, but it has a tendency to pill like a sweater.

Polypropylene: Also known as OLEFIN, this man-made fiber is strong, resists moisture and mildew, and is reasonably priced. It is a good choice for bathrooms, family rooms, dens, children's rooms, basement rooms, and even kitchens, but it has a tendency to fade.

Rag rugs: Rugs made from fabric strips that are braided or woven together, or hooked or prodded onto a backing.

Rush matting: Rushes can be woven into thickly textured or braided lengths or sold in squares. One big advantage of rush matting is that it can be laid loose over concrete and other hard floors without underlay, and it has an interesting rustic texture. It is not, however, very hard-wearing.

Saxony pile: A particularly soft, mid-length cut PILE.

Sea grass: A plant fiber grown in paddy fields and used for matting. Naturally water- and stain-resistant, it is suitable for areas of medium traffic.

Shag pile: Carpet with a 1-2 in. (2.5-5 cm.) cut pile. Once deemed the height of luxury, it is much less used nowadays. It was, and can be, used in living rooms and bedrooms, but should never be used on stairs, since heels could get caught in the pile. It gets dirtier than short pile, and the cheaper varieties tend to flatten easily.

Silk: Silk yarn can be made into extremely expensive and exotic rugs. It is one of the best of all fibers, and is usually hand-loomed.

1 *Rag rugs were much favored in the nineteenth century, when they were made – often as a hobby – by a great number of people. Modern versions are available today (look for the Portuguese rugs in particular), and their texture provides a nice contrast to any hard floor.*

2 *The crisp texture of Brussels weave is a natural background for interesting geometric and other graphic designs.*

Sisal: Tough, durable, white fiber which can be dyed easily and looks crisp. Sisal matting looks neat on any floor. It is softer than COIR but not as soft as JUTE.

Sisal-look: Term describing carpets made of wool or synthetic fibers woven to resemble sisal carpets. These carpets are much softer underfoot than sisal and often more expensive.

Staple: A relatively short textile fiber which is spun to make yarn—as opposed to a continuous filament— see also BCF.

Tapestry weave: A term applied to both carpets and rugs that are woven and have no PILE. They are generally cheaper than pile carpets and are usually made of COTTON, WOOL, or LINEN, although occasionally SILK is used. The two main types of traditional tapestry-weave are KILIMS and DHURRIES.

Tufted: The most common type of carpet; each fiber is punched into a base material, rather than woven on a loom. It is then secured with adhesive and usually sealed with a waterproof backing. It can have a LOOPED PILE or a CUT PILE.

Velvet: A short, smooth, luxurious cut pile, also called plush, which is available in a vast range of colors and designs. Also a kind of carpet loom.

Wilton: A woven carpet which, like AXMINSTER, gets its name from the loom on which it is woven. Unlike axminster, wilton is woven in one continuous length, so that the surface pile and backing are woven together for a special strength. Patterned wiltons are somewhat rare, since the number of colors in any one design is limited to five. But they do come in a very large range of solid colors.

Wool: Extremely hard-wearing as well as luxurious, wool is the only natural fiber used in any quantity in the carpet business. Wool carpets, however, are much more expensive than those made from man-made fibers and really need professional cleaning when they do become dirty. Although 100 percent wool is available, a mixture of 80 percent wool and 20 percent nylon is more common.

part two: the specifics

Hard Flooring

Brick, tiles, stone (such as flagstones, slate, and marble) and wood– the so-called hard floorings–have been used in homes over the centuries and have enjoyed renewed popularity in recent years. Handsome and hard-wearing, they are generally best if used with area rugs.

BRICK

Brick is an unexpectedly good floor treatment, especially in the country: as useful for halls, kitchens, and powder-rooms as for living rooms and dining rooms. Along with thin brick tiles, known as pavers, brick is comparable in price with a good wood or ceramic

1 Large, white ceramic non-slip tiles used for both floor and staircase make this space look particularly graphic. The gray paint on the side of the stairs looks good with the black table and the pale sand of the dining chairs.
2 Well-waxed old floorboards in a hallway lead on to equally well-worn flagstones in the living room of an old farmhouse. If a hard floor meets a softer texture, a metal or wood strip is generally required between them. But here the two hard, time-worn materials converge quite happily, while providing an interesting textural contrast.

tile floor. It should be laid on top of a solid, level base, such as a thin layer of mortar, and regular bricks can be arranged in various patterns, from basket weave to herringbone. Modern bricks, custom-made for floors, are thinner and lighter than conventional building bricks and come pre-glazed to combat stains. However, if the sub-floor is strong enough, you may prefer to use old bricks, which look mellower and are often quite a bargain. Architectural or salvage companies and local building contractors interested in old houses are good sources.

Once they have warmed up, bricks maintain a comfortable temperature, yet are agreeably cool in summer. If you are laying a brick floor and you live in a seasonal climate, consider first installing under-floor heating.

All old bricks should be sealed for easier maintenance. Then all you need to do after sweeping is to pass a damp mop over them.

FLOOR TILES

Versatile, hard-wearing, and decorative, tiles have been a deservedly popular hard flooring for centuries.

Ceramic tiles

Non-slip, floor-weight ceramic tiles can look highly decorative in the right setting and climate and are pleasantly smooth to walk on, though cold. They

come in a wide variety of colors and styles. Either hand- or machine-made from clay, they are fired at high temperatures. For outside use, choose the frost-proof, vitrified variety.

Terracotta tiles

These unglazed tiles come in several varieties. The most handsome, such as the kind produced in Mexico, are handmade out of natural clay and kiln fired. Like bricks, they retain heat. They are easily scratched, notably by grit on the bottom of shoes, but they develop a very attractive natural patina. Machine-made terracotta tiles are also available, and these are more regular in appearance.

Quarry tiles

Unglazed quarry tiles are tough and dense, and non-slip, but somewhat absorbent. Glazed quarry tiles are a little more slippery but tougher. Made from unrefined high-silica clay, all quarry tiles look rustic. They come in a range of terrracotta tones but also a variety of grays.

2

137

Encaustic tiles

Inlaid with a pattern, encaustic tiles have a soft, matte look. They look particularly stunning used in conjunction with plain "geometric" or terracotta tiles. Widely used in British Victorian and Edwardian halls, corridors, and conservatories, encaustic tiles are now popular for restoration work. They are generally smaller than other floor tiles—about 3-4 in. (7.5-10 cm.) square.

Laying and maintaining tiles

All these tiles, like bricks, need a solid, level base or concrete screed. If you want to tile over a wood floor, cover it in hardboard first or find a malleable glue that can be mixed into the adhesive, allowing movement without breaking the adhesive. If these precautions are not taken, the inevitable movement of the floorboards will someday crack the bond of the adhesive, causing the tiles to rise up.

When tiles are laid, a grout is used to fill the gaps. It is made from ground portland cement and sand, mixed with water to form a quick-drying paste. Modern grouts are much improved, with acrylic latex additives, which help prevent cracking and staining.

Most new tiles come complete with the manufacturer's instructions about sealing. Unglazed tiles, whether new or old, will benefit from a liquid resin sealant which acts like a heavy-duty polish. Alternatively, the traditional finish of one part boiled linseed oil mixed with three parts mineral spirit can be applied at regular intervals.

Like bricks, tiles can be kept clean by sweeping, then passing a damp mop with mild detergent over them.

MOSAIC TILES

These come not only in squares but in numerous other shapes and in a flooring weight. They lend themselves to all sorts of designs. There are three types—clay, marble, and glass silica—but they all act and feel much the same as conventional ceramic tiles.

Mosaic tiles are normally supplied on small sheets of plastic mesh (usually 12 x 12 in. [30 x 30 cm.], though other sizes are available). During installation, the mesh is stuck into the adhesive, leaving only the tiles visible so you don't have to stick each tile in place or grout between them. Maintenance is as for ceramic tiles, but they are easier to clean if the flooring is continued up the wall for about 6 in. (15 cm.).

1 *Old encaustic tiles in a late nineteenth-century house are original to the building. Note the small black-and-white diamond-tile border at each side.*

2 *Aged flagstones are invariably a plus in a room and will look as good with modern furniture as with old. If laying new ones, however, in whatever stone, try to install underfloor heating first. Warmth and comfort will make this kind of flooring even more appealing.*

STONE

Stone floors, whether in the form of slabs or tiles, lend elegance and a timeless quality to a home. They will last practically forever but are cold underfoot and usually quite heavy.

Flagstones

As attractive inside as outside on terraces, flagstones are used mainly in hallways or some other room on the ground floor, on top of a concrete screed or slab floor or a plywood subfloor. They can be custom-cut or bought in irregular slabs, and although somewhat cheaper than ceramic and terracotta tiles, they are more expensive to install. The term "flagstones" refers to "flagging," or slicing, stone into thin slabs. They are cut mostly from blue stone or slate, but sandstone and limestone can also be used in slabs. Some flagstones, such as limestone, are porous and need to be sealed, while others cannot be sealed.

Slate

This is often used as an alternative to marble, especially as it is much more stain resistant. Available as slabs or tiles, it generally looks best in squares or rectangles, and colors range from pale gray, green, and blue-gray to darker green, bluish-purple, and black. The slabs should be laid on a layer of mortar or a concrete or plywood subfloor downstairs, but the thin slate tiles are light enough to use upstairs over just a plywood subfloor. Slate can be left untreated, but it can equally effectively be sealed and waxed. Either way, it looks solid and handsome and is fairly easy to maintain, though it is not cheap.

Marble

Marble comes in a great range of colors, from pure white and gray (much of it quarried in New England and the South) to rust-red, green, and yellow, often with beautiful veining, and black, the colored varieties being imported especially from Italy. This looks expensive, and it is. It usually comes in 6 x 6-in. or 12 x 12-in. (15 x 15-cm. or 30 x 30-cm.) square tiles, although slabs can be ordered, too. The most fragile grades are usually the most decorative, with the most interesting veining and coloration, but they are also the most costly. The more solid grades are usually classified A and B, while the more delicate are C and D. The disadvantages of marble are that it scratches and stains easily, but to some people the aesthetics outweigh the impracticality. Lay it on a cement bed, on a concrete subfloor, or, if using the very thin tiles, on very flat plywood, or chipboard.

Terrazzo

Consisting of marble chips set in a cement or resin base and polished to a high sheen, terrazzo is reasonably non-slip, as well as being durable and handsome. Like marble, it is available in tiles or slabs, and is usually best laid in panels of about 26 ft. (8 m.). Cement-base terrazzo requires a concrete substrate; resin-based can be laid on plywood.

Granite

Less expensive than marble, granite is the hardest stone used for floors. It has an attractive grain and is less likely to stain or scratch, as well as being less slippery. Like marble, it

part two: the specifics

comes in slabs but is also available in very thin tiles, which means that it can be used in upstairs rooms, set on plywood, as long as the floor is level and firm. Granite comes in some 50 colors and in either a matte or a polished finish. The former is safer, in the sense that it is much less slippery, but the latter does look splendid.

CONCRETE

Although concrete was invented by the ancient Romans, it is still considered to be one of the most modern and malleable of materials, as it is able to take on any shape or thickness. It will make a good-looking floor in tile form, if it is painted or stained and waxed (see page 123). Concrete is also extremely practical, since it is both heat- and cold-resistant, as well as scratch-proof, and it is reasonably priced. However, concrete floors do take a month of curing to set properly, so they are best used in homes that are being built from scratch or in major renovations.

WOOD FLOORING

Wood flooring is available in every price bracket, tone, and finish, and it can be used anywhere in the house. As well as new wood, consider reclaimed beams and boards from old industrial and farm buildings. Pine, cypress, spruce, chestnut, maple and oak are some of the species available.

Types of wood

North America is richly endowed with many species of hardwood and softwood, which makes wood flooring relatively inexpensive here–compared to Britain, for example, where limited supplies of hardwood, especially, have made it necessary to import lumber from other countries.

Softwoods and hardwoods are both used for flooring, with softwood being cheaper. However, because softwood is butt-joined, it can shrink and leave gaps if it is not carefully installed. It can also be dented easily by high-heeled shoes and heavy furniture. Softwoods include hemlock, spruce, fir, and pine; they should be finished with a polyurethane or oleoresinous sealer, then polished if desired.

If you choose hardwood, you ought to make sure that the wood comes from an ecologically managed planta-tion. Among the most easily available choices of hardwood are maple, walnut, cherry, beech, and oak. Maple is particularly tough and is therefore often used for contract work. Teak, ebony, iroko, mahogany, Australian ironwood, and rosewood look splendid but are more expensive than oak. Hackberry (*Celtis*), grown in the eastern United States and southern Canada, is a light-colored wood with good shock resistance and it is sometimes used for flooring.

Among some of the more exotic tropical species now making their way into Europe are merbau, from the Philippines and Malaysia, which is a lovely chestnut color; turupay, from Papua, New Guinea, which has a yellowish-chestnut color and is extremely tough; and kwila, from the Solomon Islands, which is a black-brown and does not show water marks.

Wood flooring comes in various forms, and strips differ in width, the

1 Gleaming polished concrete makes a stunning underpinning to the neutral color scheme in this idiosyncratic loft. The flow is interrupted only by an insert of flagstones in the kitchen area—a nice textural and spatial contrast to the overall smooth monotones.

2 Bamboo floors are comparative newcomers to the increasing choice of natural wood flooring. They are both durable and handsome.

3 Nicely fitted parquet flooring made from oak.

4 Wood is as much a feature of this study as polished concrete is in the loft on the left. The light wood floor blends beautifully with the finely reeded and plain paneling and bookshelves.

first being about 8-8 in. (15-20 cm.) wide; the second being between 2½ and 3½ in. (6 and 9 cm.) Self-stick planks are also available. Parquet flooring comes in interlocking blocks, typically 12 in. (30 cm.) square, and also in a variety of patterns.

Wood flooring is available in either solid or laminated wood. The laminated type consists of a thin layer of hardwood veneer, laminated to underneath layers of plywood, blockboard, or even cork. The hardwood layer may be as thin as

part two: the specifics

means taking delivery of the boards or parquet well before installation. A solid wood floor, as opposed to the laminated variety, can be nailed directly to a wood subfloor. If the new surface is on the ground floor, it is a good idea to install some kind of moisture-retardant material, such as roofing felt between the subfloor and the new surface. If the wood is to be laid over concrete, a vapor-retardant should be used on top of the concrete, in order to act as a barrier against any moisture. Laminated flooring, however, can be set straight over concrete. And if it is one of the types that consist of interlocking pieces and are glued together rather than nailed, it should be set over a foam pad laid on the subfloor.

It is most important that installation nails not be knocked through electric cables or water pipes, so services should be mapped out with care and accuracy.

If you are attempting to lay the floor yourself, fix a line of string along the front of any fireplace, or any

⅟₁₆ in. (1-2 mm.), but thicker grades are harder-wearing and can even be sanded and refurbished a few times before the surface gets too frail. Both solid and laminated floors are sometimes used in kitchens, but neither is recommended for bathrooms.

Laying a wood floor

Even if you are employing professional floor-layers, it is useful to know what they should be doing. First, you should make certain, if you can, that the wood becomes adjusted to its new atmosphere before it is laid, which projecting walls or cabinets, then work backward from these into the recesses. Since wood expands and contracts with changes in temperature and humidity, this slight movement must be allowed for, with a narrow expansion gap around the edge. If necessary, it can be covered with beading or filled with cork. Removing the baseboards allows the new floor to be placed closer to the wall, so that the gap will be covered by the baseboards and the job will look neater. However, this is not always possible.

1 *Polished chipboard is an unusual but durable and practical surface for both general living and play space.*

2 *Wide, bleached floorboards provide a contrast to the high-beamed ceiling and tall, painted bookshelves in this mellow French living room.*

3 *Large gray diamonds painted over white have been given several coats of acrylic varnish for toughness. Such painted finishes are an inexpensive but decorative solution for battered old floorboards.*

4 *The slatted boarding used for this bathroom is more usually connected with outdoor showers, gardens, decking, and paths. It is rare to see it used inside.*

Finishes

All hardwood floorings, except pre-sealed laminated floors, need a sealer to repel moisture and dirt.

If you are finishing the floor yourself, it is much easier and more comfortable, as well as swifter, to use a water-based finish, like a urethane/acrylic combination or an organic primer with a citrus-oil base. These dry in 30 minutes and do not yellow the wood, as many polyurethane finishes do.

The traditional finish for most hard floors is tung oil and wax, and this can still be used, though the floor will need to be rewaxed once a year or so and polished regularly with an electric polisher, an essential machine for any large areas.

part two: the specifics

Flexible Flooring

Hard-wearing, easy to maintain, and relatively inexpensive, flexible floorings not only are practical but are often extremely decorative and are warmer underfoot than tiles or stone.

LINOLEUM

Made of a compound of linseed oil, pine resins, wood, ground cork, and pigment pressed onto a jute backing, linoleum comes in sheets or tiles. Non-slip, burn-resistant, and reasonably priced, it is making a big comeback. One of its biggest pluses is that the material can be inlaid and spliced to make handsome and distinctive customized designs that are a far cry from the rather sticky old brown "lino" that covered the floors of so many dreary rooms in the early twentieth century. Whether you are using the sheet form or tiles, linoleum should be glued to a spotless, level, preferably plywood underlay.

CORK

Durable and economical, cork is warm, soft, and quiet underfoot. This very resilient material is made of compressed and baked pieces of the bark of the cork oak tree. It lasts well, especially when combined with vinyl, and is efficient in bathrooms, play-rooms, kitchens, and hallways.

It comes in sheet and, much more commonly, tile form. The tiles are usually pre-sealed. If they are unsealed, they will need to be varnished after laying. Cork is available in a range of colors as well as light to dark browns.

As with wood, cork should be left in the room in which it is to be laid for at least three days prior to installation,

to allow it to become acclimatized. If the cork is being laid on old wood, cover the sub-floor first with latex-fill, hardboard or plywood. If the sub-floor is concrete, install a moisture-proof membrane first in order to prevent

moisture rising up from the slabs and lifting the flooring.

It is important to sweep cork flooring carefully to ensure that there is never any residue of grit or sand to score the surface. Avoid abrasive or alkaline cleaners. As with most floors, sealed surfaces are easily cleaned with a damp mop and mild detergent.

VINYL

Made from PVC (polyvinyl chloride), vinyl flooring is comfortable to walk on, reasonable in price, easy to clean, and available in a huge choice of colors

and designs. As with linoleum, solid colors can be combined to form good-looking patterns.

Basically, the choice is between the more expensive, longer-lasting, solid variety, and the cheaper, composition vinyl which is a mixture of fillers and pigments with a thermoplastic binder. Composition vinyl can be either cush-ioned or flat. The cushioned variety is slightly "bouncy" and more resilient underfoot, making for a softer tread, and it provides some sound insulation. The flat variety is very flexible, molding itself easily to the floor.

Solid vinyl comes in solid colors but also in realistic copies of marble, granite, terrazzo, limestone, brick, terracotta tiles, and wood. If you are purchasing composition vinyl, it is usually best to get the inlaid variety, in which the design runs through all the layers, as opposed to the rotogravure type, in which the design is merely printed on the surface.

Vinyl is available in either sheet or tile form. It can be laid on existing wood, tiled, or linoleum floors (if smooth and in good condition) or on a concrete subfloor.

RUBBER

Rubber flooring is more hard-wearing as well as softer, warmer, and quieter underfoot than linoleum or vinyl. It is resistant to burns and dents, and because in some cases it contains self-releasing wax, it can often cure itself of scratches and minor damage. It is available in sheets and tiles, in either industrial or domestic quality.

It comes in a range of colors, including primaries, pastels, and industrial black, which lends itself to a high-tech decor. Studded patterns of varying sizes are the most common, but ribbed and slate-like effects are also available. The studded and ribbed versions are very non-slip, which makes them useful in bathrooms, but they are also more difficult to clean and so not really suitable for kitchens.

1 *Cleverly cut and inlaid linoleum in quite an ambitious design makes an inexpensive but exotic and easily maintained bathroom floor.*
2 *Studded industrial rubber flooring is a perennial favorite for many minimalist installations, being non-slip, reliably tough, and relatively noiseless.*
3 *Vinyl tiles laid in a classic diamond pattern (and looking similar to the painted wood floor on page 143) are a practical choice for kitchens, dining areas, halls, and corridors. They are comparatively soft underfoot, are easier on breakages than regular ceramic, terracotta or quarry tiles, slate, or concrete, and are very easy to keep clean.*

part two: the specifics

SECTION SIX

Beautiful windows that provide equally beautiful light while looking out over an agreeable view are clearly desirable—but they are also comparatively rare. Happily, there are numerous ways to cover, treat, disguise, and enhance less-than-perfect providers of light and air. They range from the most elaborate use of fabric, tassels, fringes, edgings, tiebacks, and headings to the simplest of treatments. There is a formidable choice of shades and blinds, made not only from fabric but also from aluminum, vinyl, split bamboo, paper, and wood. And then there are alternative treatments like screens, shutters, shelves of wood or glass, trellis, stained glass, painted glass, and windows treated like paintings.

Windows

Choosing Window Treatments

It is a good idea to make a window treatment an integral part of a room, rather than designing it to stand out from everything else. I don't mean that windows should not be a focal point. Indeed, large windows and unusual or particularly handsome window treatments make very fine focal points, and in a room that might otherwise be lacking in architectural detail or interest, they can add a special quality. But curtains and draperies should be seen in the same context as the rest of the room scheme.

1 *Camel-colored roller shades at these long windows so exactly match the painted walls that they look like a paneled continuation of them.*
2 *Elaborate draperies are used at the entrance to this room, while simpler, light-colored ones are hung at the French doors, to allow some light to filter through.*
3 *Storage shelves are a bold and practical solution to this awkwardly shaped window.*

It would obviously not look right if you installed the elaborately fringed and/or swagged draperies so beloved by the Victorians in a minimalist room (though, paradoxically, it is perfectly possible to put simple but well-made curtains in an otherwise elaborately furnished and decorated room). Nor would it look good to have very bright curtains in a gently or subtly colored room. As in most things to do with decoration, it is a question of achieving a reasonable balance with all the rest of the components of a room.

Often the most decorative or unusual windows, such as arched, bay, or dormer windows or French doors, are the hardest to treat. Suggestions for their treatment are given on pages 168–71. There is, however, a vast choice of ideas for ordinary windows, ranging from draperies or shades in various styles to completely different treatments. It is easier to make a choice if your rooms are a specific period or style, or if you have already chosen the way you want a particular room to look. Much also depends, of course, on practical considerations, like how light the room is, what it is to be used for, and the money available.

PRACTICAL ASPECTS

If you want to ensure that your draperies or curtains are practical, here are some of the most important questions to ask yourself.

- **Are your windows drafty, cold or inclined to let in street noise?**
  Apart from the expensive and drastic measure of changing your present windows for well-fitting ones, or, less expensively, adding storm windows, make sure that any draperies you order are heavy and interlined. Even better, if possible, introduce an extra layer of fabric between you and the outside world with roller or Roman shades, fitted underneath the draperies. This should cut down satisfactorily on heat loss, insidious drafts, and street noise.

- **Do your windows face east or north (or west or south in the southern hemisphere) in rather dark rooms?**
  If so, you should make sure that you choose window treatments that will obscure as little of the light you get as possible. This rules out tied-back draperies that meet in the middle, deep valances, and other elaborately draped styles.

- **Do your windows face south or west (north or east in the southern hemisphere)?**
  If they do, you are likely to get a lot of light and sun, so avoid using fabrics that will fade or rot easily, like silks and very bright colors. Consider filtering the light with translucent shades or glass curtains.

- **Do you live in a town or city, or in a place where there is a lot of pollution in the air?**
  If so, avoid using light colors or treatments involving a lot of elaborate folds, so that the fabric does not need to be cleaned too often.

part two: the specifics

149

1 *Translucent panels threaded on battens at the top and bottom have a pleasantly airy feel. They also use little fabric and are inexpensive to make. However, they provide scant privacy at night when the lights are on.*

2 *Painted old interior shutters look good and are effective in their own right, which is just as well since they would be awkward to use in conjunction with most shades or draperies.*

● **Are your windows overlooked by passers-by or by houses or apartments opposite?**
Don't forget that muslin, voile, lace, and otherwise translucent curtains or shades which provide privacy during the day without cutting off light are transparent at night. As an alternative to sheer curtains, café curtains (curtains hung from a rod fixed halfway up a window) provide considerable privacy. Another way of providing some privacy is to fix several glass shelves across windows, on which you can display a collection of glass or china or plants, or all three. Densely planted window boxes can also provide a degree of privacy.

- **Do your windows have radiators under them?**

  Unless a window is tiny, draperies or curtains look best if they reach the floor; yet covering radiators with draperies causes heat loss. Therefore, if you decide to use draperies at windows with radiators, you will almost certainly want to tie them back at each side and use a shade, blind, or shutters as well. Or you could omit the draperies and just use the shade, blind, or shutters alone.

- **Do your windows have deep recesses?**

  If so, it is preferable to hang draperies or curtains outside the recesses, because this will let in the maximum amount of light by day.

3 *These toile de Jouy draperies with matching low-slung tiebacks are prettily suspended from a rod covered in the same fabric. The juxtaposition of the toile with the striped love seat is effective and, together with the miniature topiary trees on the sill behind, forms an attractive little composition.*

4 *Swedish cotton draperies are also hung from a fabric-covered rod, but with the addition of silvered finials and holdbacks, as well as a deep window seat. This seat is comfortably scattered with pillows in various patterns.*

part two: the specifics

Curtains and Draperies

Whether you are a full-scale drapery and trimmings person or prefer the simpler, modern styles, the fact remains that most rooms benefit from some sort of softness and decoration at the windows, even if it is only in the form of a top treatment.

Provided that draperies or curtains are appropriate for the style of the room and home and fulfill the practical considerations discussed on pages 149–51, they can today be as sumptuous or minimal as you like. But during the nineteenth century, the great age of draperies, the treatment in the main rooms of prosperous homes often consisted of both draperies and curtains, topped with two valances—one stiffened and one, beneath it, that might be pleated or gathered, and either a shade or shutters. The top

1 *A very long, slim rod with an elaborately swagged length of sheer fabric runs the full width of the window wall in this living room. The lightness of the fabric, allied to the pale aqua of walls and ceiling, serves to exaggerate the sense of coolness.*

2 *A curtain made from a heavily ridged fabric is here suspended by stitched leather loops from a trim steel rod. It is an unusual but effective treatment.*

3 *Breezy voile is contrasted with black rings and a twisted iron rod. The rings are spaced far enough apart to form graceful deep scallops.*

4 *Here, another light curtain is suspended by slim tabs from a rod that is held well away from the window. Note the bracket, which makes quite an interesting feature in itself.*

valances might be aligned with the room's cornice; its shelf supported the soft valance and also the rod from which the draperies were hung. Alternatively, the valance was sometimes draped around a pole, ending in a swag and cascades, which obviated the need for a stiffened valance. Generally the draperies and valance had fringe in contrasting or harmonizing colors. Tiebacks or ties were used to loop the draperies back by day, and sometimes by night, too, if a shade or shutters were used.

Today, such elaborate window treatments are seldom seen except in the most formal rooms—in fact, the opposite, a bare or minimally dressed window is much more common. But properly made draperies can still

make all the difference to a room scheme. What is more, the top treatment—whether an elaborate swag with cascades or a valance, or simply an attractive heading on draperies suspended from a pole–is as basic to the overall effect as the fabric is.

DRAPERY AND CURTAIN HARDWARE

There is a wide assortment of rods from which draperies and curtains can be hung. Curtain rods are quite simple; the white, flat-faced kind are intended to be used with curtains having a cased heading, or rod pocket, so that the rod itself is not visible, whereas the more decorative round, often brass-colored rod is designed for use with café curtains or long curtains

suspended from it with tabs or ribbons. For lightweight curtains you can use a spring-pressure curtain rod.

More substantial decorative rods, sometimes called poles, can be used for draperies where a valance is not used and where the rod itself—which may be

metal, wood, or painted or wood finish and which usually has a finial at each end–forms part of the drapery design. The draperies hang from rings, usually matching the rod. If the draperies need to be opened and closed (as contrasted with stationary panel

part two: the specifics

draperies), a rod containing a concealed traverse mechanism is used, and the rings are attached to the sliders. If the drapery heading or a valance will hide the rod, a conventional traverse rod is used. These rods come in various styles, including double rods (for both draperies and valance) and curved and angled styles, suitable for bay and bow windows. Some can be fixed to the ceiling, instead of the wall or window frame.

They are generally made of white plastic or metal, with a choice of brackets, depending upon how far away from the windows you need the draperies to hang.

CREATING ILLUSIONS WITH FABRIC

Small windows with poor views can be made to look much larger and more elegant than they are, with no sacrifice of light, by using several layers of cream or white voile, muslin, or lace.

For example, you could hang one layer of material straight over the window, suspended from the upper part of the window frame and descending to the floor, to hide the shape of the window. You could then add two separate curtains, gathered onto an overlapping rod suspended over the top of the window frame, and caught back with tiebacks at each side. The fabric could be edged with a bobble fringe or ribbon trim for added interest. Or you could simply top the first layer with a gently draped valance in similarly colored silk. If you require more privacy than the several layers of light fabric can provide at night, you could mount a roller shade beneath the under-curtain.

Another way of creating a long, graceful-looking window out of a nondescript one is to build a window seat. Fix a wood frame around the top and sides of the window and down to the floor. Next, fix a length of wood between the sides as a seat. For comfort, about 14 in. (35 cm.) deep is best; it will project beyond the frame at the front. Mount a rod across the top to hold two floor-length draperies, tied back at each side of the window. Put a foam cushion on the seat, and use scatter cushions to hide the wall between the window sill and seat.

If you have two or three such windows on a wall, you can make this arrangement look an integral part of the room, as well as adding useful storage, by building in shallow cabinets and/or shelving between the new window frames.

LININGS AND INTERLININGS

Unless you are deliberately using sheer draperies, to filter rather than block out light, you should certainly line them. And if you want a truly luxurious effect—which will also reduce heat-loss through the windows—it's a good idea to interline them also.

Lining protects the main fabric from sun, dust, and pollution, encloses hems and raw edges, and can provide decorative contrast wherever a curtain is caught back. A good lining makes draperies look better from the outside. These points also apply to valances.

If early-morning light is a problem in bedrooms, draperies (and shades) can be lined with special blackout lining fabric, which will make the window treatment much more opaque.

They can also be lined with milium, a thermal fabric which not only blocks out light (though not quite so well as blackout lining fabric) but will also help insulation.

SWAGS AND CASCADES

These are most often used for elaborate, formal treatments, and although they look as if they are made from one beautifully draped length of fabric, they usually consist of a number of different pieces that have been skillfully joined together. They are frequently trimmed with braid, piping, fringe, cord, or fabric borders, and often have contrasting or patterned linings. It is essential not to skimp on fabric, but it is equally important not to overdo it.

Proportions are crucial for this treatment. At its deepest part, the

swag needs to be between one-fifth and one-sixth of the overall height of the window, while the cascades should fall at least halfway down the window. The grander styles look best in high-ceilinged rooms on large windows, but simple treatments are quite versatile. Swags and cascades do not have to be partnered with draperies– simple swags can also be used over shades or shutters, or on their own.

A swag with cascades is fitted to a cornice board using thumbtacks or a staple gun. Instead of a cornice board, use a pole to support swags and cascades extending beyond the window on either side so as not to obscure too much light. If the fabric needs to be fixed, use a wooden pole, which will take thumbtacks, finishing nails, or staples from a staple gun.

As a simple alternative to a swag and cascades, a length of fabric can be casually draped over a pole. To make it easy to remove for cleaning, you can hold it in place with Velcro dots.

CORNICES AND LAMBREQUINS

Similar in appearance to a stiffened valance, a cornice, or a cornice board, also serves the same functions: concealing the top of the draperies and giving a finishing touch to the window. The difference is that a cornice is made of wood. It may be painted or stained to harmonize with other colors in the room, or it may be covered with padded fabric. It thus has a firmer appearance than a stiffened valance; however either can be given a decoratively shaped edge.

part two: the specifics

I This soft cotton valance has a frivolously puffy knot at each side. Such extravaganzas are generally stuffed with tissue paper to keep the shape if the fabric is very light. The gauzy fabric is edged with a fringed trim.

It is sometimes possible to find splendid old cornices in antique shops. If they fit or can be made to fit the windows, they can be a great asset to a period room. In order to be in proportion for the window treatment, however, they should be no more than one-sixth of the drapery length.

A variation of the cornice or shaped valance is the lambrequin, which reaches right down the sides of a window, sometimes as far as the floor, making an undistinguished window look far more interesting.

VALANCES

Straight and shaped valances are interlined with buckram and a soft flannel interlining, concealed with a lining. Pleated valances are lined but not interlined (unless the draperies are). They can be pleated, by hand or using heading tapes, as in many of the methods described for drapery headings (see right). They can be decorated to match the draperies, perhaps with a contrasting band or ruffle, piping, or some other trimming of your choice.

A pleated valance can be hung from a separate valance rod aligned with the main drapery rod. Either kind of valance can be attached to a shelf, which either sits above the drapery rod or has the drapery rod attached to the underside. Such shelves are usually fixed either to the top of the window frame or above the window, by means of strong, evenly spaced brackets. The boards should be at least 2 in. (5 cm.) longer than the rod at each end.

A valance known as an attached or integral valance looks much the same as the conventional variety when the draperies are closed, but is actually attached to the top of each drapery panel so that the two halves move apart when the draperies are opened. This avoids blocking incoming light, but because the drapery rod is not covered when the draperies are open, it is best used with a decorative pole.

DRAPERY AND VALANCE HEADINGS

Headings determine the style of draperies and valances, and they affect how they hang. Many are meant to be paired with decorative poles rather than being hidden. Traditionally, pleated headings are made by hand but the job is quite labor-intensive, and heading tapes are much faster.

For some window treatments, the draperies are left permanently joined at the top. The sides are held back with tiebacks, which are simply released as necessary to close the draperies. This treatment is sometimes known as a fixed heading. Any draperies can be treated in this way, but some headings have to be fixed because they are not easy to move and may look unsightly when open. They are therefore more suitable for rooms that either are very light or are used mostly at night.

Pinch pleats

This is the most commonly used heading in the United States. It allows the draperies to fall into gentle but precise folds. You can buy pinch-pleat heading tapes, but they sometimes sag, so it is generally better to hand-sew them. A single tuck is made at regular intervals, and this is then divided into triple pleats. It is important to work out the right number of pleats and spaces to fit neatly and symmetrically into the given space. This heading is fixed to a conventional or decorative rod by pin hooks placed at the back of each pleat.

French pleats

Also known as goblet pleats, this handsome heading is formed and secured in much the same way as pinch pleats. However, the three pleats are not stitched in place along their entire length but simply secured at the base of the fold. To help them keep this goblet shape, the pleats are usually stuffed with a suitable filling or interlining, and they are often further distinguished by the addition of a contrasting binding or lining. Like pinch pleats, they are best hand-sewn, although appropriate heading tapes are available from certain sources.

Flemish pleats

This handsome treatment, which needs to be treated as a fixed heading, looks infinitely better if hand-sewn. It is formed from French pleats (see pages

tip

FOR AN EVEN MORE LUXURIOUS AND PROFESSIONAL-LOOKING EFFECT ON LINED AND INTERLINED DRAPERIES, PAD EACH LEADING EDGE WITH AN EXTRA STRIP OF INTERLINING ROLLED LENGTHWISE AND INVISIBLY HAND-STITCHED INSIDE THE DRAPERY LINING.

2 Pinch pleats are here attached by rings to a classic wood pole complete with finials. Loose cord tiebacks hold back the fabric just behind the sofa.

3 Small French pleats are closely attached to a slim, slightly curved rod. The low-slung tiebacks form a good frame for the high-backed and graceful chair.

part two: the specifics

157

1 *Gently gathered draperies are suspended by rings just below rods with distressed gilded finials in this stunning bedroom. The fabric is an inexpensive Indian cotton, half-lined over the conventional lining with a woven sprigged cotton to match the blind underneath. A bit of contrasting lining like this shows nicely when the draperies are casually caught back—in this case by distressed holdbacks. The finely striped window-seat cushion and neat bolsters blend in well with the overall effect. Note the subtley painted faux paneling.*
2 *The tab heading on these curtains is made from the same dark contrasting fabric as the trim sewn onto the leading edges. The cord tiebacks have fringed tassels, and this masculine treatment looks apt with the heavy paneling.*

156–7) which are bound or trimmed at the base of the heading with a hand-sewn cord, sometimes twisted into decorative knots. Alternatively, instead of going right across the base of every pleat, attach the cord can to the base of, say, every third one, so it falls into large loops. These pleats are usually fixed to a track or board.

Box pleats

Box pleats look crisp, tailored, and elegant. They are usually formed by hand, but it is possible to buy a box-pleat heading tape, which has a pair of pull-up drawstrings, to the top of the drapery or valance. Box pleats should be treated as a fixed heading.

Smocked

Popular in Britain, this handsome heading works well in formal living rooms and dining rooms and even in bedrooms; but it does involve careful workmanship. Even with a special "smocking tape," which gives the heading a smocked outline, the smocking still has to be hand-sewn. If the whole heading is hand-stitched, it is best to plot out the smocking design on paper first, before transferring it to the top of the drapery. A smocked heading should be treated as a fixed heading.

Cartridge and pencil pleats

Cartridge pleats are small, round pleats that are stiffened with rolls of crinoline to maintain the shape. Each pleat takes up about 2 in. (5 cm.) of fabric, and there are small spaces between pleats.

A variation on the cartridge pleat, pencil pleats are smaller and are spaced close together. Very popular in Britain, they produce a softly gathered effect suitable for a more informal room. Some suppliers of decorator fabrics stock heading tapes that can be used to produce pencil pleats. Tape for gathered headings is also available.

CURTAIN HEADINGS

In recent years, as trends have moved towards less formal decorating styles, curtains have become more popular and have been given a variety of interesting new headings.

Gathered

This is still the most common heading, used especially for glass curtains and sheer tieback curtains. A casing, or rod pocket, is stitched at the top of the curtain, and this is slipped over the curtain rod. Since the curtains are wider than the length of the rod (normally at least twice the measurement), this produces a gathered effect. For an attractive finish, the casing is positioned slightly down from the folded top edge of the curtain, so that the edge stands up above the rod.

Tab

There are several variations on this style. Basically, it consists of a series of fabric tabs attached to the curtain–or sometimes part of the curtain panel itself–which are then looped over a decorative curtain rod.

The tabs can be in the same fabric as the curtain, or contrasting. Both ends of each tab can be stitched to the curtain like a loop, or just one end is stitched and the other buttoned.

Scalloped

This heading is often used on café curtains. The upper edge of the curtain is cut in a series of downward-pointing curves and backed with a matching

3 *Here a simpler tab heading in the same sheer cotton as the curtains is attached to a steel rod. The curtains puddle gracefully onto the white-painted floor.*
4 *A bold plastic pole is pushed through reinforced overscale eyelet holes in this tailored, contemporary eyelet heading.*

facing. Curtain rings are then attached to the points between the scallops and slipped over a narrow curtain rod. The curtain is only a little wider than the length of the rod, so as to display the scallops. For a fuller effect, place pinch pleats between each scallop.

Eyelet

This contemporary heading involves inserting jumbo eyelets, or grommets, along the top edge of the curtain. The curtain is folded accordian-style, and a pole is slotted through the eyelets.

part two: the specifics

TIEBACKS

Draperies can be caught back in a number of different ways, and at various heights. The usual height at which to position the hooks for a tieback is two-thirds of the way down the window, but of course they can be placed higher or lower, depending upon what seems in proportion to the window. A well-placed tieback, or pair of tiebacks, can give a splendid swoop to draperies, revealing glimpses of a contrasting lining if desired.

One of the most commonly used shapes of tieback is a long, narrow oblong, stiffened with buckram or interfacing. It can be casually tied around sewn drapery; or rings can be at the ends, each of which is then attached to a hook judiciously placed behind and to the side of the drapery. Other stiffened shapes, such as crescents, are also possible.

Another type of tieback is made from interlined tubes of fabric braided together. The fabrics might incorporate, say, one strip of the drapery fabric and two others.

Other styles include tiebacks with bows; thick cords with tassels made from silk or cotton, or a mixture of both; metal tiebacks, also known as holdbacks; and brass or silvered rosettes on a long stem, behind which you can tuck the draperies.

ITALIAN STRINGING

Another method of holding draperies back when they meet at the top is called Italian stringing, or reefing. A diagonal line of rings is sewn at the back between a point about one fifth of the way down the outside edge, and a point about one third of the way down the leading edge. Cord is then run through these rings (and, for one curtain, along a batten at the top). Pulling on the cords at the side pulls the draperies apart, as in a puppet theater. Italian stringing looks effective, and lets in more light than tiebacks placed lower down.

DRAPERY TRIMS

Most draperies look more "finished" and elegant with some sort of trim, even if it is only a self-trim—a slim roll of the drapery fabric finishing the edges. An inspiring selection is available in every price range.

Contrasting linings are a wonderful way of finishing draperies, particularly those that are tied back or Italian strung. They can include the

1 *A three-part twisted brass holdback.*

2 *Fringed tassels on a cord tieback.*

3 *A handsome gilded screw-in rosette holdback, which is easy to use and enables the drapery to be looped back as fully as desired.*

4 *French-pleated interlined linen curtains are Italian strung, with a tassel suspended just below the center of the fixed heading. Note the effective inset border, matching the white paintwork.*

same design in a different colorway, or even the same fabric used right side to front, which can be very subtle. (I find that the "wrong" side of a fabric can be much more interesting than the front, so always examine both sides.)

Sometimes when I want a contrasting fabric to show on tied-back draperies, I just face the inner half of each panel with the contrasting fabric over the top of the normal lining material. If the contrasting fabric is quite expensive, and the draperies large, this works out a lot less expensive than using the contrasting fabric for the whole panel.

part two: the specifics

Shades and Blinds

Window shades and blinds, used either in place of or along with curtains or draperies, have many advantages worth considering. Since a shade is basically just a single piece of fabric, it will show off the design of a patterned fabric much better than draperies or curtains. Also, a solid-color fabric with a border looks very crisp and architectural. Romans and rollers, in spite of sounding like a 1960s pop band, have clean lines, so are suitable for every kind of room, whether modern, period, or eclectic.

If you have a good-looking window frame, you can install a shade inside the recess to show it off, rather than hiding it with draperies. Most types of blind are good alternatives to draperies or curtains for small windows or windows with radiators or window seats underneath. You can also use them in conjunction with permanently tied-back draperies that you

cannot, or do not want to, disarrange. Apart from being a practical cover-up for a window, a shade or blind adds a sense of perspective to a room.

Shades and blinds are lowered and raised by a spring mechanism or a cord system which allows the shade/ blind to lie flat against the window, to be gathered, or to be pulled up in folds. Since blinds and shades can be lowered

1 *Plain off-white roller shades on a pair of bathroom windows look pleasingly geometric behind a scarlet-painted bathtub. Frivolous tassels attached to the roller shades repeat the color of the tub in miniature.*

2 *White silk balloon shades provide quite a contrast to the dark oriental table and collection of baskets below. But the juxtaposition of textures—silk, wood, bamboo, succulent leaves, stone and terracotta, velvet upholstery, and differing basket weaves—works well, creating a modern mood. This space is compact and utilitarian, as well as attractive to the eye.*

2

tip

MAKE A WINDOW
LOOK LONGER AND
MORE GRACEFUL BY
POSITIONING A SHADE
SO THAT THE BOTTOM
OF THE SHADE, WHEN
PULLED UP, JUST COVERS
THE TOP OF THE FRAME,
THUS DISGUISING ITS
PRECISE WHEREABOUTS.

and raised to any desired level, they can filter light or block it out.

SHADES

There are many different kinds of shade, but balloon (or cloud) shades, Austrian shades, pull-up shades, roller shades, and Roman shades are among the most popular.

Balloon shades

These were a great favorite in the Rococo period of the eighteenth century. (In Britain these are called Austrian shades.) In spite of being considered by purists as fussy upstarts, they can look entirely suitable in certain situations. They have fullness in the width–the type of heading chosen is a matter of taste; it is often simply gathered. The shade is pulled up and let down in a series of gathered, scallop-like folds. When the shade is completely down, the only fullness remaining in the length is at the base, where it is still gathered.

A balloon shade has a series of rings, usually as part of special ring tape, attached to the back of the shade in vertical lines. Each line of rings is threaded with a cord that is attached to the lower ring. The top of the shade is attached to a wooden batten or an Austrian blind track which is fixed to the top of the window frame or just above the window. Screw eyes are attached to the underside of the batten for the cords to pass through, so they will all hang together at one side. The cords are knotted together; when they are pulled, the shade rises.

A tailed balloon shade is made in much the same way, except that the cording is omitted from the sides, causing the fabric to droop at the edges. It is possible to have as many swags as liked between the edges, but just one looks less fussy.

Both kinds of balloon shade are normally made in light, airy fabrics, but they look more tailored and "serious" in heavier fabrics.

part two: the specifics

163

Austrian shades

Austrian and balloon shades are often confused, since both have a good deal of fullness in the width. However, while a balloon shade falls flat like a curtain, with its gathers or scallop effect only along the base, an Austrian shade has the fullness distributed along its entire length. (It needs twice the length of fabric of the finished drop.) It is gathered onto cords which are inserted between the fabric and lining (if any) while it is being made.

Pull-up shades or curtains

These were much in use in the eighteenth century in grand houses. Robert Adam included them, for example, in his wonderful interior for Osterley Park, near London, so they have an excellent provenance. They look somewhat like balloon shades and also work on much the same

principle, but they are made to lower right to the floor, when they look like an elegant closed drapery.

Roller shades

The earliest of all shades, these are also among the most useful. They were originally known as Holland shades because "Holland" was the name of the highly glazed, finely woven, buff- or

Manila-colored linen with which they were made. Now they can be painted, stenciled, and made in almost any fabric that can be stiffened or laminated, or that is firm enough (without being too thick) to roll satisfactorily. Roller shades can be very plain and practical or highly decorative, depending upon the design of fabric or the trim that is used at the bottom. The shades are wound around a roller which is controlled either by a cog mechanism or by a spring mechanism.

Reverse roller shades

With this type of shade, the rolled fabric is at the bottom. It works very simply with a pair of cords and screw eyes without the benefit of a roller or any mechanism. The fabric should be lightweight so that it rolls up easily.

Roman shades

A Roman shade is flat, with no fullness across the width. When down, it has no fullness in the length, either. The shade draws up into horizontal pleats, while the fabric is usually backed by a series of thin battens or dowels sewn parallel to each other in casings or pockets; the battens are pulled up by cords to form crisp folds.

A Roman shade can either be lined or unlined, but for additional warmth, it can be backed with blackout lining fabric. The shade can be edged, bordered, or trimmed with fringe or cording, and either hung by itself or dressed up with a valance, or lambrequin (see pages 155–6).

It is a good idea not to make Roman shades any wider than just under 5 ft. (1.5 m.). Otherwise, they will be heavy to pull up, and it is really important to pull them up neatly so that they do not look lopsided. If windows are much wider, make two or three narrower shades and hang them side by side.

BLINDS

There is a wide choice of blinds and of commercially made window shades in various materials.

Venetian blinds

These classic blinds are extremely versatile, allowing almost infinite gradations of light-control. They come in a huge range of styles and materials, suited to both traditional and ultra-modern rooms. Originally made of wood, they are now often made of aluminum or vinyl, sometimes painted to resemble wood. Real wood blinds can be stained in many different colors, including natural stains replicating different varieties of wood. Venetian blinds with very narrow slats, known as mini-blinds, are ideal for locations, such as large expanses of glass, where an unobtrusive window covering is desired.

Vertical blinds

Like venetian blinds, these are based on the idea of louvers –slats that can be angled to admit or close out light. Being hung vertically, however, they draw from side to side, somewhat like draw draperies, and are thus ideal for sliding patio doors. The slats are usually made of stiffened fabric, vinyl, or aluminum and are somewhat wider than the slats of Venetian blinds.

Woven wood shades

These consist of horizontal slats of wood woven with yarn in a variety of patterns. They are usually constructed along the lines of a Roman shade, so that they pull up in folds, but some hang in vertical folds.

Matchstick shades

These are made from slim spills of wood sewn tightly together with thread. They are generally rolled up and held in place with cords , although sometimes they are sold with a spring mechanism like a roller shade. They are usually sold as untreated wood, which can be either left natural, varnished, or spray-painted.

Pleated and cellular shades

Permanently accordion-pleated fabric shades gently diffuse the light. Cellular shades consist of a double layer of pleated fabric, producing small air "cells" which insulate against cold and noise. They are available in a great number of colors and several finishes.

1 Graphic fabrics like stripes lend themselves well to Roman shades.
2 Narrowly striped Roman shades, which are half let down on these long windows, look neat and tailored set right against the glass, inside the reveals. A small amount of light creeps through the sides, but the shades would not have looked nearly so graphic if they had been hung outside the frames.
3 Wide-striped Roman blinds coordinate effectively with the series of multicolored drawers fitted below the wide windowsill in this child's room.
4 Thin-slatted Venetian blinds cover a wall of windows and make intriguing striped patterns of light and shade.
5 Detail of an inexpensive matchstick blind. Though not particularly strong, they are useful combined with draperies or as protection against sunlight.

part two: the specifics

Alternative Window Treatments

In addition to conventional treatments, there are various other good-looking ways to treat windows.

SHUTTERS

These are always neat and effective, whether they are louvered and folding, or the old solid variety, which were almost *de rigueur* in late eighteenth- and nineteenth-century houses. Old wooden shutters can be stripped; and louvered wood shutters can be left as natural wood; both types can be painted any color. The old solid kind can also be painted with designs or have their panels picked out or outlined in different colors, to give them an updated geometric look reminiscent of paintings by Mondrian.

1 *American louvered "plantation" shutters in natural wood.*

2 *A pair of free-standing screens front the translucent Roman shades on this enormous window, with its tall integral French doors. The screens lend gravitas to the area, as well as literally screening some of the superabundance of light.*

3

3 *Solid shutters at this small window have been covered in fabric and, unusually, pierced with tiny diamond shapes. The juxtaposition of colors and the grouping of glass on the sill add charming detail.*
4 *Chains of irregularly shaped colored glass strung across a deep-set window reflect the sun in rainbow colors.*
5 *Here, frosted glass makes the simplest of window treatments, while the recess created by a deep window embrasure has been used to form a dressing-table area complete with storage and basin.*

5

- Glass shelves stretched across a frame are always a successful treatment for small, odd windows; windows that are difficult to open for one reason or another; corner windows at right angles to each other; and kitchen, bathroom, and powder-room windows. Like this, the window becomes an open display cabinet for items such as clear or colored glass, plants, and ceramics.
- Small windows on a stairway, landing, or corridor look chaste but interesting with one sculptural object, bud vase, plant, or small collection of objects on the sill.

- A window that frames a stunning view and is not overlooked can be treated like a painting, by making much of the window frame. This can be done by painting the frame an interesting color (which goes with the rest of the room, obviously) or even by aggrandizing the existing window frame.
- An internal window or a small window in a hall, up the stairs, or in a bathroom can be made to look highly decorative, either by replacing the glass with stained glass or engraved glass or by painting the existing glass.

part two: the specifics

Problem Windows

Ironically, some of the most interesting windows are actually the most awkward to dress. They need to be framed and shown off rather than obscured, which gives rise to the perennial conflict between aesthetics and practicality. Here are the most common problem windows, together with some possible solutions.

BAY AND BOW WINDOWS

Though usually considered an asset in a room, a bay window–or a bow window, with its continuous curve–is often a problem if it has a window seat or a radiator underneath. The answer (as, indeed, for any type of window above a window seat or radiator) is to hang shades or blinds against the glass. Permanently tied-back draperies can be hung at the sides, or the shades/blinds can be left on their own if you want a crisper look. Add a contrasting or complementary fabric element,

1 *Quantities of reasonably priced heavy Indian cotton have been made to look quite grand with elaborately fringed swags. In order not to hide the shape of the bay window, they are permanently looped back, and only the Roman shades are pulled down at night. The bay has been elegantly filled with a bolstered chaise longue.*
2 *The difficulty in finding a suitable treatment for a triangular window has been avoided here by not doing anything –the shape makes quite enough of a statement on its own.*

when there is a window seat, with scatter cushions covered in a variety of materials and textures.

You can make this type of window look as grand or as simple as you like, according to the top treatment you use. There is no reason why you cannot suspend quite elaborate swags and cascades, either across the front of the bay or on a curved rod along the top of the window if you so choose.

If there is no impediment around the windows, a traverse rod can be bent around them. The rod is best suspended from a valance shelf. Use either one pair of voluminous draperies drawn back during the day or a tied-back pair at each section of window. In this case, the window treatment is probably more expensive than awkward.

FRENCH DOORS

Many French doors open inward, which creates a problem if you want to use them while draperies are closed, but there are various ways you can overcome the problem.

If there is space, you could hang draperies across an area wider than the frame so that they can be pulled to either side to allow the doors to be opened. If there isn't room to do this, you could hang shades blinds on the glazed part of the doors, together with a good-looking top treatment fixed above the window. Or make casement curtains as for skylights.

Alternatively, for each door, hang a curtain on a Victorian-style *portière* rod, one end of which fixes to the door frame and the other to the far side of the door; the rod swivels, so that the drapery opens with the door.

2

WINDOWS WITH SHUTTERS

You can easily leave shuttered windows as they are, or you can just add a splendid valance. Alternatively, hang Italian-strung draperies or draperies permanently held back with tiebacks, closing the shutters at night. Security shutters can be a problem, though. If you have these, it is best to forget about fabric treatments and simply paint them.

ARCHED WINDOWS

Try not to lose the effect of the arch at night—or during the day, for that matter—by hiding it with a curtain heading. The traditional way to treat a Venetian, or Palladian, window (a rounded, arched window with narrow rectangular windows at each side) was

to have an Austrian shade in two parts on the center, leaving the side windows undressed or simply shuttered.

Rounded rods can be installed to follow the arch, keeping draperies permanently closed at the top and held back underneath during the day using tiebacks or holdbacks.

A simpler and cheaper approach, though it means losing the arch at night, is simply to fix a rod well over the top of the arch, so that at least you see it during the day.

Alternatively, fix a rod across the window below the semi-circular portion and cover the window beneath, leaving the arch bare. Balloon, Austrian, and pull-up shades can also be hung from a curved or arched rod, but they must be stationary and stay flat within the arch itself.

PICTURE WINDOWS AND WALLS OF GLASS

You probably will not want to obscure a picture window by day (although you will need somehow to filter or control the amount of sunlight). However, if it is a gloomy, black space at night, you will almost certainly want to cover it then. (Exceptions include high-rise city apartments, where the city lights many floors below can look magical, and windows looking out onto a garden that is beautifully lit.) Roman shades, or vertical louvers, chain, or other kinds of commercially made blinds are often the best solution for a whole wall of glass, where curtains might look rather fussy. However, you could hang a single, dramatically looped-back drapery at a picture window, if there is room to loop it back to the side.

DORMER WINDOWS

Because there is no room to the side of these windows to hang curtains, roller or Roman shades are one of the neatest solutions.

Alternatively, run hinged, slim rods through casings at the top of a pair of short curtains—the rods and curtains can swing back during the day, minimizing light loss.

SKYLIGHTS

You can buy special Venetian blinds from the manufacturers of skylights. Or use normal Venetian shade or mini-shade, a roller blind or a blind that can be held against the wall by cup hooks fixed below the windowsill.

An alternative is a casement curtain. Slip expandable spring-pressure curtain rods or adjustable

part two: the specifics

169

curtain rods through narrow casings at the top and bottom of a lightweight curtain and attach it to the frame.

CIRCULAR WINDOWS

These are really best left bare—or you could replace clear glass with etched, painted, or stained glass.

CLERESTORY WINDOWS

The best treatment for these long, narrow, horizontal strips of glass is shades or blinds. Alternatively, fit glass shelves across the frame to make a display area.

SIDE-BY-SIDE WINDOWS

These should generally be treated as one window. Hang draperies from a rod under a valance that goes across both windows, and draw the draperies to the side. Alternatively, you could use blinds or shades.

CORNER WINDOWS

When two windows are at right angles to each other in a corner, use either shades or blinds or glass shelves, which you can light from above or below by a recessed downlight or an uplight.

DIFFERENT-SHAPED WINDOWS ON THE SAME WALL

If one of the windows is particularly small, just leave it untreated with a shelf across it or a sculptural object on the windowsill. Otherwise, curtain the whole wall, tying the draperies back at either side if it is a small wall. If it is very long, you might need to have some panel draperies on the walls between the windows.

PIVOT WINDOWS AND WINDOWS THAT OPEN INWARD

If you need privacy, you can mount lightweight or sheer curtains on the window itself. For windows that pivot horizontally, attach a slim rod to the inner frame and hang café curtains from it. For vertically pivoting windows, fix casement curtains to the frames, as for skylights (see pages 169–70), or use *portière* rods as for French doors (see page **169**).

1 Fixed roller shades above with Roman shades below is the solution to the oversized windows in this cathedral-ceilinged room.

2 Old-fashioned portière rods open with the windows or can be folded away to the sides of the frame. The curtains themselves are hung from slim tabs.

3 *Awkward, shallow clerestory windows are notoriously hard to treat. This one has simply been hung with venetian blinds and balanced with a deep storage shelf of the same length.*

4 *A classic* oeil de boeuf *window has been left severely alone and looks somewhat like a landscape painting in a round frame, nicely balancing the portrait above.*

5 *An unusually shaped window— arched and slim, with a roundel tucked into the arch—has again been left untreated, and rightly so. Note how the severe "greige" walls, the bookshelves, and the single stone vase all enhance the graphic, architectural look.*

part two: the specifics

Fabrics for Windows

Almost any fabric can be used at a window, though clearly some fabrics are more appropriate for particular rooms and climates than others. But just because chintzes, light cottons, silk taffetas, and *failles* are conventionally suited to bedrooms, there is no reason why flannels, wools, or weaves of one kind or another should not be used there. By the same token, heavy textures such as wools, tweeds, and velvets, as well as chintzes, silks, *moirés*, damasks, and brocades, are thought good for living rooms–but these spaces could just as well be a riot of airy textures if it suits the situation.

Most drapery fabrics look and hang better and last longer if they are lined. In Europe, draperies are often interlined also, which makes them extra-warm and luxurious. If you

tip

IT IS FAR BETTER TO USE
A GREAT DEAL OF AN
INEXPENSIVE MATERIAL,
PERHAPS SMARTENED
UP WITH A BORDER
OR TRIMMING LIKE
CORD OR BRAID, THAN
A SKIMPY AMOUNT
OF EXPENSIVE FABRIC.

specifically want the floaty look of unlined curtains or draperies, perhaps for a delicate room scheme, or to combine with contrasting shades, use an interesting texture such as raw or watered silk, silk taffeta, softly printed voile, or lightweight linen. Lightweight curtains should be three times the width of the window, with deep hems, both to help the fabric hang better and to allow for shrinkage.

Roller shades need an easily rolled fabric, though it is possible to get a variety of fabrics specially stiffened or laminated. Roman shades, which are raised and lowered by cords, can be made in literally any material, as long as it is not too thick to pull up and pleat evenly. Austrian or similar shades need very light, soft fabrics to work well and look good.

1 Simple, inexpensive checked cotton has been lined and interlined, and beautifully designed so that the draperies look infinitely more expensive than the fabric would look otherwise. The Victorian chair and the window seat have both been covered in the same bold check.

2 Translucent shades are hung behind much heavier draperies in a paneled bay window so that the look can vary from light and airy to warmer and more enclosed.

3 Deliberately filmy curtains have been designed to blow around in romantic fashion in this country living room.

part two: the specifics

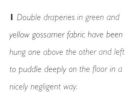

3 *A curved rod holds these voluminous voile draperies well away from the French doors. These draperies also are as generously puddled onto the floor as a sweeping bridal train.*

1 *Double draperies in green and yellow gossamer fabric have been hung one above the other and left to puddle deeply on the floor in a nicely negligent way.*

2 *In complete contrast, crisp, deeply pleated draperies barely graze the floor and are kept rigorously in place by weighted hems. Note how the exaggeratedly deep hems add to the dramatic paneled effect.*

Vocabulary of Fabric Terms

Acrylic: A type of SYNTHETIC FIBER, or a fabric made from this fiber. The properties of this fabric make it adaptable to many uses. It is stronger than NATURAL FIBERS and will not shrink or crease, but it does attract dirt.

Aniline: Term applied to dyes derived from coal tar; used in coloring fabrics.

Baize: A coarsely woven, reversible fabric with a felt-like surface. It was often used to cover doors between domestic and living quarters, but it can be used for draperies and shades.

Bark-cloth: A woven fabric with a rough texture, used primarily for draperies.

Batiste: A soft, sheer fabric, usually in white. It can be woven of COTTON, SILK, LINEN, WOOL, or SYNTHETIC FIBERS.

Bedford cord: Lengthwise, corded material of COTTON, WORSTED, or SILK.

Bengaline: A finely woven fabric with a raised horizontal rib.

Bobbinet: Curtain material made with round-hole mesh. The closeness of the mesh and the fineness of the thread determine the quality. Usually used for sheer curtains.

Brocade: Originally heavy SILK but now made of SYNTHETIC FIBERS, with elaborate pattern in silver or gold threads. A JACQUARD WEAVE, brocade has an embossed appearance.

Brocatelle: A variation of BROCADE with a higher relief, or repoussé, effect, with WARP and FILLING yarns unequally twisted, and an extra set of yarns for backing. The JACQUARD pattern stands out in raised, or blistered, effect.

Buckram: Once a rich, heavy woven cloth but now a stiffened material, usually COTTON with glue SIZING, which can be used to stiffen drapery headings, valances, and tiebacks.

Bump: British thick, loosely woven, blanket-like cotton or polyester interlining for heavy draperies.

Burlap: A coarse cloth woven from jute. Used to cover furniture springs and for wall coverings, it can also be used for draperies. In Britain, burlap is called hessian.

Butcher's linen: A coarse, HOMESPUN linen-weave cloth, originally used for French butcher's smocks.

Calico: A PLAIN-WEAVE, inexpensive, printed cotton fabric; originally from Calicut, India. Also the British term for UNBLEACHED MUSLIN.

Cambric: A fine, closely woven, white or solid-colored COTTON fabric with glazed appearance on the right side. Used primarily for curtains.

Canvas: A closely woven cloth, usually of LINEN, hemp, or COTTON.

Casement cloth: Broad term which covers many curtain fabrics, usually of a light, plain, neutral color. The weave structure is plain TWILL, satin-striped.

Challis: Soft fabric of SILK, WORSTED, or RAYON, available in solid colors or printed with small figures.

Chambray: A fine-quality PLAIN-WEAVE fabric with a LINEN-like finish that is woven in solid colors, checks, and stripes.

Chenille: Fabric made by weaving a thick, soft WEFT and a small, hard WARP, which binds weft threads together. Split into strips, this forms the chenille yarn used for weaving the fabric. The cut edges of yarn form a PLUSH-like surface.

Chiffon: A thin gauze fabric of PLAIN-WEAVE construction, made of SILK. Used mainly for curtains.

Chino: A coarse cotton fabric woven of combed yarns in a TWILL WEAVE.

Chintz: Originally any printed cotton fabric, but now a curtain fabric, which usually has a GLAZE. Associated with large floral patterns but solid-color is available.

Cotton: The fiber, or fabric made from the fiber, from the seedcase of a cotton plant. Cotton is an incredibly versatile fabric and comes in a wide range of weights and textures.

Crash: Term applied to several fabrics having coarse, lumpy, uneven yarns or rough TEXTURE. Made of jute, RAYON, LINEN, or COTTON, or a combination of them, it is available in natural or colors and is used mainly for draperies.

Crêpe: General term covering many kinds of crinkled or unevenly surfaced materials, such as wool crêpe, or crepon.

Cretonne: Printed drapery fabric of COTTON or LINEN in a variety of weaves and finishes; can include CHINTZ.

Crewelwork: Embroidery worked in colored WORSTED yarns with various stitches, especially chain, on cream-colored COTTON, LINEN, or WOOL fabrics.

Damask: Named for the ancient city of Damascus, where elaborate floral designs were woven in silk. Today this JACQUARD WEAVE is available in SILK, COTTON, WOOL, or SYNTHETIC FIBER mixtures. Flatter than BROCADE and reversible. The pattern changes color on the wrong side.

Denim: Heavy TWILL made of coarse COTTON yarn. The name, originally serge de Nîmes, comes from the French town of Nîmes. Furnishing-weight denim is finer and has a softer finish than that used for jeans. It is usually YARN-DYED.

Dimity: Crisp, lightweight, COTTON fabric usually woven with a stripe or check pattern.

Dobby weave: Cloth with small geometric pattern woven on a loom with a special attachment.

Domette: British brushed-cotton interlining, often used for swags and cascades; lighter than BUMP.

Dotted Swiss: Sheer, PLAIN-WEAVE COTTON fabric woven with dots at intervals. Used for clothing as well as for curtains.

Douppioni: A slubbed fabric made from silk; also known as dupion.

Embossing: Pressing fabric between engraved rollers with heat to give a raised effect, similar to embossed stationery. Washing or steaming will remove the design. Embossed VELVET, or PLUSH, is a fabric that is made by weaving the pile high and then shearing it to different levels.

Embroidery: A decoration in needle-work executed by hand or machine on fabric already woven.

Faille: Ribbed fabric of SILK, RAYON, or COTTON, with stripes produced by alternating fine and heavy WARPS.

Figured: Fabric with a woven-in pattern.

Filet: Square-meshed NET or LACE. Once handmade, it is now mostly machine.

Filling: Same as WEFT or WOOF. Yarn for the shuttle. Each crosswise yarn is called a pick.

Flannel: A soft fabric of PLAIN or TWILL WEAVE with a NAPPED surface on one or both sides. Heavy flannel is often used for interlining draperies.

Flock: Short, clipped fibers, glued to wood, paper, or fabric, to provide a suede-like surface.

Gabardine: A firm, tightly woven fabric with a close TWILL-WEAVE surface and a flat back.

Galloon: Narrow binding of COTTON, WOOL, or SILK, usually with fancy weaves.

Genoa velvet: A FIGURED VELVET with a SATIN ground and multicolored PILE.

Gingham: Checked PLAIN-WEAVE fabric made from COTTON yarns dyed before weaving. Originally a clothing fabric, it is used for curtains and also for covers.

Glaze: A finish on fabrics such as CHINTZ, which are treated with paraffin and calendered (pressed between rollers). Used for curtains and draperies, and also for lampshades and slipcovers.

Grass cloth: Coarsely woven fabric of vegetable fibers used as draperies, and also as wall coverings.

Grenadine: Loosely woven curtain fabric, plain or with woven dots, in SILK, RAYON, or WOOL.

Hand-woven: A term indicating that some part of the weaving has been done by hand.

Herringbone: A pattern that is made up of rows of parallel lines which, in any two adjacent rows, slope in opposite directions.

Homespun: Loosely woven fabric made to resemble hand-woven, Colonial material.

Hopsacking: A rough-surfaced COTTON, LINEN, or RAYON fabric with a basket-weave pattern.

India print: Cotton fabric with hand-blocked (or simulated) designs in bright colors.

Ingrain: Flat-weave cloth made of multi-colored threads dyed before weaving.

Irish point: Net curtain material with appliqué design.

Jacquard: DAMASK, TAPESTRY, BROCADE, and all elaborately FIGURED cloths woven on a Jacquard loom.

Jacquard weave: Weave structure of complex patterns produced on a Jacquard loom by combinations of PLAIN, TWILL, and SATIN weaves on a plain or satin-weave background.

Jaspé: French term for streaked or striped; applied to fabrics having various colored WARP threads which give a streaked appearance.

Lace: A fine, openwork fabric with patterns of knotted, twisted, or looped threads on a ground of NET or mesh.

Lambelle: A lightweight DAMASK texture having fine MERCERIZED WARP threads and slightly coarser WEFT threads of contrasting color.

Lampas: Originally an East Indian printed silk. Now applied to decorative fabric having REP ground with SATIN-like figures formed of WARP threads and contrasting WEFT figures.

Lawn: Light, thin, very smooth fabric of highly polished yarn. Originally of LINEN but now of COTTON.

Linen: A fabric made from the bark of the flax plant. Woven into cloth, it is noted for its smoothness, strength, coolness, and luster, as well as its tendency to crease.

Lisère: French silk cord fabric, made with a WEFT of BROCADED flowers and a WARP of JACQUARD figures.

Luster: Gloss finish applied to fabric by heat and pressure.

Madras: A strong COTTON fabric from India, woven with a brightly colored plaid or stripe pattern.

Madras muslin: A gauze fabric, usually white, with a design woven into it with thicker WEFT threads; used for curtains and sheer draperies.

Marquisette: A type of open-weave fabric that is used for glass curtains. Marquisette fabrics are made of RAYON, NYLON, SILK, or COTTON.

Matelassé: French, meaning cushioned or padded, hence a quilted surface produced on the loom. A FIGURED or BROCADED cloth with a raised pattern.

Mercerized: Treatment for thread or fabric to give strength and luster.

Metal cloth: Any fabric with decorative interwoven metallic threads.

Moiré: A fabric, especially SILK, having a watered or wavy pattern.

Monk's cloth: Rough, canvas-like curtain material, made of heavy COTTON yarns, often containing some flax, jute or hemp. Also called friar's cloth, it wears unusually well and is used for wall hangings, loose covers and upholstery.

Mousseline: A lightweight, MUSLIN-LIKE cotton with a crisp finish which is closely woven of highly twisted yarns.

Mummy cloth: Light, textured COTTON or SILK fabric with an irregular WARP figure; also called momie cloth.

Muslin: A PLAIN-WEAVE fabric made from COTTON, sometimes printed and varying in fineness.

Nap: Not to be confused with PILE. The downy, or fuzzy, appearance of cloth produced by raising the fibers to the surface, as in flannel. When lengths of a napped fabric are joined, the nap must run in the same direction.

Natural fibers: Fibers produced from natural sources (such as SILK, WOOL, and COTTON) as opposed to SYNTHETIC FIBERS.

Net: Open-mesh fabric of twisted, knotted, or woven construction; also British term for various sheer fabrics used for curtains.

Ninon: A type of light, transparent PLAIN-WEAVE fabric that is often used for sheer curtains.

Noil: Short fibers removed during the combing of a fiber, and spun into yarn.

Nottingham lace: Flat LACE used for curtains and tablecloths. Originally hand-made, now machine made.

Nylon: A SYNTHETIC material adapted for fashioning into filaments of extreme toughness, strength, and elasticity, then knitted into fabrics.

Oiled silk: A thin, waterproof SILK fabric, which has been soaked in oil and then left to dry.

Olefin: A trade name, this fiber is a product of the petroleum industry. It is lightweight and highly durable.

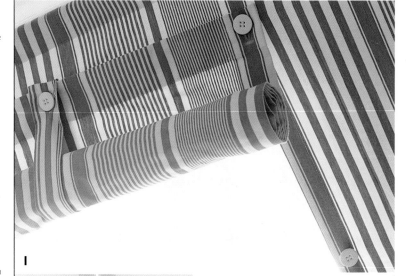

1

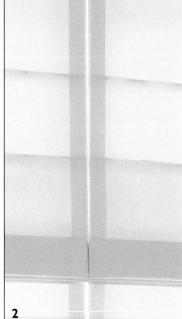

2

1 Two different kinds of blue-and-white stripes have been used for a particularly unstructured shade treatment. A batten is thrust through a casing at the top, then the shade is rolled up and kept neatly in place with buttoned tabs. Buttons are sewn to the sides for symmetry.

2 Roman shades in Indian cotton mask the strong glare of sunlight while allowing its warmth and light to filter through.

Organdy: A fine, LAWN cloth, chemically treated to produce crispness and stiffness. It is used for curtains and also for clothing.

Organzine: A thrown SILK of continuous fiber made from the unbroken cocoon of the silkworm.

Paisley: A multicolored design of Indian descent, woven or printed, usually on natural fabrics.

Panné: A term applied to PLUSH, VELVET, mohair, or SILK that has been flattened by steaming and pressure, so that the PILE lies close to the back, giving the fabric a shiny appearance.

Peau de soie: French term for soft, closely woven SATIN with a gentle luster; usually made of SILK.

Pick: The WEFT in weaving; comes from one passage of the loom's shuttle.

Pile: A fabric surface made of upright ends, as in fur, as distinct from NAP. It may be cut or uncut. Pile may be made of extra WEFT yarns, as in VELVET and PLUSH, or of extra WARP yarns, as in VELVETEEN. Warp pile can have loops on both sides, as in TERRY CLOTH. When lengths of a pile fabric are joined, the pile must run in the same direction.

Plain weave: Weave structure in which the WEFT goes under one and over one WARP. Examples include GINGHAM, VOILE, MUSLIN, and TAFFETA. Also called common weave.

Plissé: French term for COTTON fabric that has been chemically treated to give a crinkled surface.·

Plush: Cut or uncut PILE fabric having a pile of greater depth than VELVET.

Point d'esprit: French term for a BOBBINET with a small dot or woolen figure, similar to DOTTED SWISS.

Polyester: A SYNTHETIC FIBER which is strong and durable, but pills and soils easily. It blends easily with NATURAL FIBERS, such as COTTON, for both strength and versatility.

Pongee: A PLAIN-WEAVE curtain fabric of SILK or COTTON.

Poplin: Fine, cotton ribbed fabric, usually MERCERIZED. Launders and wears well, unless the weave is loose.

Ramie: A NATURAL FIBER similar to flax, obtained from the stalk of a plant native to China.

Ratine: TAPESTRY-woven fabric with nubby or bumpy surface.

Raw silk: SILK fibers as they are taken from the cocoon of the silkworm before the natural gum has been removed. Sometimes called wild silk.

Rayon: A lustrous SYNTHETIC FIBER made by converting cellulose (wood pulp or cotton linters) into a filament by means of a chemical and mechanical process. It is stiffer, more lustrous, and less expensive than SILK, but not so strong.

Rep: Closely resembles POPLIN, but rep has a heavier cord (FILLING yarn) and is wider; it is used for draperies and upholstery. When a JACQUARD figure is introduced on a REP background it is called armure.

Repeat: One complete repetition of a pattern in fabric (also in wallpaper and in rugs).

Sailcloth: Sturdy COTTON CANVAS or other material of close weave.

Sanforizing: A patented preshrinking process.

Sateen: MERCERIZED COTTON fabric of SATIN WEAVE. Better grades resemble SATIN made of SILK. Often used for lining draperies. True sateen has FILLING on the surface.

Satin: A lustrous surface fabric with broken TWILL WEAVE. Usually woven of SILK threads but may be made of RAYON.

Satin weave: Weave structure in which the WEFT is "floated" over more than one and under one WARP thread.

Seersucker: COTTON or RAYON fabric with crinkled surface.

Selvage: Tightly woven edges that prevent fabric from unraveling.

Scrim: A coarse type of VOILE used principally for sheer curtains.

Shantung: Nubby fabric, originally woven from Chinese SILK, now made also from RAYON or COTTON.

Sicilian silk: A DAMASK fabric with a SILK WARP and a COTTON or LINEN WEFT, forming a PLAIN-WEAVE ground with a SATIN-WEAVE figure.

Silk: Soft, NATURAL FIBER obtained by unraveling the cocoons of Japanese silkworms. Also applied to fabrics woven of silk thread.

Sizing: Any chemical substance applied to a fabric to provide greater stiffness, a smoother surface, and increased strength. Can be permanent (glue or clay) or temporary (starch).

Synthetic fibers: Fibers made through chemical and machine processes, as opposed to NATURAL FIBERS; also called man-made fibers. Examples include RAYON, ACRYLIC, and POLYESTER.

Taffeta: A name applied to several types of fine, crisp, PLAIN-WEAVE fabrics. May be made of SILK, COTTON, LINEN, or RAYON in mixed fibers.

Tambour embroidery: Machine embroidery in chain stitch to resemble handwork done on tambour frames.

Tapestry: Originally a HAND-WOVEN fabric made with a bobbin worked from the wrong side on a WARP stretched vertically or horizontally. A machine reproduction of tapestry is a YARN-DYED, FIGURED fabric composed of two sets of WARP and FILLING yarns woven on a JACQUARD loom.

Tarlatan: Thin, gauzy fabric of COTTON that has been glazed for stiffness. Used mostly for curtains.

Terry cloth: An absorbent fabric, woven or knitted, with a loop PILE.

Ticking: A striped COTTON fabric. Originally used to cover mattresses, it now comes in a finer grade for curtains.

Toile: A finely woven COTTON or LINEN with translucent qualities.

Toile de Jouy: Originally an eighteenth-century copperplate-printed COTTON fabric, printed with pictorial scenes in a single color on a white or cream background. Modern versions are widely available today.

Tweed: Rough-surfaced WOOL fabric of mixed, flecked colors.

Twill: A heavy COTTON fabric.

Twill weave: Weave structure in which the WEFT moves one step to the right or one step to the left with each line, producing a diagonal texture.

Unbleached muslin: A PLAIN-WEAVE inexpensive cream-colored cotton fabric.

Union: A PLAIN-WEAVE fabric in which the WARP and WEFT are of different fibers; in particular, a sturdy linen-and-cotton fabric often used for slipcovers.

Vat dye: A process of dyeing any material to obtain permanent color.

Velours: Fabrics with a short PILE.

Velvet: All WARP-PILE fabrics, except PLUSH and TERRY CLOTH.

Velveteen: A fabric with short COTTON PILE made in approximate imitation of SILK VELVET.

Vinyl: A non-woven plastic, which is capable of being embossed or printed to produce any desired finish, such as a leather or wood grain or floral pattern or textured design.

Voile: A translucent PLAIN-WEAVE fabric, often of COTTON, made of yarns that have more than the normal amount of twist. Used for sheer curtains and shades.

Warp: Set of yarns that run lengthwise of cloth, across the WEFT.

Weave: The characteristic structure of a fabric produced from interlocking strands of yarn. Common weave structures include PLAIN, TWILL, SATIN, JACQUARD, and DOBBY WEAVES.

Weft: Set of yarns running crosswise, and interlaced with the WARP, to produce a woven fabric. Also called woof, filling, pick, or shoot.

Whipcord: A ribbed material formed by floating the WARP threads over several large WEFT threads.

Wild silk: See RAW SILK.

Wool: NATURAL FIBER from sheep; also fabric woven from yarns of wool fiber. Each breed of sheep produces its own type and grade of wool, but all wool shares the qualities of warmth and elasticity which make it adaptable to blending with other fibers. It can be combined with natural or SYNTHETIC FIBERS for strength, beauty, and smoothness.

Worsted: Smooth, tightly woven WOOL fabric made from exceptionally long fibers.

Yarn-dyed: Fabrics woven of yarn dyed before it is put on the looms.

part two: the specifics

SECTION SEVEN

It is easy to become so involved with the complexities of a room's paint effects, window treatments, and flooring options that the furniture is all but forgotten. Yet remove the furniture from a room and you are left with an empty shell. Furniture, more than anything else, is what makes a home comfortable, convenient, and livable–and so should be considered carefully, whether you are about to choose new furniture or to reuse existing furniture in a more effective way. This section, therefore, deals with the most important aspects of furniture, from arranging it to choosing upholstered furniture, beds, and other modern pieces, with a brief guide to antique furniture.

Furniture

Furniture Arrangement

Apart from its style and practicality, the way furniture is arranged is of paramount importance, so your starting point should be to think about how the pieces will work together.

It might seem odd to consider furniture arrangement before discussing the furniture itself, but it is important to learn how best to place furniture, for two reasons:

1 If you are redecorating, renovating, or generally trying to improve a room, you need to have a sure idea of what to keep, what to discard, and what extra pieces, if any, you must acquire.

2 If you are designing a room from scratch, you must have a clear idea of exactly what furniture you will need, how you want to use it, what sizes will work best, and where you want to place it. All this must be decided before you go out and buy anything.

ESTABLISHING PRIORITIES

If a room does not function well, it is a failure, however good it might look. And in order to function well, the room has to be well arranged. It is as simple as that.

- If people do not feel comfortable in a room ...
- If there is nowhere to read ...
- If there is nowhere near at hand to place a glass or coffee cup ...
- If there is no easy, natural way to walk through a room without having to squeeze by and dodge pieces of furniture ...
- If the furnishings are not appropriate ...
- If there is no real focal point ...
  ...then the room is not a success.

The ideal in every room is for each piece to be placed where it works *and* looks best, but there is often a conflict between the aesthetic and the practical. An armchair, for example, might look particularly good in a corner and help to balance the other furnishings visually–but it might never actually get used there.

Therefore, if you are forced to choose between aesthetic and practical considerations, the practical must take priority. Armchairs are meant to be *sat on*, and sat on in comfort. Find something else of comparable visual bulk, like a large, bushy plant, or a side table, to give the needed balance.

Although people's needs obviously vary a good deal, there are some general criteria to follow with regard to furniture arrangement.

SEATING GROUPS

You cannot really consider any piece of seating on its own merits alone, unless it is an occasional chair or a desk and chair. Seating should be considered as part of a group. A chair on which you can sit comfortably and read easily should be partnered by a side table and a light source, preferably a lamp at the right level for reading. For deep comfort, you might also want a footstool. This arrangement, in turn, should be considered as part of a larger seating group (unless it is positioned in the corner of, say, a

1 *Upholstered pieces are arranged around a big coffee table to form a comfortable conversation area in this large space. The dining area is by the long windows.*

2 *A useful breakfast/quick-snack/ reading/writing surface has been built in on one side of a galley kitchen. The stools, which have cane tops and steel bases, are light and easily maneuverable and take up little visual space.*

3 *In this obviously comfortable bedroom, club chairs are positioned for reading or conversation. Their scale also balances the bed..*

2

study, as a relaxed place for reading and thinking). Usually, this larger group is a conversation group and includes a sofa, at least one other armchair, and possibly a love seat as well, depending on space.

These different seats will all need good lighting, as well as some sort of nearby table surface. You could, for example, combine end tables with a large upholstered stool or a good-sized coffee table in the center of the grouping. In addition, the seating should be grouped around some kind of focal point (see page 183).

MANIPULATING SPACE

Space is as much an element in a room as the objects in it. I am not, in this case, talking about the size of a room but about the space around each item –the balance between solid objects and empty space. In general, rooms that have a lot of space around the furnishings look much better than overcrowded rooms, because they seem lighter and airier.

Besides improving the aesthetics of a room, the manipulation of space plays an important part in its traffic patterns. Traffic patterns must be established when planning the positions of furniture, so that there can be easy movement throughout the room. Establishing these is mostly a matter of common sense, but there are a few guidelines to keep in mind.

- A major passageway through a room should be at least 4 ft. (1.2 m.) wide, and preferably 5 ft. (1.5 m.), to allow enough room for two people to walk side by side. For subsidiary traffic routes, allow at least 18 in. (45 cm.).

- Allow 12-18 in. (30-45 cm.) between a sofa or armchair and a coffee table, so that people can get up gracefully from a sitting position, without having to twist and sidle. At the same time, the table should not be so far away as to make it awkward to reach out and pick up, or put down, a glass or book.

- Allow about 18 in. (45 cm.) between dining chairs and at least 2 ft. (60 cm.) to pull a dining chair back from a table. There should be at least 4 ft. (120 cm.) between the dining table and a wall, to enable people to walk behind diners when serving and clearing away.

- In front of a dresser, bureau, or chest of drawers, 3 ft. (90 cm.) is necessary to allow the drawers to be pulled out. In front of a closet, at least the width of the door should be allowed for opening the door. Between beds or between a bed and a wall, 18 in. (45 cm.) is needed for bed making.

A SENSE OF BALANCE

Before you start thinking about side tables, occasional chairs, storage units, desks, dressers, pianos, and so on, you need to consider scale and balance. This involves the ratio of vertical lines (tall pieces) to horizontal lines (low pieces) and the proportion of light items relative to solid ones.

- If a room consists mainly of tall pieces, such as a wall unit or armoire, with large pictures, mirrors, tall plants, and high-backed chairs and sofas, it will look too stiff, formal, and uncomfortable.

- If it is all low lines, with low-backed seating, low storage, small plants,

part two: the specifics

The light, elegant dining table here is balanced by more solid upholstered dining chairs. The twisted wire chandelier echoes the table base, as do the tall, skinny candlesticks by the wall. The large painting nicely fills the space between the two windows.

low-hung horizontally shaped mirrors, and paintings hung low on the walls, a room will look incomplete and somehow disturbing.

- If most of the objects in a room are solid and heavy-looking—for example, a lot of upholstered pieces with a piano and an armoire—a room will look stodgy and decidedly ponderous.
- If all the furnishings are very light—say, several occasional chairs, a cane or wicker sofa and love seat, and an *étagère* (a piece of furniture with open shelves)—a room can look worryingly insubstantial.

There has to be a happy medium in a well-arranged room. This does not mean having half vertical lines and half horizontal; half solid and half light—that would look too set, too *meant*.

On the whole, most rooms look best with a predominant number of low pieces, set off here and there by taller pieces of varying heights. They could progress, perhaps, from a low, upholstered stool or sofa to a wing chair, then to a side table and lamp, and finally, to the really tall lines of an armoire, a highboy, or a painting or mirror over a side table, chest or fireplace, and tall plants.

Similarly, a sofa and armchairs, which are solid, should be balanced by the openness of occasional chairs; the lightness, perhaps of a glass table; the height and massiveness of a storage unit. A dresser or a secretary can be

balanced with tall but light and leafy plants, or indoor trees. Densely painted canvases can be juxtaposed with the reflective quality of mirrors.

Planning a room is much easier if you start with the larger, anchor pieces (the pieces you cannot move around much), balancing them carefully with permanent features, such as doorways, fireplaces, windows, bookshelves, or paneling. When all that is clear in your mind, you can decide where to fill in with the smaller pieces.

Remember that other features you have already planned for the room, like the floor, wall, and window treatments, will also count strongly in the general balance of the room. Elaborate window treatments will have much more visual weight than casual ones. A patterned wall-to-wall carpet or densely patterned oriental rug will be visually heavier and have more importance in a room than a plain wood or tiled floor with simple bordered, geometric, or needlework rugs. Dark-colored walls will look heavier than pale colors. All these factors need to be considered when you are working on the furniture arrangement and deciding how furniture should be balanced with the decoration of the room as a whole.

SUITABILITY OF POSITION

The final, and most important, key to success is how well the arrangement takes into account the environmental factors and also ease of use.

Environment

Extremes of climate, heat and cold, dryness and humidity all need to be taken into account when positioning furniture. Strong sunlight will make both wood and fabrics fade, so fabrics used for upholstered pieces placed near windows should be as fade-resistant as possible. If furniture is covered in a fabric likely to fade, do not place it near a window unless you want it to fade, or you have fitted some shades (or if the glass is the specially treated type suitable for exceptionally sunny areas, or it has been covered with a sun-filtering film).

Overzealous heating can make antique furniture (made at a time when there was no central heating) split, warp, and lose bits of veneer, as well as making doors and drawers difficult to open and shut. To help counteract this,

install a humidifier in the room. Make sure that good pieces of furniture are not placed too near radiators or heating vents.

Pianos and other large musical instruments should, if possible, be placed near an inside wall, rather than a window, and away from radiators, heat vents, sunshine, and obvious drafts. Apart from the case, which in older pianos is as vulnerable as antique furniture, sound mechanisms can be affected by extreme humidity.

Listening and viewing

Stereo equipment should be placed near, or against, a hard wall, facing soft surfaces like curtains and upholstery, or an upholstered wall (see page 112), because the combination of hard and soft surfaces produces the best acoustics. A television screen should not, except in the case of a media room, be a dominant part of a space. But it should be placed so that it can be seen by at least four people.

Creating a focal point

If a living room does not have a natural focal point, like a fireplace or large or interesting window, you will need to create some central interest around which you can form various furniture groupings. A large painting or a group of smaller ones, a tapestry, or a rug mounted on a wall might be suitable. If there is a suitable outside wall, you might be able to put in a decorative wood-burning stove; it is worth finding out.

Other possibilities include an interesting bookcase or a "media wall" (an attractive built-in storage system for television, video recorder, sound

system, and videos and CDs). Even a low table holding an assortment of interesting objects could be a suitable focal point. Whatever you choose, it will help to unify the seating area.

CREATING ARRANGEMENTS

The next stage is to check that your proposed arrangement will work, by drawing it to scale on a floor plan. Do not be tempted to skip this stage, as it is an invaluable way to check that the arrangements will work. Living rooms are by far the most difficult to do—most other rooms more or less arrange themselves, unless they are particularly large. Therefore, planning out your own living room will be good practice, whether it is for real or just for experimentation.

Start by drawing your room plan on graph paper (see page 16). Most pieces of furniture have fairly standard measurements, and so you can use the templates of the most common furniture pieces, drawn to scale; these are available as kits from some home centers. You will need to supplement them with templates you make yourself (to the same scale) for non-standard items—or you could make them all yourself.

Look at the photographs in this book to get ideas for possible arrangements. Analyze why some are more suitable for your room than others, taking into account the points covered in this chapter.

Try your hand at some arrangements. There is no need to think in terms of style at this stage—just scale, comfort, practicality, and suitability. Move the templates around on the

FURNITURE PLACEMENT CHECKLIST

Before finalizing the furniture placement in a room, use this checklist to remind yourself of all the factors you need to take into account. With just a little practice, you will find yourself thinking of all these aspects automatically.

PRACTICALITY—Will it work well?

AESTHETICS—Will it look good?

ORGANIZATION OF SPACE—Have you allowed enough space around individual items of furniture?

TRAFFIC PLANNING—Can people move around easily?

SCALE AND BALANCE—Will the furnishings look interesting and varied, and without any individual item dominating?

ENVIRONMENTAL ASPECTS—Will furniture get too much sun, heat, cold, humidity, dryness, or drafts?

EASE OF USE—Will people be able to hear music and see television properly, and is there a good focal point?

plan until you find the best arrangement, then trace their outlines onto the final plan.

Doing a floor-arrangement plan helps you to see if there is anything left out, what should be left in, and what should be purchased new. If you abide by such a blueprint, you are less likely to go astray later with unsuitable impulse purchases.

Upholstered Furniture

The most important point to learn about upholstery is that what you see is not necessarily what you get. What you *cannot* see is the key to the piece's comfort. An upholstered piece should *feel* as good as, or better than, it looks, because the inner construction is what counts. Therefore, always look at the label detailing the construction of an upholstered piece before you are beguiled into buying it; in most countries, the law requires that the contents be listed in detail. More often than not, the label will detail care instructions also.

CONSTRUCTION METHODS

To ensure that you know what to look for and whether the construction is all it is made out to be, it helps to understand a little about how upholstered furniture is constructed. There are two types of upholstery:

1 Fully upholstered pieces, such as sofas, love seats, armchairs, slipper chairs and upholstered stools. These are completely covered with upholstery, with no frame showing, except possibly the lower part of the legs.

2 Exposed-frame pieces, like occasional chairs, *chaises longues,* and stools that have parts of the frame showing.

The *frame* is constructed first. A good-quality piece of furniture should be made from oak, teak, or walnut, or some other kiln-dried hardwood, not from softwood such as pine. It should be straight, with no warpage. The joints should be glued, and double- or triple-doweled, corner-blocked, and screwed.

Next comes the *webbing,* which is the bottom-most material used on an upholstered piece, to hold the other layers. Good strong webbing should be made from jute, flax, or a synthetic material, and woven into a basket-weave design, which is tacked to the bottom of the frame.

In top-quality furniture, after the webbing come the *springs.* Such furniture incorporates coil springs, which are set close enough together to provide good support without actually touching each other, and which are hand-tied in place. About eight springs are used for one chair seat. Cheaper furniture makes use of more rigid "sagless" springs, which are far more cost efficient because they do not need to be hand-tied; or else it eschews springs altogether, as in the case of foam upholstery.

On top of the springs goes a tough layer of *canvas* or *burlap,* which is firmly sewn in place as a base to hold the *padding.* This padding consists of polyurethane foam, polyester, rubberized hair, foam rubber, feathers or down, according to the quality of the furniture. Down is the most expensive type of padding, but a popular filling nowadays is a "sandwich" which consists of down with a layer of foam

in the middle. This prevents the soft down from sagging too much and gives it a certain firmness.

The best-quality furniture then has a final layer of *cotton felt* (also called *linterfelt*), which is eased just below the upholstery fabric. Sometimes even that layer has a protective covering of muslin to reduce the tension on the covering and thus maintain the shape.

When the *upholstery fabric* is stretched over the piece of furniture, it is often trimmed with self- or contrast piping to give it more "fit" and definition. Loose cushions are treated in the same way.

COMMONLY USED FABRICS

The upholstery fabric itself has to be firm and durable, since it will have to withstand a great deal of wear and tear. The toughest-wearing upholstery fabrics are densely woven cotton, sailcloth, denim, ticking, cotton rep, twill, brocade, and corduroy, which are all cotton-based; linen union, which is linen mixed with cotton and is a traditional slipcover material; velvets, which can be cotton or linen-based; and woven, textured, or plain damask.

Wool is a softer but still excellent upholstery fabric and is the basis for tweeds, wool reps, jacquards, and some tough, shaggy textures. Never buy a loosely woven wool, or a loosely woven texture of any kind, for upholstery. Leather and suede, while expensive, always look luxurious and are extremely long-lasting, so they remain enduringly popular. Ultrasuede (imitation suede) is cheaper and can easily be spot-cleaned, so it is a good substitute.

To prolong the life of upholstery fabric, it is advisable to have it treated with one of the protective finishes available. It is better to have such a finish applied by the upholsterer or the fabric producer, since the do-it-yourself aerosol finishes, in less than skilled hands, can be something of a disaster (and some have been withdrawn for safety reasons). In any event, such a treatment should be tested on a small portion of the fabric first. A further refinement is to get the fabric quilted, which also prolongs its life.

CHECKING FOR QUALITY

First test for comfort. Are there firm cushions to give back support? Is the chair or sofa of standard height? (Too-low seats are difficult for the elderly, people with back problems, and those who are overweight.)

If the piece is covered in a patterned, striped, checked, or plaid fabric, make sure that the designs are centered, lines and checks are straight, and the pattern matches at the seams. All seams and piping should be neat and straight. Any buttons should be sewn right through the filling, not just attached to the fabric. You can test this by gently pulling on the button; if there is a slight tension, it has been properly done.

Check any loose seat cushions (these are a good idea because they can be regularly reversed, thus prolonging the life of the seating). Good-quality items should be stuffed with feathers or down and should be closely fitted to the chair or sofa.

Now run your hands over the piece to be sure there are no lumps or bumps. You should not be able to feel

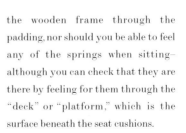

1 Brightly checked cotton upholstery matches the various colors of the collection of glasses and finger bowls on the shelves next to the chairs.

2 A 1920s modern classic leather and steel sofa has a useful filing cabinet placed beside it as a side table.

3 A gray-painted frame on a piece of French furniture. Note the studs edging the upholstery fabric.

4 A pair of luxurious-looking French fauteuils upholstered in nicely worn linen velvet. Again, notice the finishing touches of the metal studs edging the material.

the wooden frame through the padding, nor should you be able to feel any of the springs when sitting—although you can check that they are there by feeling for them through the "deck" or "platform," which is the surface beneath the seat cushions.

Check that casters are smooth-running and sturdy. Finally, as mentioned earlier in the book, don't forget to check measurements—of both the piece you are thinking of buying and your doorways, elevators, and any turns in stairs and passageways. Make sure the piece can actually be delivered into its destined room.

part two: the specifics

Non-upholstered Furniture

Whether in beautifully grained wood or sleek modern plastic, tables, chairs, and storage pieces have a wonderfully tactile quality. However, it is important to check the quality behind the beguiling surface.

1 Red and black curved Italian plastic chairs look good set around a pale wood dining table.
2 A painted dresser with glass-fronted bookshelves goes well with the Louis Seize-style chair covered in a small check, and with the white-painted iron headboard.
3 Light steel chairs around a refectory table in a pale natural wood tie in with the steel-fronted range in the background.

WOOD FURNITURE

Wood furniture, whether new or old, is made either of hardwoods, such as mahogany, rosewood, oak, maple, walnut, teak, yew, or cherry, or of softwoods such as pine.

Wood veneer is generally a thin sheet of fine, attractively grained wood glued to a base of inexpensive solid wood, plywood, or chipboard. While old wood veneer on antique furniture is inclined to crack and come loose from its base in hot, centrally heated rooms, modern veneers rarely do so. Nevertheless, antique furniture is often in very good condition and has a beauty, patina, and rarity value that everyone will appreciate.

All wood furniture, whether new, antique (technically, over a hundred years old) or–that nebulous third category–secondhand, should be checked for stability and the quality of construction and finish.

Chairs

It is important to check the joints of chairs, new or old. They should be constructed with corner blocks, preferably with ribs; these are meant to strengthen the joints, which come under considerable pressure. There should be no gaps, and the joints should be smooth. Dining chairs, because they come under daily strain, generally have stretchers (cross pieces connected to the legs) to reinforce them. Straight legs have the greatest strength.

To test the stability of a chair, lean on the piece to see if it tips easily.

4

Next, push it a little to see if it wobbles. Finally, inspect the finish, which should be perfectly smooth with no bubbles or streaks.

Tables

Like chairs, these should be constructed with corner blocks to strengthen the joints, and the legs should be secure. The grain of the wood should be well-matched, and if there are extending leaves, they should obviously match the grain and color of the main part of the table. Check, too, that any extending leaves are easy to fit and to remove.

Case goods

These are storage pieces like desks, armoires, breakfronts, dressers, secretaries, sideboards, and chests of drawers. (They are called case goods, incidentally, because, up until the eighteenth century, people kept all their clothes and personal belongings in wooden cases or chests.)

Examine any inset panels in doors, in drawers, and on the sides of the piece, to see that they feel solid. Doors should swing freely and fit well. Apply slight pressure to the tops of doors to make sure that they do not sag when they are pressed. Drawers should slide smoothly and fit well, and their bottoms should be firm enough not to buckle when pushed upward. The insides should be smoothly finished and the corners joined by dovetail or tongued-and-grooved joints. Fine-quality furniture has thin layers of wood, or "dust panels," between drawers to protect them from dust. Check too for matching color and wood graining on the fronts, tops, and sides of all pieces.

4 *A large-scale colonial-style chair of the kind made in Indonesia looks both comfortable and sculptural. It also appears very much at home against the white-painted floorboards and the floaty white voile curtains.*

HARDWARE

Another important item to examine carefully on both new and old furniture is the hardware (the knobs, handles, hinges). Make sure it is of an appropriate scale, shape, and material, and, in the case of old furniture, that it is right for the period. Good hardware is cast mainly from heavy metal, such as brass, and the edges must be smooth. Knobs also come in porcelain, wood, glass, copper, brushed steel, chrome, and resin.

GLASS, PLASTIC, OR METAL FURNITURE

Furniture, particularly occasional pieces, can also be made from glass, Lucite or other plastics, metals, or combinations of these materials. Well-designed pieces are deservedly popular, because they can fit in any room alongside most periods of furniture with a pleasing anonymity and will generally take up less "visual" space than wood pieces.

Glass

This is particularly used for table tops and shelves. (Some nineteenth-century Indian and Far Eastern princes and potentates actually had entire sets of elaborately ornamented, completely glass or mirrored furniture for their palaces.) The glass should have a thickness of at least ¼ in. (5 mm.), preferably ½-¾ in. (1.2-2 cm.) for practical use. It must be smoothly ground and beveled at the edges.

Plastics

These include fiberglass, Lucite, laminated plastic, polystyrene, polyvinyl, and acrylics. The disadvantages of plastic are that it collects dust (although you can polish or spray it with an anti-static solution which helps that problem) and scratches easily. Always choose pieces that are thick enough to stand up to heavy use. Joints should be smooth and bonded together with a heavyweight adhesive or sturdy bolts.

Metals

Brass, copper, stainless steel, chrome-plated tubing, plastic-covered steel tubing, angle iron, and wrought iron are all used for furniture, mainly in conjunction with canvas, heavy cotton, or open-weave plastic in the case of seating, and glass in the case of tables. Always check metal to make sure it is smooth, with no bubbles, and free of weak spots along seams. If the piece is collapsible, test the mechanism for durability, safety, and easy operation.

CANE, WICKER, RATTAN, AND BAMBOO

This is a useful category of furniture for porches, sunrooms, and garden rooms, bedroom occasional furniture, and fill-ins. Check that it is sturdily constructed, that joints are bound well, and that it is not shedding too many little "tails," which can later unravel. All of these materials take paint well and generally age gracefully.

part two: the specifics

Beds

Because you spend around a third of your life in bed, it is hardly extravagant to buy a good-quality one. But because they all look much the same, it is sometimes difficult to know what to look for.

Like upholstery, beds have "hidden" value, and the more expensive the mattress and box spring, the better they should be. Obviously, box springs should be steady, sturdy, and non-squeaky, and mattresses should both support and "give" easily, with the degree of firmness that best suits the user (who, incidentally, should always try out a bed by lying on it first).

Bed length is usually determined by adding 16-10 in. (5-25 cm.) to the height of the user. In the case of a couple, the length is dictated by the taller person. As with other large pieces of furniture, remember to check the sizes of doorways, elevators, and narrow turns on stairs and corridors before ordering a bed. If a large bed will be impossible to get into the house or apartment, you could substitute twin-bed box springs, set side by side with mattresses that zip together.

MATTRESS TYPES

There are several types of mattress, all of which are quite different from each other, though the first three types are all covered in ticking and look similar. Like upholstery, mattresses should bear a label describing their contents and construction.

Innerspring mattresses

This type of mattress, like a good over-stuffed chair or sofa, consists of 800 or so coiled springs, covered with insulating cotton, polyester or foam. Usually

you buy one in conjunction with a box-spring divan, which is about 7 in. (18 cm.) thick, as is the mattress. This is the most popular type.

Foam mattresses

This lightweight mattress is made of urethane or latex foam. It should be 4-6 in. (10-15 cm.) thick, and firm. Usually foam mattresses are sold with slightly deeper box-springs.

Stuffed mattresses

These mattresses are for beds not large enough to hold innerspring or foam mattresses. They are much thinner and consist of polyester or cotton topped by foam.

Water beds

As the name implies, the mattress on a water bed is filled with water. The mattress sits inside a plastic lining set within a wooden frame. Water beds are supposed to be especially good for the circulation, to encourage restful sleep and to be effective for burn victims, as well as discouraging bed sores in invalids and the bedridden. Make sure that the bed has a sturdy frame, a puncture-resistant mattress (many a bad flood has been sustained without such a precaution), and a thermostatically controlled water heater.

A recently introduced variety of water bed has a good-quality, high-density polyurethane foam frame instead of the wooden variety, and is

1 A black-painted iron bed is softened by the luxurious-looking white bed linen. The heart-shaped chair back beside it echoes the bed's design.

2 A French lit en bateau, so-called because of its boat-like shape, dates from the French Empire period. Such beds look extremely elegant and are certainly pieces to reckon with in their own right, but they are always somewhat tough to keep tucked in and neat.

3 An exotically framed daybed looks handsome in any room, whatever the style, as well as being relaxing to lounge around on.

4 Another twentieth-century classic chair and matching stool balance the low, modern bed in this room. Notice the length of yellow cotton used as a decorative panel behind the bed.

covered with padding and ticking so it looks more like a normal mattress.

GUEST BEDS

Certain types of bed are particularly useful for the occasional guest:

• A *sofa bed* can be a sofa most of the time and open out to become a spare bed when necessary. (Make sure the mattress is thick enough for comfort; some are quite thin.)

• A traditional *daybed*, of the kind shown on this page, can accommodate the average-size guest for a night or two. More useful for long-term or frequent guests is a twin-size daybed with a second bed underneath, which can be pulled up level with the first to make either a double bed or two twin beds.

• A *Murphy bed* folds up against a wall behind a panel; excellent for a studio or one-room apartment.

HEADBOARDS

Most beds are sold with a headboard attached. There is an enormous choice, including padded fabric, wood, brass, chrome, cane and white- or black-painted iron.

part two: the specifics

189

Period Furniture

In theory, any piece of furniture over 100 years old can be called antique, but in practice, more modern pieces are also very collectible now. As in styles of architecture and decoration, furniture designs have been cyclical, appearing and reappearing in different guises, in different woods, with different decoration, in different countries. Sometimes styles have coincided exactly with a ruler, at least in the country of origin, but have reappeared some years later on another continent. Leading designers produced pattern books, which were copied, with varying degrees of success, by cabinetmakers all around the world, often decades later. Nor do styles necessarily run in neat chronological order, since many are concurrent with each other or are reactions to a prevailing look. Then, too, there are the umbrella terms, such as Georgian and Victorian, covering a variety of styles over many decades.

English Renaissance oak cupboard

RECOGNIZING STYLES

Very early period furniture, and really beautiful pieces from the eighteenth century or earlier, are seldom to be found outside museums, grand houses open to the public, and the more rarefied antique shops. Nevertheless, it is useful to have a shorthand knowledge of the styles, if only to recognize influences, reproductions, and reintroductions.

On the following pages you will find capsule descriptions of furniture-style periods for both sides of the Atlantic. To place each furniture style in context, see the Chronology of Style Periods on pages 76–7, and also see pages 78–83 for details of the style periods themselves. Technical terms are defined as briefly as possible in the Vocabulary on pages 198–203.

BRITISH FURNITURE

Throughout the seventeenth and eighteenth centuries, the furniture of the British Isles remained the strongest influence on American furniture styles.

Tudor

The relative peace and stability that accompanied the reigns of the Tudor monarchs enabled people to begin furnishing their homes with an eye to comfort and beauty rather than use the basic furniture that preceded that time. However, Tudor furniture was still sturdy and rectilinear and consisted of staple pieces like, chests, dressers, four-poster beds, wardrobes, stools and benches.

- Most tables were still of the temporary trestle type.
- Cabinet furniture was primitively decorated by simple surface grooving, narrow strips of inlay in contrasting wood, a checkered effect, or crudely carved patterns.

Elizabethan

More Renaissance ideas filtered into Britain during this period.

- Oak was the principal wood. Elaborate carving, especially strapwork, was popular.
- Court cupboards, or buffets, were used for displaying pewter.
- Chairs were either "turned" or "wainscoted."
- Furniture legs were often bulbous, carved at the top with a gadroon and at the bottom with an acanthus leaf.
- Beds for the rich were very grand, with carved corner-posts, a canopy, and long velvet hangings.
- Solid-topped refectory tables replaced the makeshift trestle tables of Tudor times.

Stuart (Jacobean and Carolean)

Classicism was now better understood, which was reflected in the furniture. A sense of comfort also crept in, with chairs beginning to have upholstered backs and seats.

- Lighter chairs were made for smaller houses, along with gateleg tables.
- The farthingale chair and the dresser (initially without the shelf section) were introduced.
- The bulbous turning of the Elizabethan period became more elongated.
- Knobs and drawer pulls were often carved, sometimes in a caricature of the human head.

Jacobean oak wainscot armchair

Cromwellian

Decoration became less important than function in this period.

- Moldings were applied, rather than carved from solid wood.

- Leather was used for upholstery.
- Exaggerated ornament disappeared.
- The first chests of drawers appeared, and probably the first stick-back (Windsor) chairs.

Restoration

The prevailing feeling of extravagance was reflected in the furniture.

- Walnut veneer replaced solid oak.
- Chair seats, and sometimes backs, were often caned and covered with loose cushions. Spiral turnings for legs and stretchers were used frequently, as was the Flemish scroll.
- Frames were sometimes gilded and were very often silvered. Handsome upholstery, leather, and heavy hand-made silk fringes all became fashionable.
- The wing chair was introduced. At that time, its back was capable of being lowered to an almost horizontal level, hence its alternative name of "sleeping chair."
- Upholstered stools and benches in elaborate designs were also now popular.
- Round tables appeared, as did gaming tables, smaller occasional tables, and bookcases.
- Japanese lacquer ornamentation started to become popular, along with floral marquetry.
- Painted wooden fire screens in the form of life-sized human figures dressed in contemporary clothes became fashionable.

William and Mary

Immigrant French Huguenot and Dutch craftsmen injected a new vigor into British craftsmanship.

William and Mary ormolu-mounted japanned cabinet on stand

- Splendid pieces were made of walnut, with marquetry using holly, ebony, satinwood, and ivory.
- Lines became simpler, with more delicate proportions and less carving.
- Thin wood veneers and cross-banding were often applied to flat surfaces.
- Oriental lacquer finishes became more prevalent.
- King William's attachment to his Delft pieces galvanized the incipient passion for blue and white (already started by the new oriental porcelain imports).
- The legs and feet of furniture changed radically once again. They became straighter, and the bun foot made its appearance, although spiral and trumpet legs were still being made.
- The newest piece of case furniture was the tallboy. Drop-front writing cabinets appeared at this time, along with the first occasional tables, tea, and card tables. Lighter armchairs were also made. Other new pieces to emerge were clocks, cabinets, dressing tables, and mirrors.

Queen Anne

Inspired by the Dutch version of Baroque, Queen Anne furniture was nevertheless a uniquely British style. It was based particularly on walnut veneer and subtle curves.

- Furniture innovations were secrétaires and other desks and china cabinets. Card and tea tables were developed further.
- Comfort became more of a priority, and this was the first time that the properly upholstered armchair made an appearance. The wing chair became more comfortable, while the spoon-back chair was a conscious attempt at ergonomics.

Queen Anne walnut wing chair

part two: the specifics

- Almost all pieces had the newly perfected, double-curved cabriole legs ending in Dutch or claw-and-ball feet.
- The hoop-back chair was introduced. Splats in the middle of chair backs had different shapes in the form of fiddles or vases.
- Typical pieces were tall, often double-domed cabinets, such as bureaus (desks) surrounded by bookcases or cabinets, in walnut veneer with fine moldings.
- Carved shell shapes were much in evidence, as were elegant brass handles on drawers, and curving swan-necked pediments.

Early Georgian

The gentle curves of the Queen Anne era gradually gave way to the more severe lines and architectural details of classicism. To match the Neo-Palladian architecture, furniture was on a grand scale.

- Heavy carved and gilded pieces were upholstered in velvet and damask. Massive cabriole legs and claw-and-ball feet added to the stately, throne-like look of the chairs. Settees became popular.
- Solid-looking mahogany slowly replaced walnut.
- Bookcases now had pedimented tops, thereby echoing the exterior of the house.
- Drop-front bureaus and tables on cabriole legs were typical. The drop-leaf dining table appeared.

Mid-Georgian

A time of almost unparalleled experiments in design, this was also the era of the pattern books, nobly produced

by great cabinetmakers like Thomas Chippendale (whose *The Gentleman and Cabinet Maker's Director* was first published in 1754) as well as lesser luminaries. They gave inspiration and instruction to aspiring cabinetmakers and joiners in Britain, in the North American Colonies, and, indeed, all over the world. The various publications gave a choice of fashionable styles to follow, from pure Rococo to its offshoots, Chinese and Gothick.

Chippendale

The master of them all, Chippendale anglicized the Rococo. Having studied many sources–Classicism, Rococo, Louis Quinze, Gothick, and Chinese–he combined them and refined them with a stunning sense of harmony.

- Chippendale's early seating made much use of the cabriole leg, with carved foot, and splat backs with a yoke form (i.e., a frame similar to a yoke used for carrying pails). In ornament he used Rococo motifs such as "C" scrolls, flowers, and foliage, shells, and rocks.
- He later turned to the straight Marlborough leg, and intricate imitations of Gothic tracery for chair backs.
- He also worked in a Chinese style, incorporating pierced legs on chairs and fret carving, lattice-work, and *faux* bamboo. His carved and gilt Chinoiserie mirrors were ornately decorated with Rococo scrolls and oriental motifs.

The Adam brothers

Great as Chippendale's influence was, that of Robert Adam, together with his brother James, was probably greater. The Adam period is considered one of the triumphs of the glorious

Early Georgian giltwood mirror

eighteenth century, and although the Adam designs were made exclusively for the super-rich, their ideas eddied out to the mainstream. Spearheading the new Neoclassical style, the Adam brothers were not cabinetmakers, but they cooperated with Chippendale and Hepplewhite, among others. Sheraton was also greatly influenced by the Adam motifs and ornaments.

- Satinwood, and other pale and elegant woods imported from the East, started to come into favor.
- Inlay was used for both wood and marble.
- Dining chairs and tables grew lighter and were supported by slim, tapering legs.
- Desks started to have fitted drawers.
- Very fine mirrors often became an integral part of the decoration or paneling.
- The Adam brothers did not make chairs, but they produced beautiful side tables, cabinets, bookcases, settees, and, above all, sideboards.

- Another Adam piece was the console table, which was often gilded, with a top of scagliola or marble set on four straight, tapered legs. It was generally set between tall windows, with a long mirror above it, and often it was decorated with festoons, or with plaques, like Wedgwood's Jasper-ware medallions, or with inlaid colored woods.
- Adam furniture also included commodes, with either painted decoration or marquetry; bookcases with broken pediments and narrow beading; and *torchères* in Etruscan shapes, with tripods of satinwood ornamented with painting, gilding, or marquetry.
- Robert Adam is credited with the fashion for flanking a serving table with pedestals supporting classic urns, frequently made of the same wood. These urns were often fitted with lead containers so that cutlery and glasses could be washed between courses, while the pedestals were used as plate warmers or as storage bins for wine. Other pedestals were designed to take classical busts.
- Adam motifs included the Grecian honeysuckle and fret, the fluted frieze or apron, the patera and rosette, and the various urns and ears of grain.

Hepplewhite

George Hepplewhite adapted the rarefied Adam designs for a larger, middle market. His furniture, characterized by lightness and elegance, free of unnecessary ornament, bridged the period between the decline of Georgian mahogany and the rise to fashionable prominence of satinwood.

- Hepplewhite's shield-back chairs, with their spade-shaped feet and sober lines, became widely popular.
- His bow and serpentine fronts for sofas, chairs, sideboards, and chests of drawers had a wide influence.
- Hepplewhite's carvings, like Adam's, relied mainly on Roman motifs, such as elongated laurel leaves, honeysuckle, and pateras. Carving reached its apogee in the 1750s and 1760s–at no age has the woodcarver been more technically ingenious.

Late Georgian

Many changes took place during this period, when formality began to give way to romanticism. Furniture was now arranged not for display but in small, functional groups. The period began more or less with Thomas Sheraton, a designer whose work was to influence much of the best Regency furniture, as well as thousands of cabinetmakers in the New World. Sheraton adapted many French designs, and the French appropriated an equal number of new English furniture ideas, including dumbwaiters and tripod tables.

- Sheraton's furniture was light and delicate, with narrow tapering legs. His preferred forms of ornamentation were inlay, crossbanding, and stringing, as well as painted decoration.
- Carving practically disappeared in Sheraton's furniture, although it reappeared again in Adam's later designs, and then with Thomas Hope.
- Nautical motifs were popular as a result of Nelson's victories at sea.

- Satinwood continued to be the favorite veneer until around the end of the period, but many other exotic woods were also used.
- Elaborate wood marquetry was briefly revived during this period but was then replaced with cheaper, painted decoration.

Regency

Regency furniture had its roots in the Neoclassicism of the late eighteenth century, but was also strongly influenced by the French Directoire and Empire styles, as well as by Greek classicism, which had taken over from the Roman vogue. Thomas Sheraton, Thomas Hope, and Thomas Chippendale Jr. were all leading Regency furniture makers.

- Mahogany remained the most popular wood and rosewood the most popular veneer, contrasted with inlays of ebony, brass, or boxwood. Gilding was used only as a relief.

- There was a revival of japanning.
- Furniture became less sturdy, and chairs were smaller than previously. Often made of cheaper beechwood that had been grained to look like rosewood, they had broad splat backs.
- Large breakfront bookcases gave way to smaller book cabinets.
- Much furniture was based on Greek pieces, as seen on painted Greek vases, and included the X-frame stool and the Klismos chair, with saber legs and a broad crest rail, often decorated with Etruscan-style paintings.
- The Grecian sofa, with its curved ends, bolsters, and carved feet, and the English version of the *chaise longue*, with its saber legs, are typical Regency pieces.
- Regency carving repeated a lot of Greek and Egyptian motifs, including caryatids and sphinxes, lions and eagles.

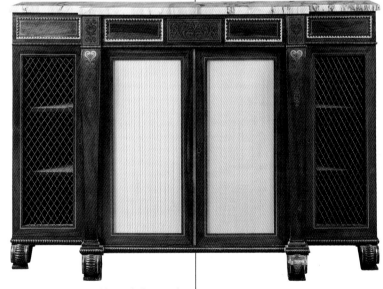

Regency ormolu-mounted, brass-inlaid rosewood breakfast side cabinet

- Toilet tables and dressing tables became very popular, along with the sideboard. Occasional tables proliferated, such as sociable round tables, sofa, and games tables.
- The writing desk known as a davenport was introduced.

William IV

The reign of William IV produced some simpler, rather more solid, mahogany furniture. The Grecian sofa, in particular, remained popular. This simple solidity has proved to be especially popular today, since it fits in well with modern pieces.

Victorian

Furniture producers turned indiscriminately to the past for inspiration, sometimes incongruously mixing several styles in one piece. Among the prosperous on both sides of the Atlantic, Neo-Rococo held considerable sway, surrounded by Neo-Gothic, Neo-Elizabethan, Neo-Tudor, Neo-Baroque, Neo-Renaissance, Medieval, and Moorish, among others.

- Rooms were much more densely furnished than previously.
- Mahogany was the favored wood, along with rosewood, ebony, and a good deal of gilding.
- Buttonbacked and tufted, overstuffed sofas and chairs added to the comfortable and sumptuous atmosphere.
- Characteristic pieces included chiffoniers and sideboards, often carved and inlaid with engraved ivory; large, mirrored hall stands; chesterfields and ottomans; occasional tables of all kinds; balloon-back chairs; and whatnots.

part two: the specifics

Arts and Crafts movement

The first vigorous protest against the mass-produced, machine-made furniture of the Victorian era, the Arts and Crafts movement, spearheaded by William Morris, advocated the reintroduction of craftsman-made furnishings. Morris's company produced sturdy oak furniture (along with wallpapers, fabrics, pottery, and metalwork), of which the "Sussex" chair was one of its best-known pieces.

- Furniture was simple, robust, and rectilinear. Carving was kept to a minimum. Wrought iron decoration was common.
- Pieces were often painted in pale colors, especially green. Painted leather panels might be added.

Aesthetic movement

E. W. Godwin, a leading figure of the Aesthetic movement, was largely responsible for its two main styles of

Art Nouveau chair by C. R. Mackintosh

furniture, "Anglo-Japanese" and "Queen Anne revival." Godwin simplified structure and decoration down to their essential elements. Light and well-proportioned, often in ebonized wood, the furniture was easy to mass-produce and so was widely imitated. Much of the Queen Anne revival furniture was produced by Collinson & Lock in Britain, and by the Herter brothers in the United States. Typical pieces include the small kidney desk, the overmantel, and the glass-fronted display cabinet.

Art Nouveau

Curving, sinuous forms drawn from nature were used for Art Nouveau furniture. Designs were stripped down to elegant

Ebonized Arts and Crafts chair by William Morris with Morris's original "Bird" woolen tapestry

bare curves, and many pieces were ornamented with carving, marquetry, ivory, gilt, or brass. Entire chair backs, arms or legs could be carved to represent plant forms. In Britain, Charles Rennie Mackintosh's furniture, with its exaggerated verticals, lacquered, ebonized, or painted finishes, and Japanese feel, was a rectilinear version of Art Nouveau.

FRENCH FURNITURE

French furniture had an enormous influence on both European and American furniture.

Louis Quatorze

It was Louis XIV who brought French furniture design to a pinnacle of Baroque grandeur and ornamentation. There were many introductions in the seven decades of his reign that were to have a profound influence on the future of furniture.

- The most costly materials were used for furniture, from rare woods to solid silver and lacquerwork.
- Rich brocade fabrics were used for upholstery.
- Carved and gilded furniture was made in walnut, as well as the ubiquitous oak. Some pieces were inlaid with ebony.
- Typical Louis Quatorze pieces include rectilinear gilt upholstered sofas; heavy, high-backed chairs with scrolled arms and legs; tall cabinets, bureaus, and commodes decorated with floral marquetry.
- Ornamentation on tables and case furniture often consisted of heavy ormolu mounts depicting mythological scenes, masks, lions, and acanthus leaves.

- André-Charles Boulle was France's most celebrated cabinetmaker. His finely veneered furniture was elaborately inlaid with tortoiseshell and brass.

Louis Quatorze-style walnut fauteuil

Régence

During this early phase of the Rococo, furniture was lighter but retained some of the Louis Quatorze grandeur.

- The *bergère*, the first really comfortable padded armchair, was developed at this time.
- Chinese motifs such as dragons and parasols began to be used alongside Classical motifs.
- Slipcovers for chairs were another innovation of this period.
- Chair armrests were set back and the backs lowered so as not to interfere with the panniered skirts and large, elaborate coiffures.

Louis Seize tulipwood marquetry bureau

Louis Quinze

Rococo is synonymous with the first half of Louis XV's reign. Thanks to the pattern books so prevalent in the eighteenth century, the French Rococo furniture designs were diligently copied in Spain, Austria, Hungary, Portugal, Poland, Bohemia, Russia, Scandinavia, to a lesser extent in Britain, and, most of all, in Germany, where the style was grand, stately, and elaborate.

- Rococo furniture was light, with gracefully curving legs and delicately carved floral or shell motifs, and was often gilded.
- Whole sets of furniture would often be made for a room, to create a lighthearted synthesis between fixed and movable decoration and furniture.
- The comfortable, curvaceous Louis Quinze armchairs were agreeable both to look at and to sit on.
- Typical pieces were the serpentine-fronted commode, with ormolu mounts, and the *bergère*.

Louis Seize

Under the reign of Louis XVI, as rooms began to be smaller and more intimate, furniture became simpler.

- The legs were tapered and fluted and almost invariably crowned at the top by a small, square block on which was carved a rosette.
- Cabinet pieces were rectangular and were enriched with either wood or metal moldings.
- Many small tables and smaller case pieces were topped with colored marble.
- For the first time, English taste began to infiltrate across the

Channel, especially the designs of Robert Adam.
- Mahogany was used extensively, and ebony became more common, as did painted furniture.
- Ornamentation was Greek (e.g., scrollwork, Greek fret, palmette, anthemion) but the forms of the furniture were not.

Directoire

This period was characterized by the austere, severely simplified furniture of Neoclassicism.

- Wood carvers were inspired by military symbols: spears, drums, stars, and the Liberty cap of the revolutionary armies.
- Because the French kings had nothing to do with Greece, Pompeii, or Egypt, motifs from those sources were still allowed.

- New motifs like scythes and sheaves of wheat were meant to show the growing power of the agricultural workers.
- Greek curves were introduced wherever possible, giving a slight backward roll at the top of a chair back and an outward curve to sofa arms. Front legs on seating often curved forward and rear legs backward. On case furniture, the short supports had a slight outward curve.
- Sometimes Greek or Egyptian heads were used at the tops of legs, which ended with two human feet.
- Bent wrought iron and bronze furniture with tripod supports, also designed in the Greek manner, became popular.

Directoire fauteuil

Empire Style

Furniture, as with other design in this late Neoclassical period, was geometrical in form and Classical in ornament. The principal furniture maker was Jacob-Desmalter, whose patterns influenced many others, both in France and abroad.

- Nearly all tables were round or octagonal with marble tops, and many were supported by a central pedestal leg which rested on a triangular block.
- Beds were usually designed to be placed sideways, military-style, against walls. Boat or sleigh beds appeared, with roll-over ends of swan's necks supporting muslin draperies suspended from above.
- Curved Greek-style chair backs and sofa arms were still popular.
- For the first time, spring seats were used for upholstery.
- The most popular wood was mahogany, but yew, elm, maple, and fruitwood were also used, with veneers like amboyna, thuya, amaranth, palisander, and rosewood imported from Africa and the West and East Indies.
- Carving was largely eliminated, but there was a prodigious use of ormolu mounts of classical motifs for hardware and details.
- Sphinxes with upraised wings, winged griffins and lions, cobras, vultures, palms, obelisks, and hieroglyphics were all motifs taken from Egypt. Caryatids, bees, swans' necks, and the ubiquitous acanthus leaves were other much-used motifs.

part two: the specifics

OTHER EUROPEAN FURNITURE

Elsewhere in Europe, the style-periods were much the same as in France and Britain, though each country had its own interpretations and own unique furniture. There are two styles in particular that are of considerable interest today.

Gustavian

This was Sweden's Neoclassical style-period, but the furniture was more pared down than elsewhere.

- Furniture tended to be painted *en suite* with the walls in cool, pale colors, such as muted blue, pearl gray, and straw yellow. It was usually gessoed before being painted, in order to produce a smoother surface.
- Chairs were straight-legged, with restrained carved ornament.
- Furniture was arranged symmetrically in a room.

Biedermeier

Although contemporary with France's Empire period style, Biedermeier, which prevailed in Germany, Austria, and, to a lesser extent, Scandinavia, was more practical and somewhat less pretentious.

- It is characterized by black-trimmed light-toned wood (elm, ash, maple, or fruitwood), though mahogany was used a lot, too, and by solid, clean, geometric lines.
- The discreet, understated Neoclassical detailing consisted mainly of columns, pilasters, and palmettes.
- Saber legs or straight legs were used on chairs.

Biedermeier drop-front desk with decorative urns on top

AMERICAN FURNITURE

The most important influence on the development of American furniture has been the varied social and cultural origins of its people. The English settlers in Virginia, New England, and elsewhere; the Dutch in the Hudson River Valley, in what is now New York State; the Germans in Pennsylvania; the French in Louisiana and South Carolina; the Swedish in Delaware; and the Spaniards in Florida and the Southwest all have contributed to generic American furniture.

Yet despite the disparate backgrounds of the settlers, the North American climate, terrain, and natural resources, particularly the plentiful supply of timber, meant that the indigenous furniture, like the architecture and interiors, developed uniquely American characteristics.

Early Colonial

This period was characterized by unpretentious furniture made in local materials by not-especially-skilled carpenters. In the North, most were copies of Jacobean or William and Mary styles, or German, Dutch, or Scandinavian pieces. In the South, a great deal of English and French furniture was imported.

Queen Anne

By the beginning of the eighteenth century, the Colonial had had a chance to settle, traditions were established, and industry strengthened. New settlers began to arrive, among them expert cabinetmakers and carpenters.

The American Queen Anne style tended to be lighter and more delicate than the British original, and the American version often used solid walnut rather than veneer. However, the claw-and-ball foot was not much appreciated until later in the century —instead, the pad or pad-and-disks foot was preferred.

Georgian

In the wealthier homes, furniture became increasingly sophisticated, with very skillful copies of Queen Anne, early Georgian, Chippendale, Sheraton, and Hepplewhite designs.

- The vase-like outline of solid splats on the back of Queen Anne-style chairs; the claw-and-ball feet based

American late eighteenth-century mahogany elbow chair

on early Chinese carvings of dragons' claws clutching pearls; the carved shells of the Rococo; the acanthus leaves of Rome and Greece–all became popular motifs. Though simpler than the original versions, the pieces produced by American craftsmen, especially those in Philadelphia, were handsome and also very well made.

- Handsome side chairs, tables, highboys, lowboys, bureaus and drop-front desks were combined with new upholstered sofas, armchairs, and daybeds.
- The Martha Washington chair, with its high back, low seat, and open arms, was introduced.

Simple country homes, however, were still equipped mainly with solid, rustic furniture, often painted with hearts, flowers, leaves and other Dutch, German, or Scandinavian motifs, as well as the roses, thistles, and crowns associated with Britain. Numerous pattern books were brought over from London, but regional styles were particularly individualistic because of the variety of colonizing groups.

Federal, Empire, and Greek revival

Following the War of Independence, there was a growing demand for more sophisticated home furnishings. In particular, the European devotion to Neoclassicism, together with George Hepplewhite's *The Cabinet Maker and Upholsterer's Guide* (published in 1788), inspired some splendid post-Colonial furniture in the last years of

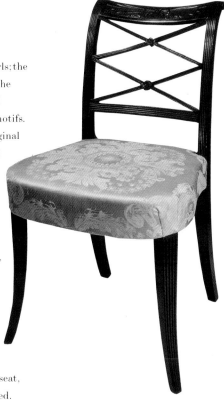

American Federal mahogany scroll-back chair, c.1807, by Duncan Phyfe

the eighteenth century and the first years of the nineteenth.

American cabinetmakers revived the habit of using veneer and inlay on predominantly mahogany furniture. Painted furniture, decorated with landscapes, flowers, or trophies, also became extremely popular, particularly if it was from Baltimore. Carved motifs included the usual Neoclassical references–caryatids, acanthus leaves, griffins–plus the American bald eagle and other patriotic symbols.

The three leading cabinetmakers of the day were all immigrants: Duncan Phyfe from Scotland, Charles-Honoré Lannuier from France, and Joseph B Barry, who was from Ireland but had trained in England. Barry worked out of Philadelphia, and the other two worked from New York. Although

Duncan Phyfe's designs ranged from the Hepplewhite and Sheraton styles through to Empire, and finally to early Victorian, he is thought of mainly as the preeminent designer of the Federal style-period, and his lyre-back chairs and caryatid-based consoles were, and are, highly prized.

By the early 1800s, the elegance and purity of the Federal period was giving way to the heavier, more opulent Empire style, with its deeper carving and more elaborate ornamentation, such as stenciling, graining, gilding, and ormolu mounts.

Empire style, in turn, evolved into the Greek revival. Americans favored this style as much as the French did, and Greek revival furnishings and architecture were extremely fashionable, especially on the East Coast.

Simple cherrywood Shaker tripod table, c.1820

Victorian

On the East Coast, there was much the same eclecticism as in Europe. In the Midwest and West, however, very simple pieces were still produced, including unpretentious chests, chairs, and cupboards, which tended to be either in the cheerful Pennsylvania-German or Dutch eighteenth-century tradition, or country Windsor, rocking, and Hitchcock chairs.

Another profound influence came from the various religious and utopian socialist communities that proliferated in the nineteenth century, particularly the Shakers. Strict rules governed both the decoration and the manufacture of their furniture, and Shaker tables, chairs, and case furniture were beautifully crafted, with clean, spare lines.

With the 1876 Centennial, a new spirit of nationalism provoked a Colonial revival, and manufacturers quickly turned from their French-inspired Louis-whatever pieces to the reproduction of simple "Early American" furniture.

Mission

Produced in the 1890s and the first decade of the twentieth century, Mission furniture was similar to English Arts and Crafts pieces. Strong, straight-lined, with exposed joinery and canvas or leather coverings, it was usually made from oak. Mission furniture was made at the Craftsman Workshops by Gustav Stickley, a disciple of William Morris, and at the Roycroft workshops, a craftsmen's community founded by Elbert Hubbard. Like English Arts and Crafts furniture, it is highly prized today.

part two: the specifics

Vocabulary of Period Furniture Terms

Acanthus leaf: The thick, scalloped leaves of *Acanthus spinosus,* used since Classical times in stylized form on the tops of columns (notably the capital of the Corinthian column) for architectural moldings, and, on a smaller scale, as carved decoration on furniture.

Acorn turning: A knob, foot, or drawer-pull shaped like an acorn.

Adirondack furniture: Rustic furniture produced in the middle of the nineteenth century in upper New York State, made from roughly hewn and bent branches and logs. Adirondack chairs are made from slats with a slant back and wide arms (excellent for setting drinks on) and are much reproduced today for garden furniture.

Angel bed: A bed with a wooden top CANOPY shorter than the bed and no front support.

Anthemion: Decorative motif of Greek origin, the radiating pattern of which resembles honeysuckle. Often used in Classical ornament.

Apron: A strip of wood at the base of cabinets, seats, and table tops extending between the tops of legs or of bracket feet. Also known as a FRIEZE.

Arabesque: Decorative SCROLLWORK or other intricate ornament, using interlaced branches, foliage, abstract curvilinear shapes etc. The name derives from the fact that it was adapted by Muslim artists around a thousand years ago, becoming a traditional part of Arab ornament. It was used in Europe from the early Renaissance, after arabesques were found in Roman tombs. European versions also included animals and human figures.

Arcading: A series of arches with supporting columns or piers. Used to decorate panels on chairs and chests from the sixteenth century onward.

Architrave: In Classical architecture, the lowest of the three parts of the ENTABLATURE. Can also refer to a decorative frame surrounding a door, window, mirror, or other opening.

Armoire: Large, two-door cupboard, originating in France, for storing clothes.

Arrow-back chair: An American form of the WINDSOR CHAIR in which the SPINDLES flare outward. It was popular after about 1830.

Astragal: A small convex beaded molding sometimes placed at the junction of a pair of doors on a cabinet.

Ball foot: The rounded end of a turned leg, with a slightly hooded effect.

Balloon back: Chair back in which the uprights merge into the top rail in one continuous curve and there is no upholstery in the back. Very popular in Victorian times.

Baluster: A turned supporting column in a series supporting a rail.

Balustrade: A series of BALUSTERS with a rail along the top forming a low wall or barrier, usually made of stone or wood.

Bamboo: Light, cheap oriental furniture, first popularized in the late seventeenth century by the Dutch East India Company. *Faux* bamboo was sturdier, since proper wood, often mahogany, was used and either TURNED or painted to give a bamboo effect. Particularly popular in the Regency period.

Banding: Decorative INLAY or MARQUETRY with a color or grain to contrast with the surface it is decorating.

Banister-back chair: American chair often made of EBONIZED maple with vertical split BALUSTERS at the back.

Banjo clock: An American wall clock slightly resembling an inverted banjo, dating from the early nineteenth century.

Banquette: An upholstered bench or SETTEE. Also the ledge at the back of a BUFFET.

Barrel chair: A nineteenth-century American upholstered chair shaped like an old rustic chair; it was originally based on half a wine barrel. The back is usually upholstered in vertical ribs.

Bead: A small convex molding with a nearly semicircular section.

Beau Brummell: Georgian dressing table for men, named after the early nineteenth-century fashion arbiter.

Bergère: Comfortable French armchair with a rounded upholstered back and sides and a wide seat, which appeared in the Régence period and was popular in the Louis Quinze and Louis Seize periods. It was the antithesis of the majestic, uncomfortable chairs of the Louis Quatorze period.

Bibliothèque-basse: French term for low cabinet fitted with shelves for books, with doors fronted either with glass or with grilles.

Bird's-eye maple: Wood of the sugar maple, with small, dark knots, around which the grain forms rings.

Blanket chest: Old English or Colonial chest used for storing blankets and clothes, and often doubling as a bench.

Block foot: A square foot at the base of a straight, untapered leg.

Blockfront: A chest with a recessed center panel, flanked by two projecting panels.

Bobbin twist: Design for TURNED chair STRETCHERS, backs, and legs from the seventeenth century on; the name derives from their resemblance to bobbins.

Boiserie: Carved wooden panels which were used for walls and pieces of French furniture from the seventeenth century onward. In the Louis Quinze period, they were often painted white and gilded.

Bombé: French term (literally, "blown out") for an outward curve or convex front to a COMMODE, BUREAU, or ARMOIRE. Particularly prevalent on Louis Quinze furniture.

Bonheur du jour: French term for a small writing table, usually with tall, slim legs, and sometimes fitted to hold toilet accessories as well. Popular in the eighteenth and nineteenth centuries.

Bonnet top: A broken-arch PEDIMENT covering the top of a piece of CASE FURNITURE, from front to back.

Boston rocker: An American nineteenth-century rocking chair with a downward curved seat, SPINDLE back, and wide top rail.

Boulle: Brass and tortoiseshell MARQUETRY. It is named after Louis XIV's cabinetmaker André Charles Boulle (1642–1732), who perfected the technique. It was highly prized from the late seventeenth to the nineteenth centuries, when the effect started to be reproduced by machine.

Bow back: A type of WINDSOR CHAIR.

Bowfront: An outwardly curving front forming a convex curve.

An English oak buffet designed by Thomas Jeckyll c.1865 for The Old Hall, Heath, Yorkshire in England.

Bracket foot: One of the most common of all feet on CASE FURNITURE. It runs both ways from the corner, forming a right angle.

Breakfast table: See PEMBROKE TABLE.

Breakfront: A bookcase or china cabinet consisting of three sections, with the center one projecting forward beyond the two end sections. It also denotes an upper bookcase set back from cabinets or shelves beneath.

Brewster chair: Chair with large turned posts and SPINDLES, first made in Colonial America in the seventeenth century and named after a governor of the Massachusetts Bay Colony.

Buffet: French term for small sideboard or place for keeping dishes.

Bun foot: A flattened ball or bun-shaped foot with a slender ankle above. Popular in the William and Mary period.

Bureau: A low chest of drawers. In Britain the word designates a writing desk with a sloping DROP FRONT. The term is French and derives from the Latin *burras*, meaning "red," for the red leather covering originally used on the tops of writing tables.

Bureau-bookcase: British term for a DROP-FRONT WRITING CABINET surmounted by a bookcase.

Bureau-plat: French term for a flat-topped writing desk, usually with a leather top.

Burjar: A large upholstered armchair originally made by Thomas Chippendale.

Burl: A knot in a tree which shows beautifully patterned markings when sliced. Used for VENEERS and INLAYS, particularly in burr walnut and burr elm.

Butterfly table: A DROP-LEAF TABLE originating in the United States in the eighteenth century. The brackets that support the leaves are shaped like a butterfly's wings.

Cabinet: Either a cupboard, with solid doors, or a display case, usually glass-fronted.

Cabinetmaker: Umbrella term for a maker of fine furniture as opposed to a joiner. In the seventeenth, eighteenth, and nineteenth centuries, cabinetmakers made CASE FURNITURE, while joiners made chairs and tables.

Cabriole leg: Furniture leg that swells outward at the knee and inward at the ankle. Originally used in ancient Greece, it was much in use in the first half of the eighteenth century.

Camelback: A SOFA back with an irregularly curved shape like a hump. This design was much used by Chippendale and Hepplewhite.

Canapé: French word for a SOFA or DIVAN, first associated with the Louis Quinze period.

Cane furniture: Cheap, light, durable furniture made from the rattan palm. It was introduced into Europe and Britain in the seventeenth century by the Dutch East India Company and into North America at the end of that century.

Canopy: A covering, usually of fabric stretched on a frame, used above a bed.

Canterbury: Originally a type of music stand, then a partitioned trolley, said to have been made for an archbishop of Canterbury. Now used mostly for storing magazines.

Card table: First appeared in reign of Charles II in England. A walnut version with CABRIOLE LEGS and candlestick corners appeared in the Queen Anne period. Now generally a baize-topped, square, collapsible table.

Carlton House table: An eighteenth-century writing table with an adjustable top, originally made for Carlton House, the London home of the Prince of Wales in the Regency period.

Cartouche: Ornament in scroll or tablet form, usually oval, containing a motif such as Egyptian hieroglyphs or a coat of arms; used on the back of a chair, a fire surround, or similar.

Carver chair: Seventeenth-century American armchair usually made of maple or ash, with a rush seat, named after John Carver, governor of the first Plymouth Colony. Also a dining chair with arms, sometimes called an elbow chair.

Caryatid: Female figure derived from Greek architecture; it is used as a decorative support.

Case furniture or pieces: Pieces used for storage, such as bookcases, cabinets, armoires, and sideboards, as opposed to seat furniture. Also called case goods.

Cassone: Italian Renaissance chest, elaborately carved, inlaid, or painted, and often used as a DOWER CHEST.

Cellaret: A case on legs or a stand for wine bottles.

Chaise longue: French term for, literally, a long chair, like a couch with a chair back. Very popular in France in the late eighteenth and nineteenth centuries. Also known as a DAYBED.

Chamfered: A faceted edge, often on furniture legs that are turned outward.

Channeling: A grooved or furrowed effect in wood.

Chesterfield: A deep, often button-backed SOFA with high upholstered arms. Named after Lord Chesterfield in nineteenth-century England.

Cheval glass: A long mirror suspended between vertical posts.

Chiffonier: French word (originally chiffonière) for a narrow chest of drawers. It often has shelves and a mirror above it.

Chinoiserie: European designs that freely interpreted oriental motifs. Fretwork, pagodas, dragons, birds, landscapes, trees, and rivers were common decorative devices, as was a LACQUER finish. Chinese, Indian, and Japanese influences were frequently intermingled. Fashionable from the late seventeenth century.

Claw-and-ball foot: A leg, usually on a chair, ending in the shape of a claw holding a ball. In oriental furniture, from which it derives, the claws are talons or dragon's claws. In European and American pieces they are more often an eagle's claws.

Coffer: Box or chest covered in leather or material and banded with metalwork.

Commode: A low chest of drawers which originated in mid-seventeenth-century France and became widely popular in the eighteenth century. During the nineteenth century, the piece was designed for living rooms, but the term came to apply to a chair that disguised a chamber pot.

Console table: A form of side table that is supported by wall brackets and two front legs.

Corner chair: Chair designed to fit into a corner, with a low back on two adjoining sides of a square seat. Also called a roundabout chair.

Corner cupboard: Triangular cupboard that fits into a corner. It can be free-standing or suspended from the wall, and either small or tall.

Cornice: In Classical architecture, the top part of the ENTABLATURE. In furniture, the horizontal molding that projects from the top of some CASE PIECES.

Cornucopia: The horn of plenty used as a design motif for carved furniture.

Couch: A late seventeenth- and eighteenth-century term for a DAYBED with a single head, usually in the shape of a chair back. Nowadays the term is used for a SOFA as well.

Court cupboard: A low cupboard (the name comes from *court*, the French word for "short"), used for displaying plate or other precious goods, dating from the late sixteenth century.

Credenza: Italian term for a SIDEBOARD or BUFFET table, usually ornate Italianate or French-style.

Cross-banding: Decoration on furniture using thin strips of VENEER cut across the grain.

Cross-stretcher: X-shaped stretcher found on some chairs and tables.

Curule legs: X-shaped legs used on a folding chair with no back.

Davenport: A large SOFA or COUCH named after a Boston upholsterer. In Britain, a small chest of drawers with a sloped top for writing.

Daybed: A COUCH with a single head, usually in the shape of a chair back, sometimes with arms. First made in the seventeenth century. Also called a CHAISE LONGUE.

Dentelles or dentils: A series of rectangular blocks with spaces in between them, used as a molding on a CORNICE.

part two: the specifics

Desk box: An early form of desk consisting of a box for holding writing materials and a hinged, sloping lid.

Diaper motif: A trellis design of squares or rectangles sometimes containing a carved leaf or flower, or other design.

Disk foot: A flat, literally disk-shaped, foot for chairs and tables.

Divan: An upholstered bench of oriental origin, popular in the Victorian era as part of a Turkish style of room. Also, British term for a bed base.

Dovetail joint: A right-angled joint with interlocking dovetail or fan-shaped TENONS. From the eighteenth century on, these were often concealed (at least in furniture of high quality) by an overlapping piece of wood.

Dowel: A headless wooden peg used in furniture construction.

Dower chest: A chest made to store a trousseau. Examples include Hadley chests, Connecticut chests, and painted PENNSYLVANIA DUTCH or GERMAN chests.

Dresser: A SIDEBOARD with shelves and sometimes cupboards above, for storing and displaying china; most often made from pine or oak.

Drop front: A hinged cover on a desk which, when lowered, serves as a surface for writing. When closed, it may be slanting or vertical.

Drop-leaf table: A table with hinged leaves, such as a BUTTERFLY TABLE, GATELEG TABLE, PEMBROKE TABLE, or SOFA TABLE.

Drop-front writing cabinet: A cabinet in which the front, when open and supported, can be used as a desk. The front may be vertical or sloping.

Drum table: A Neoclassical round table with a TRIPOD base and a FRIEZE beneath the top, sometimes containing drawers; normally used for writing.

Dumbwaiter: A dining-room stand consisting of circular trays set on a central column with a TRIPOD base. Diners were able to help themselves to china, cutlery, or food from the trays, which diminish in size from bottom to top and may revolve. Introduced early in the eighteenth century.

Dust board: Thin, horizontal boards placed between the drawers of a COMMODE or chest of drawers to keep out dust.

Dutch dresser: A cabinet with open shelves above and drawers or a cupboard below.

Dutch foot: A pad used as the foot on a CABRIOLE LEG. Also called a duck foot.

Ébéniste: A French term for a cabinetmaker.

Ebonized wood: Wood stained black to look like ebony; also called *bois noir* in French. Used frequently on Victorian oriental-style cabinets and for the trim on Biedermeier furniture.

Egg-and-dart molding: A classic design made up of alternating egg-like ovals and dart shapes, said to symbolize life and death, and carved onto quarter-round or half-round molding.

Elbow chair: See CARVER CHAIR.

Entablature: In Classical architecture, the whole section above the capital of a column, consisting of the ARCHITRAVE, FRIEZE, and CORNICE. The term is also applied to the equivalent part of a cabinet or cupboard.

Escritoire: A French term for a DROP-FRONT WRITING CABINET. Usually it refers to one made before 1720 and with a vertical, rather than sloping, front. Many had secret compartments among the drawers and pigeonholes.

Escutcheon: A shield or emblem upon which a coat of arms or other special devices are emblazoned.

Étagère: A set of shelves, freestanding or attached to a wall, used for displaying objects. It may have glazed doors.

Farthingale chair: An armless, wide, upholstered chair especially designed in Elizabethan times to accommodate voluminous skirts.

Fauteuil: French term for an armchair that has open spaces between the arms and seat.

Festoon: Also known as a swag. This design appears on Renaissance as well as Neoclassical furniture and imitates a loop of drapery or a garland of fruit and flowers.

Fiddle back: A chair splat that is shaped like a fiddle.

Fire screen: A screen to give protection from the heat of a fire. It may be either a POLE SCREEN (an oval or round screen set on a TRIPOD base) or a cheval screen (which consists of a panel enclosed by two uprights, each on a pair of legs). Fire screens were in use from the eighteenth century.

Flambeau: French term for a carved decoration in the shape of a flaming torch.

Flemish scroll: A Baroque form of double SCROLL, where the curve is broken by an angle. It was used on late seventeenth-century chair legs and stretchers.

Fleur-de-lis: A motif representing a stylized lily or iris, consisting of three petals bound together near the bottom. It was once the royal arms of France.

Fluting: Parallel grooved lines on any horizontal or upright surface; the opposite of REEDING, it was particularly popular in Neoclassical furniture.

Fly rail: A folding bracket to support a DROP LEAF of a table.

Foliated: Decoration composed of leaf designs.

Four-poster: A style of bed that originated in medieval times, with four posts, one at each corner, usually supporting a canopy.

Fretwork: A form of decoration used on woodwork (especially with CHINOISERIE) formed from interlaced geometric designs carved into thin wood. Blind fretwork has a backing, often of a contrasting wood or color; open fretwork does not.

Frieze: In Classical architecture, the middle part of the ENTABLATURE, between the ARCHITRAVE and CORNICE. In furniture, a decorative, wide horizontal band just below a cornice or a table top, also called the apron or the skirt.

Functionalism: In furniture design, an emphasis on efficiency rather than looks.

Gadroon: A curved molding in an olive or ruffle shape, sometimes used on the edges of table tops or chairs.

Gateleg table: A form of DROP-LEAF TABLE with rounded, hinged flaps. When lifted, these are supported by gate-like legs that swing out from the center of the table. Very popular in seventeenth-century Britain, the Netherlands, and Colonial America.

Gesso: A white substance traditionally made of chalk and size, which is applied to furniture. Once it has hardened, it produces a smooth, porous surface for gilding, painting, or lacquerwork. It can be generally cast to make repeating ornamental forms.

Girandole: An ornate candelabrum, or a wall mirror to which candle sconces, or brackets, are attached.

Glastonbury chair: A Gothic chair with a sloping, paneled back and arms with a drooping curve. First used by the abbots of Glastonbury in the sixteenth century, it was widely copied in the nineteenth century.

Griffin: A chimerical or fanciful beast, employed in early Georgian decoration.

Guéridon: A small table with a round top for holding candlesticks.

Guilloche: A continuous figure-eight motif used on a band or border. Originally used in Classical architecture, it was popular for furniture decoration from the sixteenth century.

Hadley chest: A type of Early American DOWER CHEST on four feet with one or more drawers, decorated with flat carving. Named for its place of origin, Hadley, Massachusetts.

Highboy: An early eighteenth-century American version of the TALLBOY, often on CABRIOLE LEGS and with a broken PEDIMENT or CORNICE moldings.

High relief: Deep carving found on any plain surface.

Hitchcock chair: American chair with an oval turned top rail and a rush, cane, or wooden seat. The chair was usually painted black, and the top rail and back splat were decorated with colored or gilded flowers, fruit, or similar motifs. Named after the designer Lambert Hitchcock, it was produced between 1820 and 1850.

Hoof foot: The end of a leg in the shape of a goat's hoof.

Hoop-back chair: Wooden chair with upholstered seat with a rounded front rail, CABRIOLE LEGS, and a back with a rounded top and solid SPLAT; associated with Britain's Queen Anne period.

Inlay: A decorative technique using contrasting woods, and sometimes small pieces of ivory, horn, metal, or MOTHER-OF-PEARL, sunk into holes of similar shape cut into another material, usually solid wood.

Intaglio: Incised, or countersunk, decoration made by cutting into the surface of a material.

Intarsia: Italian type of decoration similar to INLAY in which a design is sunk into another surface.

Jasperware: A kind of hard biscuit-ware introduced by the Wedgwood company in the eighteenth century. Occasionally used for medallions set into chair backs.

Joinery: The craft of assembling woodwork by means of a DOVETAIL JOINT, tongue-and-groove, MORTISE and TENON, dowels, etc. Joiners make furniture like chairs and tables, more than CASE PIECES.

Key pattern: Also known as Greek key or fret pattern. A repeated design of straight lines at right angles, creating a maze-like effect. It originates from Classical Greek architecture and is often used as a border.

Kidney desk: A small desk or writing table with a curved front that is shaped like a kidney.

Klismos: A chair used by the ancient Greeks and Romans, and revived in the late eighteenth and early nineteenth century. It had a concave, curved back rail and curved legs.

Kneehole desk: A desk with a space through the middle of it, to allow a person's knees to be accommodated comfortably when seated at the desk.

Ladder back: A chair back with horizontal cross rails instead of a splat. The style was adopted by Chippendale and other cabinetmakers of the eighteenth century.

Lattice: Open FRETWORK decoration using crisscrossed lines forming diamonds or squares.

Linenfold: Wood carved to represent vertical folds of drapery. It was popular in the fifteenth and sixteenth centuries on furniture, particularly chests and wardrobe doors, and on wall paneling, and during the nineteenth-century Tudor revival.

Lit en bateau: French term for a distinctive boat-shaped bed with curving ends, popular during the Empire period.

Loo table: A nineteenth-century round pedestal table for playing the card game Loo.

Lotus: Ancient Egyptian motif based on the water lily of the Nile.

Love seat: A SETTEE, or small SOFA, designed for two people.

Lowboy: An eighteenth-century American chest of drawers, usually with one long drawer and three short ones. It was often made to match a HIGHBOY.

Low relief: Shallow carving on any plain surface.

Lozenge: A diamond-shaped motif or panel.

Lunette: Semicircular shape used to decorate furniture; often filled with ornamental carving or inlaid or painted decoration in the Neoclassical period.

Lyre back: The back of a chair in the form of a lyre. It is roughly the shape of a horseshoe with outwardly scrolled ends, and a horizontal bar between its arms. It was popular in the late eighteenth century.

Marlborough leg: Heavy, straight, grooved leg with a block foot, used by Thomas Chippendale and others in the eighteenth century.

Marquetry: A flush pattern in a veneered surface, produced by inserting contrasting wood veneers and sometimes tortoiseshell, ivory, MOTHER-OF-PEARL, or metals.

Martha Washington chair: Late eighteenth-century American armchair with a low upholstered seat, open arms, and a high upholstered back. Also known as a lolling chair.

Martha Washington table: A work-table, usually octagonal, with drawers and two deep receptacles for needlework.

Medallion: A decorative oval or circular plaque, with an ornamental motif inside.

Modillion: A projecting bracket that is used to support a Corinthian cornice. It is also often used as an independent decorative device.

Rococo console table with elaborate ormolu, by Cuvilliés, c.1739.

Morris chair: A large Arts and Crafts easy chair with arms usually extending slightly beyond the back, which can be adjusted to various angles. Designed in 1883, it was produced by William Morris's firm.

Mortise: A hole cut in wood to take a TENON projecting from another piece.

Mother-of-pearl: The iridescent inner layer of some shells, pieces of which were inlaid into furniture from the seventeenth century onward. In the nineteenth century it was a popular inlay in PAPIER-MÂCHÉ furniture.

Mounts: Ornamental or utilitarian metalwork such as handles or drawer pulls, used on CASE FURNITURE.

Ogee: A double curve which is convex above and concave below, as in an ogee molding. An ogee arch is composed of two mirror-image ogees, whose sides come together before curving in the opposite way. Identified with Gothic forms, and used in Neo-Gothic furniture for chair backs, paneling, and architectural moldings. Also often found on the feet of Georgian furniture. A reverse ogee is concave above and convex below.

Ormolu: Gilt-bronze decoration or mounts. The name derives from the French term *bronze doré d'or moulu* ("bronze gilded with ground gold"); it is also known as *bronze doré.*

Ottoman: An upholstered bench without a back, often used as a footstool. The name is taken from the Ottoman (Turkish) Empire.

part two: the specifics

201

Oxbow front: Reverse SERPENTINE front (i.e., concave in the center, and convex on either side) used in eighteenth-century CASE FURNITURE.

Pagoda: A Chinese or Japanese tower with several stories, often used as a motif in oriental furniture.

Palmette: Classical motif resembling a palm leaf, used as carved or painted ornament on furniture.

Panel: A surface enclosed by a frame. It may be sunk (below the frame), flush (at the same level), or fielded (raised above the frame).

Papier-mâché: French term for pulped paper that is mixed with glue and molded while wet into various shapes; used for lightweight furniture, often japanned and inlaid with MOTHER-OF-PEARL, in the nineteenth century.

Parcel-gilt: Partly gilded.

Parquetry: A geometrical MARQUETRY pattern, which often produces a three-dimensional effect.

Patera: A round or oval disk, often surrounding a rosette or other ornament; particularly used in Neoclassical ornament.

Patina: The natural sheen and softening of color that develops on wood over the years; also the greenish film that forms on bronze through a chemical reaction.

Paw foot: Furniture leg ending in the shape of a paw. Used in ancient Egypt, Greece, and Rome, and popular again in Neoclassical furniture.

Pedestal: A supporting base or block for a statue or vase, usually treated with moldings at the top and a base block at the bottom. Without any moldings, it is called a plinth.

Pedestal table: A table on a round, center support within a wide base.

Pediment: In architecture, the triangular space at each exterior end of a Greek temple. In furniture, an ornamental feature on top of a CASE PIECE. It can be "broken," "scrolled," or "segmental."

Pembroke table: A DROP-LEAF TABLE with oval or rectangular ends, usually with a drawer in the FRIEZE. Named after a

Lady Pembroke, it was used in the eighteenth and nineteenth centuries for writing, card games, needlework, and meals. Also known as a BREAKFAST TABLE.

Pennsylvania Dutch or German: Furniture made by German settlers ("Dutch" is a corruption of "Deutsch") in Pennsylvania between 1750 and 1850. Made mostly in softwood, it was painted with colorful folk-art motifs.

Piecrust table: A small table with its edge carved or molded with scallops, like the crimped edge of a pie crust. Popular in the eighteenth century.

Pier glass: Large window-height mirror.

Pietre dure: Italian decorative technique, using inlaid semiprecious stones. The technique was used in ancient Rome and then revived during the Renaissance.

Pilaster: Flattened, rectangular column, often with REEDING, superimposed on a surface. Used to decorate the façade rather than for any structural support.

Pillar: Popular term for a column.

Pineapple: Carved pineapple-shaped ornament often found on bedposts on early nineteenth-century American beds, as well as on gateposts and the newel posts of stairs. It symbolized hospitality.

Pinnacle: Small cone-shaped turret, often used in Gothic decoration.

Plaque: Plate or panel inserted into wood; it is usually made of metal, glass, or pottery and treated with some sort of surface enrichment.

Plinth: See PEDESTAL.

Pole screen: Adjustable panel mounted on a vertical pole, used as a FIRE SCREEN.

Pomegranate: Decorative motif, symbolizing fertility.

Poudresse: French term for small table with mirrored lid that covers a space for cosmetics.

Pouffe: French/English term for large, round, stuffed cushion used as a seat; fashionable from early nineteenth century.

Primitive: Early, simple, naïve furniture.

Quatrefoil: An ornamental figure or leaf motif, divided by cusps or featherings into four foils, leaves, or lobes. Much used in Gothic decoration.

Quattrocento: The fifteenth century in Italy; Renaissance furniture of the fifteenth century.

Rail: Any horizontal strip forming a portion of a frame in paneling (vertical strips are STILES); also the top member of a chair.

Récamier: French name for a CHAISE LONGUE with curved ends in the Neoclassical style. The name was adopted after the appearance in 1800 of Jacques-Louis David's portrait of Mme. Juliette Récamier reclining on a *chaise longue* while receiving visitors.

Reeding: Decoration consisting of parallel, usually vertical, narrow convex moldings; the opposite of FLUTING. It is often found on chair and table legs. Sheraton, Adam, and Duncan Phyfe used it extensively.

Refectory table: A long, narrow table, used for dining in medieval houses, monasteries, and convents. Also called a hall table.

Relief: A type of decoration made prominent by raising it from the surface or background of the material. See also HIGH RELIEF and LOW RELIEF.

Repoussé: Embossed relief decoration on metal.

Ribbon back: Chair back designed with pattern of interlacing ribbons, often used by Chippendale.

Rinceau: French term for Classical, ornamental device made of intertwining stalks of ACANTHUS or other scrolling foliage. It is sometimes used in combination with CARTOUCHES.

Rolltop desk: Desk in which the writing table and fittings are enclosed by a curved, slatted panel.

Romayne work: Carved medallion heads or knobs used as furniture ornaments or drawer pulls; characteristic of the Jacobean and Restoration periods.

Rondel or roundel: Round outline or object in a surface pattern.

Rope bed: Bed with rope laced to the frame to support a mattress.

Rosette: Ornamental motif formed by a series of leaves or petals around a central point.

Roycroft furniture: American Arts and Crafts furniture produced by the Roycroft community, founded by Elbert Hubbard, from 1896. Designs were plain and made from ash, oak, or mahogany, often with copper fittings, prominent MORTISE and TENON joints and tapering legs.

Rush seat: Rushes plaited to form a chair seat, a style that was common in Europe and America in the eighteenth and nineteenth centuries, especially for country furniture.

Saber leg: Curved leg in the Classical style, generally with REEDING.

Saddle seat: Chair seat hollowed to resemble a saddle.

Sausage turning: TURNED legs or STRUTS resembling a string of sausages.

Sawbuck table: A table with an X-frame, either plain or scrolled.

Scagliola: Imitation marble surface formed from hardened and highly polished plaster or GESSO and marble fragments. It was used for tabletops as well as columns and pilasters.

Scallop: A carved ornament in the shape of a shell that was widely used in Rococo pieces.

Sconce: Ornamental wall bracket, or candleholder, used for candles or electric lightbulbs.

Scoop seat: A chair that has been especially hollowed out in order to fit the human body.

Scroll or scrollwork: A spiral, or convoluted, line used for ornamental purposes, as in an ARABESQUE. A representation of a parchment roll used as an ornament.

Scroll foot: A foot in the form of a spiral line.

Scroll pediment: Broken PEDIMENT with each half shaped in the form of a reverse curve and ending in an ornamental scroll.

Seaweed marquetry: MARQUETRY utilizing woods with a figured grain, such as holly or boxwood, to produce patterns resembling seaweed; often used in the William and Mary period and also in the eighteenth century.

Secretary: A drop-front desk with drawers below and a cabinet or bookshelves above—the latter style called, in Britain, a BUREAU-BOOKCASE.

Sedan chair: Enclosed eighteenth-century chair, with two poles, usually carried by four men.

Serpentine curve: Undulating curve used for the fronts of commodes, chests or bureaus. The center curve is convex and the curves on either side concave.

Serving table: A long, narrow table with drawers.

Settee: A seat or bench with a high back, and often with arms, large enough to seat two or more people. Originally it was more formal than a SOFA, but today the terms are sometimes used interchangeably. It was widely in use in Britain from the early seventeenth century to the nineteenth.

Settle: A wooden bench with a back and solid arms, produced from the sixteenth century onward. Having developed from the chest, it sometimes had a hinged seat for storage (and was then known as a box-settle).

Sgabellow: Italian term for small wooden Renaissance chair with a carved splat back, octagonal seat, and trestle supports.

Sgraffito: Italian term for a pattern that is first scratched onto a surface and then colored.

Shaft: Central portion of a column or pilaster.

Shaker furniture: Simple, functional, nineteenth-century American furniture with tapering legs, swallowtail joints, much prized today for its spare and elegant lines. Usually made in pine, maple, walnut, or fruitwood. Derived from English country furniture, a Shaker chair was a taller, slimmer version of a LADDER BACK chair, often with a practical bar on top from which to suspend a cushion. Well reproduced today.

Shield back: Chair back shaped like a shield; much used in the eighteenth century by Hepplewhite.

Sideboard: Dining-room serving table with a long, flat top and drawers and cupboards underneath. First popularized by the Adam brothers in the 1760s.

Singerie: French term for eighteenth-century design showing monkeys (*singes* in French) at play, usually dressed up and behaving like humans. Popular as CHINOISERIE decoration.

Skirt: See FRIEZE.

Slant-top desk: A desk with a drop-front cover which lies at a slant when it is closed.

Slat back: Late seventeenth-century chair with slats—wide, horizontal, ladder rails—between the back uprights, like a simplified LADDER BACK.

Slipper chair: A short-legged chair, often upholstered, used especially in bedrooms.

Sofa: The sofa, which was large enough to recline on and was more upholstered and informal than the SETTEE, gradually took over from the settee during the nineteenth century. Nowadays it is a general term for upholstered seating for two or more people.

Sofa table: Narrow, rectangular table with two front drawers and hinged leaves at either end. Originally put in front of a sofa, it is now generally placed behind it, instead.

Spade foot: Rectangular-shaped tapered foot, like a spade.

Spandrel: Arched form bounded by a horizontal and vertical frame, often used by Sheraton for chair backs.

Spanish foot: Foot in the shape of an inward-curving SCROLL.

Spindle: A long, slender rod, ornamented with TURNED moldings.

Spiral leg: A leg carved in the shape of a rope twist.

Splat: A plain, shaped, or carved vertical strip of wood, usually forming the center of a chair back.

Splayed: A surface canted outward, or on a slant.

Split spindle: Spindle cut in half lengthwise, so that each half has one flat and one rounded side. Used as applied decoration in seventeenth-century English and American furniture, particularly chests and cabinets.

Spoonback: A chair back shaped to fit the human back.

Stile: The vertical strips of the frame of a panel.

Strapwork: Furniture decoration of narrow bands of wood folded, crossed, and sometimes interlaced; popular in the Netherlands in the sixteenth century, and in Elizabethan England.

Stretcher: A brace, or support, horizontally connecting the legs of a piece of furniture.

Stringing: A decorative border for furniture, especially tabletops, consisting of a narrow line or lines of wood or metal INLAY.

Sussex chair: A late nineteenth-century chair produced by William Morris, with a rush seat.

Tabouret: French term for a low, upholstered stool made from the seventeenth century onward.

Tallboy: A small chest of drawers placed on top of a larger one; also known as a chest-on-chest.

Tambour: A desk with a shelved top and sliding panels replacing a glass or grilled front.

Taper leg: A leg that narrows as it reaches the foot.

Tavern table: Small, sturdy rectangular table, usually braced with STRETCHERS, and generally with a drawer or two in the FRIEZE. Used in eighteenth-century taverns.

Tenon: A projection at the end of a piece of wood, intended to fit into a corresponding shape in another piece of wood (MORTISE). Hence "mortise and tenon" construction.

Tester: Top framework of a canopy bed.

Tilt-top table: Small table with the top hinged to a pedestal base so that it can be tilted up when not in use.

Torchère: Originally a stand that held a candle or lamp; also known as candle-stand. Today, a floor lamp designed to throw light upward.

Trefoil: Motif with three leaves, or foils, usually contained within a circle. Typical of Gothic decoration.

Tripod: Three-legged stand for a PEDESTAL TABLE.

Triptych: Three-part, hinged mirror or small screen.

Trumeau: Generally, French term for the decorative treatment of the space over a mantelpiece. More specifically, overmantel panel treatment popular in the Louis XV and XVI periods.

Trumpet leg: A conical leg with a flared end or foot.

Trundle or truckle bed: A low seventeenth-century bed which was rolled under a larger bed.

Tudor arch: Flat-pointed arch that is characteristic of Gothic and Renaissance decoration.

Tudor rose: Decorative motif composed of a five-petaled rose, often a red one encircling a white, symbolizing the Tudor dynasty.

Turning: A type of ornamentation produced by rotating wood on a lathe, and shaping it into various forms with cutting tools.

Veneer: A thin sheet of finishing wood, or other material, applied to a surface for decorative effect.

Wainscot chair: An early seventeenth-century Colonial wooden chair which has a back paneled like the wainscoting of a wall.

Wardrobe: Developed in the seventeenth century as a cupboard for storing clothes.

Washstand: Adapted for bedroom use after 1750, this consists of a cupboard on legs with a basin sunk in the top.

Welsh dresser: A cabinet with a large, enclosed storage base and an upper section of open shelves.

Whatnot: A portable, open cabinet with shelves for books, ornaments, etc., developed about 1800. Popular from the Regency period onward.

Wheat: Carved ornament representing ears of wheat, much used by Hepplewhite.

Windsor chair: Usually oak, elm, or yew, with a back of TURNED SPINDLES, plus pegged legs and a wooden or rush seat. Produced from the seventeenth century in Britain, and popular in America from the eighteenth century.

part two: the specifics

Once you have created a good background, or framework, in a room, you can fill in the final details, which will give the space its particular character. "God is in the detail" was one of the twentieth-century architect Mies van der Rohe's design aphorisms. Certainly the final detailing makes all the difference between a room that barely holds the attention and one that is distinguished, memorable, and idiosyncratic—in other words, truly personal. This is the really fun part, the icing on the cake, when you can choose the accessories that reflect your own and your family's personality and bring a room to life.

The Finishing Touches

Finessing a Room

There are, of course, many aspects to detailing. All the groundwork will already have been done, and this is the stage when it is all finalized and enhanced. The furnishings and finishes need to be completed and then maintained as well as possible. And finally, the art and objects, flowers and plants, and general accessorizing can be decided upon.

This kitchen with its splendid ecclesiastical window is an excellent example of finesse. Surfaces gleam, and everything appears to work as well as it looks, from the range and its hood to the drawers and work surfaces. Yet the room does not look too perfect to be used, which is the fate of all too many beautifully planned kitchens. Surely anyone would want to cook here.

COUNCIL OF IMPERFECTION

There is a fine line between finessing a room–grooming it, as it were–and making it so perfect that it is positively discomforting to look at. Perfect rooms are as irritating as perfect people. The ideal room is one that manages to look both interesting and relaxing–used, but not abused.

Upholstery should look neat and smoothed, probably piped or edged in some way to keep its shape, and cushions should be plumped and well arranged. But that same upholstery should also look deeply comfortable and welcoming–never too pristine to put one's feet up.

ATTENTION TO DETAIL

If draperies are held back with tie-backs, these should be positioned at just the right height for the folds to look graceful. Blinds and shades should be pulled up so that they are straight; it's surprising how many otherwise well-groomed people fail to notice when blinds are crooked.

Carpets, matting, or hard flooring should all look as clean as possible. Rugs should lie flat. Polished wood should be kept polished; marble, glass, plastic, and any metals should be free of spots and smears.

Tabletops, windowsills, mantelpieces, display units, and shelves look best with some sense of arrangement, rather than cluttered with papers and paraphernalia all over the place. Plants, collections, and art should be carefully chosen and arranged. But above and beyond these concerns, they should not look so well arranged (or artificial) that one is nervous about putting down a glass or a cup for fear of spoiling an artistic effect.

It is good if door furniture matches and paintwork is clean and free of finger marks. Ultimately, though, a little imperfection here and there is a reminder that people live in and relax in the room, and so is not a bad thing.

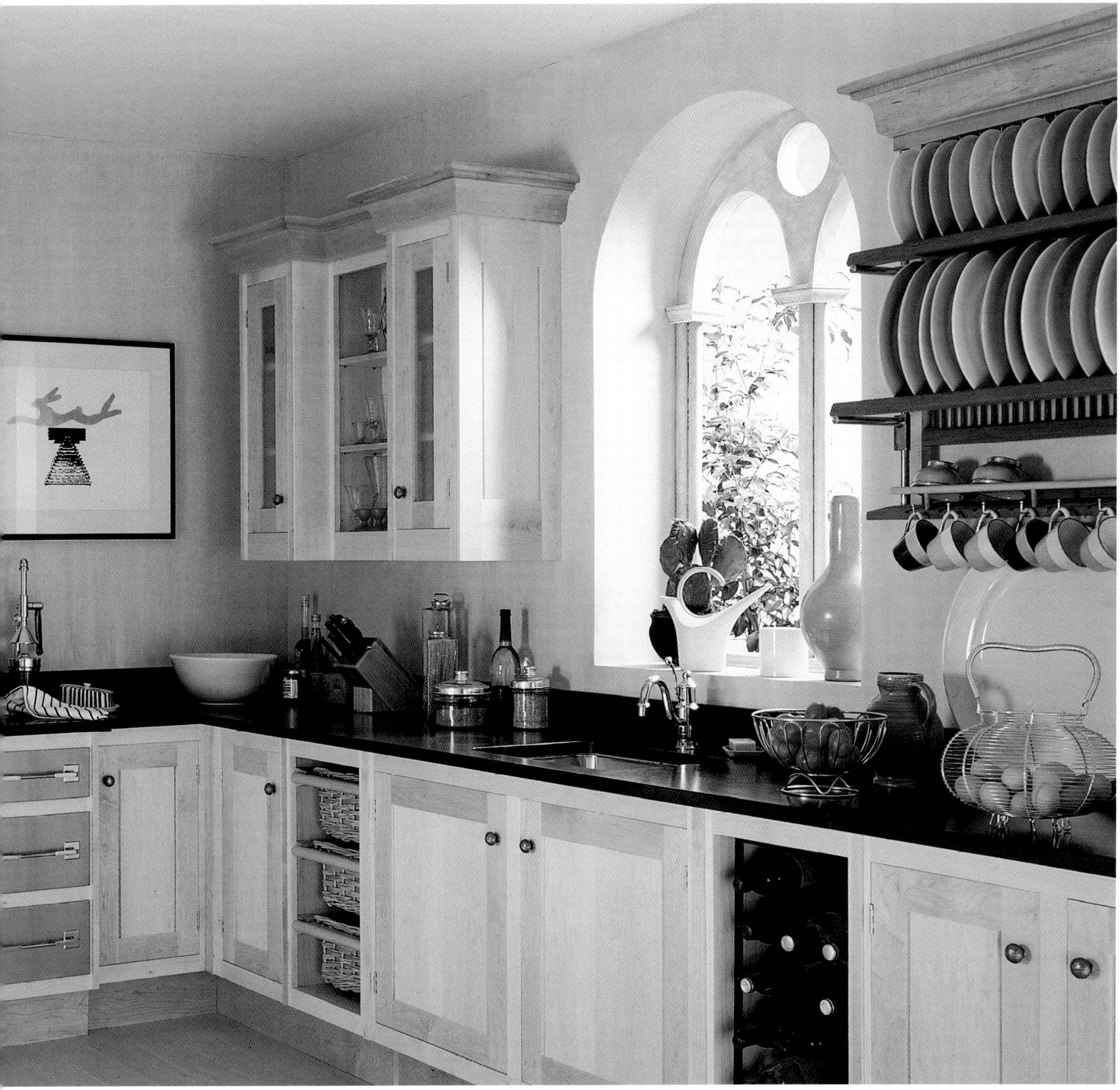

Accessories

If good lighting, color schemes, window and floor treatments, and the choice of furniture and upholstery are what make a room comforting, then the paintings and objects, plants and flowers, and other embellishments are the elements that make it special, idiosyncratic, and memorable. For a truly individual room, the objects must be personal and enjoyed for their own sake. They should have been thought about carefully and put together for some reason, not just to fill the space.

SIMPLICITY VERSUS CLUTTER

There are two schools of thought on the possession and display of objects: the school for simplicity, and the school for clutter. The first approach is typified by just one or two exquisite and interesting pieces, while the second favors an accretion of possessions and collections that can be called, rather aptly, memorabilia.

The trouble about the "simple" school is that the few beautiful objects really must be beautiful or unusual, or at least made to appear so. The difficulty about the "cluttered" school is that the collections—or the disparate amassing of objects that amounts to clutter—must be organized to display the possessions to their best advantage. This involves a careful assemblage of texture and shape and color, for you are virtually creating "still lifes" in just the same way as a painter or a photographer does.

Collections of small objects are far more effective when grouped together, rather than scattered thinly around a room or home. For example, very small objects like shells, pebbles, or polished fragments of stones from the beach

can be put into bowls or goblets and displayed on windowsills or shelves. Slightly larger objects, however different, should be grouped so that they have something in common, like color, texture or national origin. Alternatively, they can be juxtaposed with larger or smaller objects to create extra interest and balance. Add a

plant or some dried flowers, or even a selection of single blossoms in specimen jars for contrast.

If arrangements are grouped on low tables that are also used for

books, magazines, glasses, and so on, leave space so that the composition will not be ruined by putting down a tray, drink, or book. If arrangements are placed on a glass shelf, or table,

1 There is clearly an overload of disparate objects on and around this mantelpiece, including two lamps and a candlestick. But they work successfully together because all are in much the same neutral tones, quite apart from each being interesting in its own right.

2 Again, very different objects share the common denominator of color against the white woodwork and the pale fawn painted wall, though these are carefully spaced.

3 Everything on these neatly arranged shelves has been chosen for its own merit or memories.

lighting them from underneath with an uplight is effective. If they are not on a transparent surface, try lighting them from above with a downlight or spot, to add extra brilliance.

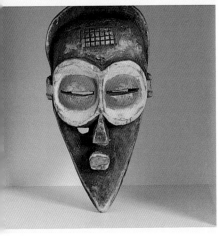

UNUSUAL COLLECTIONS

Collections of ordinary but unexpected objects often make for more memorable rooms than much rarer and more expensive items. Perhaps this is because one is less impressed by the effect of something one knows to be especially good than by that of something one had not necessarily thought about. I can think back with pleasure on massed assemblies of old irons, shoe lasts, medicine bottles, and pill jars with their different-colored glass, eighteenth- and nineteenth-century eyeglass cases, old locks and keys, toast racks, wine glass rinsers, pen boxes, card cases, old matchbox cases and tinder boxes, different ivory objects, old hats, old baskets... the list could go on and on.

SCULPTURE

Sculpture will always add distinction to a room. It might be a classical bust, a figurative bronze, or an abstract design; it could be Chinese, Oceanic, or pre-Columbian. Almost all sculpture, apart from life-size or freestanding pieces, looks better on some kind of plinth, whether it is stone, wood, fiberglass, marble, plaster, or clear plastic.

1 *Here the shelving adds almost as much interest as the objects displayed, which in turn are as interesting for their blocks of color as for themselves. The whole effect is of some Miró-like abstract, practically floating in the middle of the expanse of white wall.*

2 *Two pieces of primitive art—a shield and a horse—are shown to good advantage against the yellow wall.*

3 *One way to treat awkward, shallow, horizontal windows is to use them as a backlit display area. Here a window displays a collection of cameras, which can be lit from the front when the daylight fades. Note that even the light – a photographer's lamp – sustains the theme.*

4 *A collection of amethyst glass on glass shelves stretched across a small window is matched by pinkish-purple chrysanthemums.*

5 *No one could deny the decorative value of hats hung on a wall. This collection is hung rather rakishly askew to good effect.*

Arranging Art

The schools of thought on hanging art are as varied as the objects on display. Broadly speaking, however, they can be divided into two categories: people who want to make room for their serious collections, and people who want to use their wall space to its most decorative advantage.

People in the first category are always thinking of a wall as a means to an end –a support, a background–and moving paintings around as their collection expands or contracts, or changes direction. These people guard every bit of wall zealously. The second group need to find some unifying factor for their disparate and often undistinguished possessions. This especially applies to first-time householders, as well as to new partnerships, in which both partners bring their own collections to a new joint home.

tip

IF ONE PAINTING OR PRINT IS MUCH LARGER THAN THE OTHERS, PUT IT AT ONE END OF A GROUPING, RATHER THAN IN THE MIDDLE SURROUNDED BY SMALLER WORKS, WHICH CAN GIVE THE IMPRESSION OF TAILING OFF. BALANCE IT AT THE OTHER END WITH SOMETHING ELSE TALL: A PLANT, A PIECE OF SCULPTURE, OR A FLOWER ARRANGEMENT ON A TABLE BELOW.

UNIFYING A SET

A miscellaneous set of prints can be given a unity it otherwise lacks if each print is given a mat of the same distinctive color–buff, gray, blue, yellow, deep red, or whatever fits the room or space–and is framed with the same material, whether chrome, brass, or gilded, silvered, or natural wood. Again, an odd assortment of different subjects will have a unity of their own if they share a color: all sepia tints, or all black and white, or all green, ivory, or terracotta.

1 An eclectic collection of different-sized and framed mirrors is hung along with varied prints and photographs, all on wide, white mats. The varying convex mirrors, with their somewhat distorting reflections, adds a most interesting twist.
2 This collection of ancient Greek images, all framed in terracotta and black is hung as a carefully

measured central block of 15, with two smaller groupings of three apiece on adjacent walls. They look especially arresting in an otherwise sparsely decorated, all-white bathroom. Though a bathroom is not an obvious (or always practical) location to hang an art collection, the result is gratifyingly spectacular.

2

HANGING HEIGHTS

When there are a lot of different things to hang, try not to hang them too high or too far apart. Do not fix anything so low over a sofa or chair that people will knock their heads on it, and try to hang as much as possible at eye level (taking either sitting or standing levels into account). When there are very large groupings, keep at least the central pieces at eye level. But when the seating in a room consists of low-level couches and chairs, and stools or benches, there is no reason why some paintings, prints, or posters should not be hung somewhat lower than usual.

There are certain tenets to follow, which, as always in interior design, are mostly common sense:

- Most artwork stands out on dark walls, although drawings and graphic art look good, even rather serious and gallery-like, on gray and neutral colors.
- If walls are strongly patterned, it is best to give prints and drawings very deep mats so that the subject is becalmed in an area of its own and does not get lost in the surrounding background design.
- Before hanging different sizes of pictures, juggle them around on the floor to find the layout that works best with other arrangements in the room and the wall space available.
- Decide on the overall shape of the arrangement and mark out the area on the wall in pencil before you attempt to hang several things together. This will save a lot of unwanted nail holes.
- Vertical arrangements of art will make rooms look taller.
- Horizontal arrangements will make rooms look longer.
- A lot of small works of art can be hung as a block to balance a larger painting or plaque, or as a substitute for a large painting.

part two: the specifics

ALTERNATIVE ART

There are plenty of alternatives to conventional art, whether old or current. Framed bits of fabric such as antique lace; square pieces of fabric pinned together like a patchwork; interesting bedspreads or rugs; samples of all manner of things, from different crops to riding crops; ceremonial Chinese and Japanese robes; old plaques; collections of chains; old pieces of jewelry, such as necklaces, earrings, and brooches; old advertisements;

collections of postcards; book covers– anything, in fact, that can be pinned up and can look decorative or interesting.

- Suspend heavy fabrics on a slim curtain rod hung on hooks. Unless the fabric is very rare, turn over the top to make a casing for the rod.
- Frame lighter fabrics under clear plastic or glass, or stretch them like canvas over thin wood frames.
- Hang smaller items on top of a square of felt, velvet, or canvas, again stretched on a frame.

1 Black-and-white photographs are rested, propped, or otherwise fixed against black-painted paneling. The only color is the touch of green leaves.

2 Paper memorabilia is effectively arranged in a long, envelope-like, transparent holder.

3 Old sepia prints are similarly propped against the wall on this mantelpiece in a deliberately casual manner. Propping paintings and drawings is often an effective alternative to hanging.

4 The ornate but empty picture frame above the carved oak chest shows off the brick wall very nicely. Notice, too, the clever balance of the tall candlestick with the tray, books, and balls, and the trug filled with wooden shoe trees.

Plants in the Home

I would find it hard not to use plants in a room. Tall plants, wide-spreading plants, clusters of small plants, flowering plants, indoor trees, and, of course, flowers all add a new dimension, a liveliness and freshness that are gratifyingly cheap in relation to the pleasure that is given. Moreover, plants, like books, always seem to furnish a room.

There is almost no gap in a room that a plant cannot fill and improve; no piece of furniture that cannot be balanced and made to look better by a spread of leaves, no corner that is not softened by foliage. Conversely, the sight of sick, uncared-for plants is immediately offputting.

LIGHT AND ASPECT

The choice of plants is governed by the amount of light a room gets and its aspect (the direction in which its windows face). If the aspect and light are not right for a plant, no amount of cosseting, fertilizing, spraying, and careful watering can prevent its slow demise.

Most people who care for plants maintain that they can tell in a week if the location is appropriate by the gloss on the leaves, and a certain indefinable air of well-being. And if the setting is right, most plants seem to thrive with remarkably little attention, except for repotting as they grow and spread.

USING PLANTS CREATIVELY

Put plants in baskets, stainless steel planters, stone or terracotta pots, Versailles boxes, or an urn on a pedestal –anything that best suits the prevailing mood of the room.

Make a group with plants and sculpture. Mass single flowers in specimen jars and old bottles.

Tall plants and indoor trees make subtle room dividers, and planters can be set on small casters or wheels for moving around easily. I have also seen them massed on shallow trolleys for easier maneuverability.

A bushy indoor tree or a well-planted hanging basket set in front of an unshuttered, uncurtained window can make it look completely dressed.

Rows of plants on shelves, strung across awkwardly shaped or placed windows, solve the problem of unity in a minute.

LIGHTING PLANTS

Place uplights behind plants to throw dramatic shadows onto walls and ceilings, as well as illuminating the foliage on a dull day and at night. Or place small spots so that they shine through the leaves–but be careful not to put them so close that they burn them. Put plants or massed flowers directly under a downlight (again, placed a suitable distance away), for a special brilliance.

Be as generous as possible with anything you have to do with the plant world. Indoor landscaping can be just as exciting, and considerably less work, than the outdoor variety.

I *Stone jars of grass, twigs of blossom, and a paper lampshade make a nicely nuanced contrast of textures.*
2 *The grouping of old suitcases and an oriental statue is greatly enhanced by the oversize basket of scarlet flowers and greenery.*
3 *A huge plant in a pot looks calmly stunning seen through tall double doors. The foreground is softened by a large fern.*

part two: the specifics

Index

Acknowledgements

PICTURE CREDITS

1 Ken Hayden/Red Cover; 2 Simon Upton (Designer: Marja Walters/Michael Reeves)/Interior Archive; 4 Simon Upton (Designer: Rupert Spira)/Interior Archive; 5 above left Ray Main/Mainstream/Designer: Roger Oates; 5 above right Deidi von Schaewen; 5 center left Paul Ryan/International Interiors (Designer: James Gager); 5 center right Edina van der Wyck (Designer: Jenny Armit)/Interior Archive; 5 below Andreas von Einsiedel (Designer: Charles Rutherfoord); 6: Nadia Mackenzie/Interior Archive; 7: Paul Ryan/International Interiors (Designer: Alexander Vetners) ; 8 left Ray Main/Mainstream/Designer: Jasper Conran ; 8 center Ken Hayden/Red Cover ; 8 right Verne/Houses and Interiors; 9 left Dennis Gilbert/VIEW (Conran Design Group); 9 center Jake Fitzjones/Houses and Interiors; 9 right Ray Main/Mainstream/Architect: Gregory Phillips; 10 Paul Ryan/International Interiors (Architect: Barnes & Coy); 12:1 Paul Ryan/International Interiors (Designer: Charles Rutherfoord); 12:2 Ray Main/Mainstream; 13:3 Roger Brooks/Houses and Interiors; 14:1 Chris Gascoigne/View (Architects: Lifschutz Davidson); 14-15:2 Roger Brooks/Houses and Interiors; 15:3 Ray Main/Mainstream; 18-19 Verne/Houses and Interiors; 20-21:1 Arcaid/Richard Glover/Architect: Ben Mather; 21:2 Tim Beddow/Interior Archive; 22:1 Deidi von Schaewen; 23:2 Christl Rohl (Owner: Volker Classen)/Interior Archive; 23:3 James Morris/Axiom Photographic Agency; 24:1 Wayne Vincent (Owner: Dykman)/Interior Archive; 24:2 Ray Main/Mainstream/Designer: Lawrence Llewelyn-Bowen; 25:3 Dennis Gilbert/VIEW (Blauel Architects); 26:1 Laura Resen for Lachapelle Representation; 26:2 Ray Main/Mainstream; 27:3 Ray Main/Mainstream/Designer: Jasper Conran; 28: Ray Main/Mainstream; 29: Dennis Gilbert/VIEW (Conran Design Group); 30:1 Christl Rohl (Owner: Pilz)/Interior Archive; 31:2 Ray Main/Mainstream/Architect: Chris Cowper; 32-33:1 Nathan Willock/VIEW (Circus Lofts); 33:2 Paul Ryan/International Interiors (Designer: Caroline Breet); 34:1 Paul Ryan/International Interiors (Designer: Christian Liaigre); 35:2 Andrew Wood (Architect: Spencer Fung)/Interior Archive; 35:3 Robert Harding Syndications/Polly Wreford/GE Magazines: Inspirations; 36:1 Lu Jeffery; 37:2 Heidi Grassley/Axiom Photographic Agency (Architect: Seth Stein); 37:3 Nadia Mackenzie/Interior Archive; 37:4 Verne/G Fiorentino; 38:1 Paul Ryan/International Interiors (Designer: Frances Halliday); 39:2 Andrew Wood (Designer: The Holding Company)/Interior Archive; 40:1 Deidi von Schaewen; 41:2 Robert Harding Syndications/ Tim Imrie/GE Magazines: Inspirations; 42:1 Dennis Gilbert/VIEW; 43:2 James Morris/Axiom Photographic Agency; 44:1 Robert Harding Syndications/Lucinda Symons/GE Magazines: Inspirations; 45:2 Luke White/Axiom Photographic Agency; 46:1 Richard Waite/Arcaid; 47:2 Chris Gascoigne/VIEW (Architect: John Kerr); 48:1 Robert Harding Syndications/Debi Treloar/GE Magazines: Inspirations; 49:2 Robert Harding Syndications/Sandra Lane/GE Magazines: Inspirations; 49:3 Deidi von Schaewen; 50:1 Paul Ryan/International Interiors (Designer: Barbro Grandelius); 51:2 Ray Main/Mainstream; 52:1 Nick Hutton/VIEW; 52:2 Deidi von Schaewen; 53: Ray Main/Mainstream; 54:1 Ray Main/Mainstream/Designer: Roger Oates; 55:2: Deidi von Schaewen; 56:1 Richard Bryant/Arcaid; 57:2 Ray Main/Mainstream; 57:3 Verne/St Peiters; 57:4 Verne/G Pattun; 58:1 Jake Fitzjones/Houses and Interiors; 58:2 Ray Main/Mainstream; 59:3 Ray Main/Mainstream/Designer: Jasper Conran ; 60-61: Ken Hayden/Red Cover; 62:1 Earl Carter/Belle/Arcaid; 63:2 Ianthe Ruthven; 64:1 Ianthe Ruthven; 65:2 Deidi von Schaewen; 66:1 Ken Hayden/Red Cover; 66:2 Ianthe Ruthven; 67:3 Ray Main/Mainstream; 68:1 James Morris/Axiom Photographic Agency; 69:2 Laura Resen for Lachapelle Representation; 69:3 Jonathan Pilkington (Owner: Rotheston)/Interior Archive; 70:1&3 Ben Johnson/Arcaid; 71:2 Ianthe Ruthven; 72:1 Angelo Hornak; 72:2 Deidi von Schaewen; 73:3 John Bethell/Bridgeman Art Library ; 74:1 Richard Bryant/Arcaid; 74:2 Angelo Hornak; 75:3 Andrew Wood (Designer: Nicholas Haslam)/Interior Archive; 78:1 Jeremy Cockayne/Arcaid; 79:2 Mark Fiennes/Arcaid; 79:3 Richard Bryant/Arcaid; 80:1 James Mortimer (Architect: Le Corbusier)/Interior Archive/(FLC/ADAGP, Paris & DACS, London 2000; 81:2 Christie's Images Ltd; 82:1 Ianthe Ruthven/(ARS, New York & DACS, London 2000; 83:2 Angelo Hornak; 84 left Henry Wilson (Designer: Leslie Goring)/Interior Archive; 84 center Winfried Heinze/Red Cover ; 84 right Simon Upton (Designer: Ann Boyd)/Interior Archive; 85 left Lu Jeffery; 85 center Laura Resen for Lachapelle Representation; 85 right Andreas Von Einsiedel; 86-87 Andreas von Einsiedel (Designer: Tara Bernerd); 88:1 Mary Gilliatt; 88:2 Verne; 89:3 Laura Resen for Lachapelle Representation; 90:1 Paul Ryan/International Interiors (Designer: Kathy Gallagher); 90:2 Jonathan Pilkington (Designer: Dido Farrell)/Interior Archive; 91:3 Tim Clinch (Designer: Borja Azcarate)/Interior Archive; 92 left: Alan Weintraub/Arcaid; 92:1 Paul Ryan/International Interiors (Designer: Marcel Wotterinck); 93:2 Ray Main/Mainstream; 93:3 Andreas von Einsiedel; 94:1 Andreas von Einsiedel (Designer: Frederic Mechiche); 95:2 Robert Harding Syndications/Lucinda Symons/GE Magazines: Inspirations; 96:1 Brian Harrison/Red Cover; 96:2 Lu Jeffery; 97:3 Julia Pazowski/Houses and Interiors; 98:1 Andrew Wood (Owner: David Quigley)/Interior Archive; 98:2 Winfried Heinze/Red Cover; 98:4 Jeremy Cockayne/Arcaid ; 99:3 Roger Brooks/Houses and Interiors; 100:1 James Morris/Axiom Photographic Agency; 100:2 Andreas von Einsiedel (Designer: Annie Constantine); 100:4 Jonathan Pilkington (Owner: Hinchcliffe)/Interior Archive; 101:3 Richard Waite/Arcaid; 102: Deidi von Schaewen; 105:1 Edina van der Wyck (Designer: Mimmi O'Connell)/Interior Archive; 105: Wayne Vincent (Designer: Dyckman)/Interior Archive; 105:3: Simon Upton (Owner: Christine Davies)/Interior Archive; 106:1 Paul Ryan/International Interiors; 106:2 Andreas von Einsiedel (Designer: Ina Lindemann); 107:3 Mary Gilliatt; 108:1 Mary Gilliatt; 108:2 Andreas von Einsiedel; 109:3 Andreas von Einsiedel; 110:1 Deidi von Schaewen; 110:2: Steve Hawkins/Teresa Ward/Houses and Interiors ; 111:3 Mark Bolton/Red Cover; 112:1 Andreas von Einsiedel (Designer: Michelle Halard); 112:2 Simon Upton (Designer: Sasha Waddell)/Interior Archive; 113:3 Earl Carter/Belle/Arcaid; 114:1 Deidi von Schaewen; 115:2: Ray Main/Mainstream/Designer: Kelly Hoppen; 116:1 James Morris/Axiom Photographic Agency; 117 center Richard Powers/Redback/Arcaid; 117:2 Verne; 118:1 Tim Beddow (Designer: Bill Amberg)/Interior Archive; 118:2 Tim Clinch (Owner: Handelsmann)/Interior Archive; 119:3 Robert Harding Syndications/Sandra Lane/Inspirations/GE Magazines; 119:4 Simon Butcher/Houses and Interiors; 119:5 Simon Upton/Interior Archive; 120-121 Eduardo Munoz (Designer: Ferruccio Laviani)/Interior Archive; 122:1 Andreas von Einsiedel; 122:3 Simon Upton (Designer: Bill Amberg)/Interior Archive; 123:2 Paul Ryan/International Interiors (Designer: Sasha Waddell); 124: 'Artistry' carpet, by Stoddard/Carla Reid-Adam; 126:1&3 The Carpet Foundation, UK tel: 01562 755568; 126:2&4 Blenheim Carpet Company/Barbara Douglass; 126:5 Natural Flooring Direct/photo: Peter Johnston/Theo Woodham-Smith; 127:6 The Carpet Foundation, UK tel: 01562 755568; 127:7 Woodstock Blenheim by Fired Earth; 127:9 Natural Flooring Direct/photo: Peter Johnston/Theo Woodham-Smith; 127:8: Richard Bryant (Architect: Spencer Fung)/Arcaid; 128: Ken Hayden/Red Cover; 130-131: Christie's Images Ltd; 132-133: Christie's Images Ltd; 134:1 Robert Harding Syndications/Sandra Lane/GE Magazines: Inspirations; 135:2 Blenheim Carpet Company/Barbara Douglass; 136:1 Richard Powers/Redback/Arcaid; 137:2 Simon McBride (Owner: Katy Brown)/Interior Archive; 138:1 Paul Ryan/International Interiors (Designer: Frances Halliday); 139:2 Brian Harrison/Red Cover; 140:1 Winfried Heinze/Red Cover ; 141:2&3 Natural Flooring Direct/Theo Woodham-Smith; 141:4 Alberto Piovano/Arcaid; 142:1 Roger Brooks/Houses and Interiors; 142:2 Andreas von Einsiedel (Designer: M. Antonin); 143:3 Paul Ryan/International Interiors (Designer: Sharone Einhorn); 143:4 Andrew Wood (Owner: Mandy Coakley)/Interior Archive; 144:1 Ray Main/Mainstream; 144:2 James Morris/Axiom Photographic Agency; 145:3 Christopher Drake/Red Cover; 146-147 Henry Wilson (Architect: Voon Yee Wong)/Interior Archive; 148:1 Laura Resen for Lachapelle Representation; 149:2 Houses and Interiors; 149:3 Richard Waite/Arcaid; 150:1 Ray Main/Mainstream; 151:2 Ray Main/Mainstream; 151:3 Winfried Heinze/Red Cover; 151:4 Andreas von Einsiedel; 152:1 Paul Ryan/International Interiors (Designer: Sasha Waddell); 153:2 Ray Main/Mainstream; 153:3 Paul Ryan/International Interiors

(Designer: Victoria Hagan); **153::** Roger Brooks/Houses and Interiors; **155:1** Andreas von Einsiedel (Designer: Nona von Haeften); **155:2** Laura Resen for Lachapelle Representation; **156:1**: Richard Felber; **157:2** Andrew Wood (Designer: Christine Rucker/The White Co.)/Interior Archive; **157:3** Andreas von Einsiedel (Fabrics and design by 'Les Olivades', France); **158:1** Andreas von Einsiedel; **159:2** Ray Main/Mainstream; **159:3** Winfried Heinze/Red Cover; **159:4** Henry Wilson (Designer: John Plummer)/Interior Archive; **160:1** Paul Ryan/International Interiors (Designer: Jan des Bouvrie); **160:2** Simon Upton (Designer: Colefax and Fowler)/Interior Archive; **160:3** Paul Ryan/International Interiors (Designer: Harriet Anstruther); **161:4** Andreas von Einsiedel (Designer: Annie Constantine); **162:1** Simon Upton (Designer: Carol Thomas)/Interior Archive; **163:2** Lu Jeffery; **164:1** Robert Harding Syndications/Rowland Roques-O'Neill/GE Magazines: Inspirations; **164:2** Ray Main/Mainstream/Architect: Mary Thum ; **164:3** Ray Main/Mainstream; **165:4** Henry Wilson (Designer: Denise Lee)/Interior Archive; **165:5** Laura Resen for Lachapelle Representation; **166:1** Verne/Houses and Interiors; **166:2** Tim Beddow (Architect: Craig Hamilton)/Interior Archive; **167:3**: Nadia Mackenzie (Property: Ivy Cottage)/Interior Archive; **167:4** Henry Wilson (Designer: Ian Dew)/Interior Archive; **167:5** Paul Ryan/International Interiors (Designer: Kastrup & Sjunnesson); **168:1** Andreas von Einsiedel (Designer: Annie Constantine); **169:2** Ray Main/Mainstream; **170:1** Henry Wilson (Designer: Brett Muldoon)/Interior Archive; **170:2**: Paul Ryan/International Interiors (Designer: Sabina Streeter); **170:3** Eduardo Munoz (Architect: Sobejano/Nieto)/Interior Archive; **171:4** Christopher Drake/Red Cover; **171:5** Ray Main/Mainstream; **172:1** Andreas von Einsiedel (Designer: Annie Constantine); **172–173:2** Simon Upton (Designer: John Wright)/Interior Archive; **173:3** Tim Beddow/Interior Archive; **174:1** Erika Lennard; **174:2** Andreas von Einsiedel; **174:3** Christl Rohl (Owner: Mathias Schrunder)/Interior Archive; **176:1** Laura Resen for Lachapelle Representation; **176:2** Tim Beddow (Architect: Craig Hamilton)/Interior Archive; **178**: Paul Ryan/International Interiors (Designer: Lee Mindel); **180:1** Winfried Heinze/Red Cover; **180–181:3** Andreas von Einsiedel (Designer: Reed/Boyd Partnership); **181:2** Winfried Heinze/Red Cover ; **182** Paul Ryan/International Interiors (Designer: Jan des Bouvrie); **185:1**: Andreas von Einsiedel (Designer: Mark Weaver); **185:2** Andreas von Einsiedel (Designer: Grant White); **185:3** Tim Beddow (Designer: Kathryn Ireland)/Interior Archvie; **185:4** Brian Harrison/Red Cover; **186:1** Christl Rohl (Owner: Rueter)/Interior Archive; **186:2** Winfried Heinze/Red Cover; **186:3** Bob Smith (Owner: Ricardo)/Interior Archive; **187:4** Paul Ryan/International Interiors (Designer: Sabina Streeter); 188:1 Jake Fitzjones/Houses and Interiors; **188:2** Paul Ryan/International Interiors (Designer: Lee Mindel); **189:3** Andreas von Einsiedel; **189:4** Paul Ryan/International Interiors (Designer: Kathy Moskal & Ken Foreman); **190–191** Christie's Images Ltd; **192–193:** Christie's Images Ltd; **194 above** Christie's Images Ltd; **194 below** Victoria and Albert Museum, London, UK/Bridgeman Art Library; **195** Christie's Images Ltd; **196 above** Mark Fiennes/Arcaid; **196 below** American Museum, Bath, Avon, UK/Bridgeman Art Library; **197 above** Henry Francis Dupont Winterthur Museum, Delaware, USA/Bridgeman Art Library; **197 below:** American Museum, Bath, Avon, UK/Bridgeman Art Library; **198** Christie's Images Ltd; **201** Angelo Hornak; **204–205:** www.elizabethwhiting.com; **206– 207:** Andrew Twort/Red Cover; **208:1** Andreas von Einsiedel (Designer: Yves Taralon); **208:2** Andreas von Einsiedel: (Designer: Grant White); **209:3** Wayne Vincent (Designer: Howard Green)/Interior Archive; **210:1&2** Ray Main/Mainstream; **211:3&5** Ray Main/Mainstream; **211:4** Andreas von Einsiedel; **212:1** Laura Resen for Lachapelle Representation; **213:2** Andreas von Einsiedel (Michael Daly); **214:1** Laura Resen for Lachapelle Representation; **214:2** Andreas von Einsiedel (Designer: Grant White); **214:3** Melanie Acevedo; **215:4** Paul Ryan/International Interiors (Designer: G Pensoy); **216:1**: Laura Resen for Lachapelle Representation; **216-217:2** Ray Main/Mainstream; **217:3** www.elizabethwhiting.com.

AUTHOR'S ACKNOWLEDGEMENTS

I first wrote some of the basic material for this course for the enterprising and fast-growing US franchise company, Decor and You. I am most grateful to Karen Powell and Josie Cicerale for their instigation and for their friendship and for allowing material to be incorporated into this venture. It has been a real pleasure to have worked with Caroline Proud, Muna Reyal, Mary Staples, Jo Walton and Alison Wormleighton who made up the team from Conran Octopus and I thank them so much for their sensitivity to, and understanding of, the material and for their enthusiasm. I certainly have to acknowledge the patience, efficiency, enormous hard work and general agreeableness of Lin Prior, who helped so much with the preparations and organisation. And I most particularly want to thank Kate Coughlan, the best magazine editor I have ever had the good fortune to work with, for her belief in me and her support.

Since the course is the sum total of my own experience in a long working life connected with design and journalism, there are certain people – mentors, employers, friends, colleagues, clients – whom I have learnt a great deal from, or have been greatly helped by, or who have been a particular pleasure to work with. In one way or another, they have all contributed to this work, even if quite unknowingly, and I am deeply thankful to them all, some of them, alas, posthumously. In alphabetical order they are: Mike Adams, David Aldridge, Pam and Larry Barnett, Virginia Bredin, Felicity Bryan, Druscilla Beyfus, Alison Cathie, the late Debbie Christian, John, Carole and Brian Collins, Sam Cohn, Ralph and Amanda Congreve, Virginia Lo Faro Cooper, Katie Couric, John Cresswell-Turner, Kurt Dolnier and Allessandra Manning Dolnier, Michael Dunne, Andreas von Einsiedel, Vicky Ellerton, Dick and Judy Felber, Colin Gee, Jane Gelfman, Annie and Christopher Cruice Goodall, David Gough, Sally Griffiths, Mark Griffiths, Lord and Lady Griffiths, Susie Hanmer, Helene (Fesenmaier) Hodgson, D'Arcy and the late John Howell, Winefride Jackson, Carmel and John Jones, Philip Kendell, Jan Kern, Alex Kroll, Liz and Jack Lambert, Judy and Jim Lance, Alex and Eileen Lari, Sarah Tomerlin Lee, Larry Lehman, Stephen Long, Angela (Caccia) and Taffy Lloyd, John Ludovici, Katherine Manisco, the late Billy McCarty, Joy and George McWatters, Jim and Meredith Mercer, Bobbie Middleton, Michael Middleton, Beatrix Miller, Brian Morris, Filippa Naess, Sue and Paul Neale, Liam Neeson, Toby Nuttal, Barbara Plumb, Polly Powell, Helen (Robinson) Preston and the late Desmond Preston, Max Reinhardt, Natasha Richardson, Ray Roberts, Regina Ryan, Antonia Salvato, Jim Seabrook, Harry and Penelope Seidler, Gloria Steinhem, the late Comtesse Rosa Tarnowska, Ladislas Tarnowski, Angela and Wade Thompson, Jane Turner, Dr Steve Udem and Dr Sharon Nathan Udem, Graham Viney, Fred Weiss and Jeanne Wilkins.

The publisher and author would also like to thank Paul Williams for the floor plans on page 16; Laney Loughridge, of Old Village Paint, Ltd.; Kathryn Sellers, of the Carpet and Rug Institute; and the Blenheim Carpet Company (+44 20 7823 5215/20 7225 3393) for the photographs on page 126 (no. 2 and 4) and page 135 (no. 2).